T0330578

Advanced Data Science and Analytics with Python

Chapman & Hall/CRC
Data Mining and Knowledge Series

Series Editor: Vipin Kumar

Text Mining and Visualization
Case Studies Using Open-Source Tools
Markus Hofmann and Andrew Chisholm

Graph-Based Social Media Analysis
Ioannis Pitas

Data Mining
A Tutorial-Based Primer, Second Edition
Richard J. Roiger

Data Mining with R
Learning with Case Studies, Second Edition
Luís Torgo

Social Networks with Rich Edge Semantics
Quan Zheng and David Skillicorn

Large-Scale Machine Learning in the Earth Sciences
Ashok N. Srivastava, Ramakrishna Nemani, and Karsten Steinhaeuser

Data Science and Analytics with Python
Jesús Rogel-Salazar

Feature Engineering for Machine Learning and Data Analytics
Guozhu Dong and Huan Liu

Exploratory Data Analysis Using R
Ronald K. Pearson

Human Capital Systems, Analytics, and Data Mining
Robert C. Hughes

Industrial Applications of Machine Learning
Pedro Larrañaga et al

Automated Data Analysis Using Excel
Second Edition
Brian D. Bissett

Advanced Data Science and Analytics with Python
Jesús Rogel-Salazar

For more information about this series please visit:

https://www.crcpress.com/Chapman--HallCRC-Data-Mining-and-Knowledge-Discovery-Series/book-series/CHDAMINODIS

Advanced Data Science and Analytics with Python

Jesús Rogel-Salazar

CRC Press
Taylor & Francis Group
Boca Raton London New York

CRC Press is an imprint of the
Taylor & Francis Group, an **informa** business

A CHAPMAN & HALL BOOK

First edition published 2020
by CRC Press
6000 Broken Sound Parkway NW, Suite 300, Boca Raton, FL 33487-2742

and by CRC Press
2 Park Square, Milton Park, Abingdon, Oxon, OX14 4RN

© 2020 Taylor & Francis Group, LLC

CRC Press is an imprint of Taylor & Francis Group, LLC

ISBN: 978-0-429-44661-0 (hbk)
ISBN: 978-1-138-31506-8 (pbk)
ISBN: 978-0-429-44664-1 (ebk)

To A. J. Johnson

Then. Now. Always.

Contents

List of Figures

List of Tables

Preface

WRITING A BOOK IS AN exhilarating experience, if at times
a bit hard and maddening. This companion to *Data Science
and Analytics with Python*[1] is the result of arguments with
myself about writing something to cover a few of the areas
that were not included in that first volume, largely due to
space/time constraints. Like the previous book, this one
exists thanks to the discussions, stand-ups, brainstorms and
eventual implementations of algorithms and data science
projects carried out with many colleagues and friends. The
satisfaction of seeing happy users/customers with products
they can rely on is, and will continue to be, a motivation for
me.

[1] Rogel-Salazar, J. (2017). *Data Science and Analytics with Python*. Chapman & Hall/CRC Data Mining and Knowledge Discovery Series. CRC Press

The subjects discussed in this book are complementary and
a follow-up to the ones covered in Volume 1. The intended
audience for this book is still composed of data analysts and
early-career data scientists with some experience in
programming and with a background in statistical
modelling. In this case, however, the expectation is that they
have already covered some areas of machine learning and
data analytics. Although I will refer to the previous book in

The book and its companion are
a good reference for seasoned
practitioners too.

parts where some knowledge is assumed, the book is written to be read independently from Volume 1. As the title suggests, this book continues to use Python[2] as a tool to train, test and implement machine learning models and algorithms. Nonetheless, Python does not live in isolation, and in the last chapter of this book we touch upon the usage of Swift[3] as a programming language to help us deploy our machine learning models.

[2] Python Software Foundation (1995). Python reference manual. http://www.python.org

[3] Apple Inc. (2014). Swift programming language. https://swift.org

Python continues to be, in my view, a very useful tool. The number of modules, packages and contributions that Pythonistas have made to the rest of the community make it a worthwhile programming language to learn. It is no surprise that the number of Python users continues to grow. Similarly, the ecosystem of the language is also evolving: From the efforts to bring Python 3.x to be the version of choice, through to the development of the computational environment that is the Jupyter Notebook and its evolution, the JupyterLab.

Visit https://jupyterlab. readthedocs.io for further information.

For those reasons, we will continue using some excellent libraries, such as Scikit-learn[4], Pandas[5], Numpy[6] and others. After all, we have seen Nobel prize winning research being supported by Python, as have been a number of commercial enterprises, including consultancies, startups and established companies. The decision to use Python for this second volume is therefore not just one of convenience and continuity, but a conscious adoption that I hope will support you too.

[4] Pedregosa, F., G. Varoquaux, A. Gramfort, V. Michel, et al. (2011). Scikit-learn: Machine learning in Python. *Journal of Machine Learning Research 12*, 2825–2830
[5] McKinney, W. (2012). *Python for Data Analysis: Data Wrangling with Pandas, NumPy, and IPython*. O'Reilly Media
[6] Scientific Computing Tools for Python (2013). NumPy. http://www.numpy.org

As I mentioned above, the book covers aspects that were necessarily left out in the previous volume; however, the readers in mind are still technical people interested in moving into the data science and analytics world. I have tried to keep the same tone as in the first book, peppering the pages with some bits and bobs of popular culture, science fiction and indeed Monty Python puns. The aim is still to focus on showing the concepts and ideas behind popular algorithms and their use. As before, we are not delving, in general, into exhaustive implementations from scratch, and instead relying on existing modules.

I sincerely hope the most obscure ones do make you revisit their excellent work.

The examples contained here have been tested in Python 3.7 under MacOS, Linux and Windows 10. We do recommend that you move on from Python 2. For reference, the versions of some of the packages used in the book are as follows:

Maintenance for Python 2 has stopped as of January 2020.

Python - 3.5.2   Pandas - 0.25

NumPy - 1.17.2   Scikit-learn - 0.21

SciPy - 1.3.1   StatsModels - 0.10

BeautifulSoup - 4.8.1   NLTK - 3.4.5

NetworkX - 2.4   Keras - 2.2.4

TensorFlow - 1.14.0

As before, I am using the Anaconda Python distribution[7] provided by Continuum Analytics. Remember that there are other ways of obtaining Python as well as other versions of

[7] Continuum Analytics (2014). Anaconda 2.1.0. https://store. continuum.io/cshop/anaconda/

the software: For instance, directly from the Python
Software Foundation, as well as distributions from
Enthought Canopy, or from package managers such as
Homebrew. In Chapters 4 and 5, we create conda
environments to install and maintain software relevant to
the discussions for those chapters, and you are more than
welcome to use other virtual environment maintainers too.

Python Software Foundation
https://www.python.org

Enthought Canopy https://www.
enthought.com/products/epd/

Homebrew http://brew.sh

We show computer code by enclosing it in a box as follows:

```
> 1 + 1 # Example of computer code


  2
```

We use a diple (>) to denote the command line terminal
prompt shown in the Python shell. Keeping to the look
and feel of the previous book, we use margin notes, such
as the one that appears to the right of this paragraph, to
highlight certain areas or commands, as well as to provide
some useful comments and remarks.

This is an example of the margin
notes used throughout this book.

As mentioned before, the book can be read independently
from the previous volume, and indeed each chapter is as
self-contained as possible. I would also like to remind you
that writing code is not very dissimilar to writing poetry.
If I asked that each of us write a poem about the beauty of
a Jackalope, we would all come up with something. Some
would write odes to Jackalopes that would be remembered
by generations to come; some of us would complete the task
with a couple of rhymes. In that way, the code presented
here may not be award winning poetry, but the aim, I hope,

I hope Sor Juana would forgive
my comparison.

will be met. I would welcome to hear about your poems. Do get in touch!

We start in Chapter 1 with a discussion about time series data. We see how Pandas has us covered to deal with the fiendish matter of date data types. We learn how to use time series data similar to that found in stock markets and see how Pandas lets us carry out resampling, slicing and dicing, filtering, aggregating and plotting this kind of data. In terms of modelling, in this chapter we see how moving averages and exponential smoothing let us get a first approach at forecasting future values of the series based on previous observations. We look at autoregression and see how it can be used to model time series.

Time series data and analysis is covered in Chapter 1.

In Chapter 2, we take a look at processing text data containing natural language. We look at how we can obtain data from the web and scrape data that otherwise would be out of reach to us. We take a look at the use of regular expressions to capture specific patterns in a piece of text and learn how to deal with Unicode. Looking at text data in this way leads us to the analysis of language, culminating with topic modelling as an unsupervised learning task to identify the possible subjects or topics that are addressed in a set of documents.

Natural language processing is covered in Chapter 2.

In Chapter 3, we look into some fundamental concepts used in the analysis of networks, whether social or otherwise. We look at graph theory as a way to discover relationships encoded in networks such as small-world ones. We have a chance to talk about measures such as degree centrality,

Chapter 3 covers the use of graphs and network analysis, a topic that will inevitably make us more social.

closeness, betweenness, and others. We even do this with
characters from a galaxy far, far away.   :)

Chapter 4 is probably the deepest chapter of all, pun
definitely intended. It is here where we turn our attention to   Chapter 4 looks at neural
the "unreasonable effectiveness" of neural networks. We   networks and deep learning.
look at the general architecture of a neural network and
build our own from scratch. Starting with feedforward
networks, we move on to understand the famous
backpropagation algorithm. We get a chance to look at the
effect of the number of layers as well as the number of
nodes in each of them. We then move on to the
implementation of more complex, deeper architectures, such
as convolutional and recurrent neural networks.

Finally, in Chapter 5, we look at the perennial issue of   Chapter 5 looks at the deployment
bringing our models, predictions and solutions to our   of machine learning models.
customers, users and stakeholders. Data products are the
focus of our discussion, and we see how the availability,
processing, meaning and understanding of data should be
at the heart of our efforts. We then look at the possibility of
bringing our models to the hands of our users via the
implementation of a model inside a mobile device
application in an Apple device such as an iPhone via Core
ML.

Remember that *there is no such thing as a perfect model, only
good enough ones*. The techniques presented in this book,
and the companion volume, are not the end of the story,
they are the beginning. The data that you have to deal
with will guide your story. Do not let the anthropomorphic

language of machine learning fool you. Models that *learn, see, understand* and *recognise* are as good as the data used to build them, and as blind as the human making decisions based on them. Use your Jackalope data science skills to inform your work.

As I said before, this book is the product of many interactions over many moons. I am indebted to many people that have directly and indirectly influenced the words you have before you. Any errors, omissions or simplifications are mine. As always, I am grateful to my family and friends for putting up with me when I excuse myself with the old phrase:*"I have to do some book... I am behind"*. Thank you for putting up with another *small* project from this crazy physicist!

You know who you are!

Do some work on the book of course...

London, UK   *Dr Jesús Rogel-Salazar*
                                          March 2020

Reader's Guide

THIS BOOK IS INTENDED TO be a companion to any Jackalope data scientist that is interested in continuing the journey following the subjects covered in *Data Science and Analytics with Python*[8]. The material covered here is fairly independent from the book mentioned above though.

[8] Rogel-Salazar, J. (2017). *Data Science and Analytics with Python*. Chapman & Hall/CRC Data Mining and Knowledge Discovery Series. CRC Press

The chapters in this book can be read on their own and in any order you desire. If you require some direction though, here is a guide that may help in reading and/or consulting the book:

- Managers and readers curious about Data Science:

    - Take a look at the discussion about data products in Chapter 5. This will give you some perspective of the areas that your Jackalope data scientists need to consider in their day-to-day work.

    - I recommend you also take a look at Chapters 1 and 3 of the companion book mentioned above.

    - Make sure you understand those chapters inside-out; they will help you understand your rangale of Jackalope data scientists.

- Beginners:

  - Start with Chapters 2 and 3 of the companion book. They will give you a solid background to tackle the rest of this book.

  - Chapter 1 of this book provides a good way to continue learning about the capabilities of Pandas.

  - Chapter 2 of this book on natural language processing will give you a balanced combination of powerful tools, with an easy entry level.

- Seasoned readers and those who have covered the first volume of this series may find it easier to navigate the book by themes or subjects:

  - **Time Series Data** is covered in Chapter 1, including:

    * Handling of date data

    * Time series modelling

    * Moving averages

    * Seasonality

    * Autoregression

  - **Natural Language Processing** is covered in Chapter 2, including:

    * Text data analysis

    * Web and HTML scraping

    * Regular expressions

    * Unicode encoding

    * Text tokenisation and word tagging

    * Topic modelling

– **Network Analysis** is discussed in Chapter 3,
including:

* Graph theory

* Centrality measures

* Community detection and clustering

* Network representation

– **Neural networks and Deep Learning** is addressed in
Chapter 4, where we look at:

* Neural network architecture

* Perceptron

* Activation functions

* Feedforward networks

* Backpropagation

* Deep learning

* Convolutional neural networks

* Recurrent neural networks

* LSTM

– **Model Deployment and iOS App Creation** is covered
in Chapter 5, including:

* Data products

* Agile methodology

* App design

* Swift programming language

* App deployment

About the Author

Dr Jesús Rogel-Salazar is a lead data scientist with experience in the field working for companies such as AKQA, IBM Data Science Studio, Dow Jones, Barclays and Tympa Health Technologies. He is a visiting researcher at the Department of Physics at Imperial College London, UK and a member of the School of Physics, Astronomy and Mathematics at the University of Hertfordshire, UK. He obtained his doctorate in Physics at Imperial College London for work on quantum atom optics and ultra-cold matter.

He has held a position as senior lecturer in mathematics, as well as a consultant and data scientist, for a number of years in a variety of industries, including science, finance, marketing, people analytics and health, among others. He is the author of *Data Science and Analytics with Python* and *Essential MATLAB® and Octave*, both also published by CRC Press. His interests include mathematical modelling, data science and optimisation in a wide range of applications, including optics, quantum mechanics, data journalism, finance and health.

Other Books by the Same Author

- **Data Science and Analytics with Python**
  CRC Press, 2018, ISBN 978-1-138-04317-6 (hardback)
  978-1-4987-4209-2 (paperback)

  Data Science and Analytics with Python is designed for
  practitioners in data science and data analytics in both
  academic and business environments. The aim is to
  present the reader with the main concepts used in data
  science using tools developed in Python. The book
  discusses what data science and analytics are, from the
  point of view of the process and results obtained.

- **Essential MATLAB® and Octave**
  CRC Press, 2014, ISBN 978-1-138-41311-5 (hardback)
  978-1-4822-3463-3 (paperback)

  Widely used by scientists and engineers, well-established
  MATLAB® and open-source Octave provide excellent
  capabilities for data analysis, visualisation, and more.
  By means of straightforward explanations and examples
  from different areas in mathematics, engineering, finance,
  and physics, the book explains how MATLAB and Octave
  are powerful tools applicable to a variety of problems.

1

No Time to Lose: Time Series Analysis

HAVE YOU EVER WONDERED WHAT the weather, financial prices, home energy usage, and your weight all have in common? Well, appart from the obvious, the data to analyse these phenomena can be collected at regular intervals over time. Common sense, right? Well, there is no time to lose; let us take a deeper look into this exciting kind of data. Are you ready?

Not obvious? Oh... well, read on!

Or is it Toulouse, like "Toulouse" in France?

A time series is defined as a sequence of data reading in successive order and can be taken on any variable that changes over time. So, if a time series is a set of data collected over time, then a lot of things, not just our weight or the weather, would be classed as time series, and perhaps that is true. There are, obviously and quite literally, millions of data points that can be collected over time. However, time series analysis is not necessarily immediately employed.

A lot of data is collected over time, but that does not make the data set a time series.

Time series analysis encapsulates the methods used to understand the sequence of data points mentioned above

and extract useful information from it. A main goal is that
of forecasting successive future values of the series. In this
chapter we will cover some of these methods. Let us take a
look.

1.1   *Time Series*

KNOWING HOW TO MODEL TIME series is surely an
important tool in our Jackalope data scientist toolbox.
Jackalopes? Yes! Long story... You can get further
information in Chapter 1 of *Data Science and Analytics with
Python*.[1]. But I digress, the key point about time series data
is that the ordering of the data points in time matters. For
many datasets it is not important in which order the data
are obtained or listed. One order is as good as another, and
although the ordering may tell us something about the
dataset, it is not an inherent attribute of the set.

However, for time series data the ordering is absolutely
crucial. The order imposes a certain structure on the data,
which in turn is of relevance to the underlying phenomenon
studied. So, what is different about time series? Well, Time!
Furthermore, we will see later on in this chapter that in
some cases there are situations where future observations
are influenced by past data points. All in all, this is not a
surprising statement; we are well acquainted with causality
relationships.

Let us have a look at an example of a time series. In Figure
1.1 we can see a financial time series corresponding to the

[1] Rogel-Salazar, J. (2017). *Data Science and Analytics with Python*. Chapman & Hall/CRC Data Mining and Knowledge Discovery Series. CRC Press

See for instance the datasets analysed in the book mentioned above.

What is different about time series? —Time!

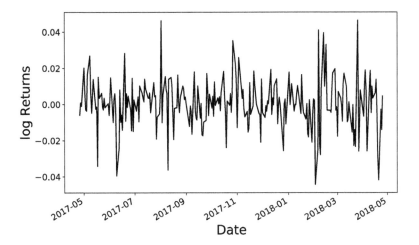

Figure 1.1: A time series of the log returns for Apple Inc. for a year since April 2017.

log returns of Apple for a year starting in April 2017. The log returns are used to determine the proportional amount you might get on a given day compared to the previous one. With that description in mind, we can see how we are relating the value on day n to the one on day $n-1$.

The log return is given by $\log\left(\frac{FV}{PV}\right)$, where FV is the future value and PV is the past value.

In that way, a Jackalope data scientist working in finance may be able to look at the sequence provided by the time series to determine a model that can predict what the next value will be. The same train of thought will be applicable to a variety of other human endeavours, from agriculture to climate change, and from geology to solar dynamics.

And hop all the way to the bank...

In contrast, in many other cases the implicit assumption we may be able to make is that the observations we take are not a sequence and that the values obtained are independent from each other. Let us consider the Iris dataset that we have used in Chapter 3 of *Data Science and Analytics with*

Python[2]. The dataset records measurements of three species of iris flowers in centimetres, including sepal length, sepal width, petal length and petal width. In collecting the information, there is no reason to believe that the fact the current iris specimen we measure has a petal length of, say, 6.1 cm tells us anything about the next specimen.

In a time series the opposite is true, i.e., whatever happens at time t has information about what will happen at $t + 1$. In that sense, our observations of the phenomenon at hand are at the same time both outcomes and predictors: Outcomes of the previous time step, and predictors of the next one. I know what you are thinking—*cool!!*— and now how do we deal with that situation‽

You will be happy (although not surprised perhaps) that there is an answer: There are various ways to deal with this input/output duality and the appropriate methodology very much depends on what I call the *personality* of the data, i.e. the nature of the data itself, how it was obtained and what answers we require from it. In this chapter we shall see some of the ways we can analyse time series data. Let us start with a few examples.

1.2   *One at a Time: Some Examples*

IN THE PREVIOUS SECTION WE have seen a first example of a time series given by the log returns of Apple (shown in Figure 1.1). We can clearly see a first maximum on August 2nd, 2017. This corresponds to the day Apple released

[2] Rogel-Salazar, J. (2017). *Data Science and Analytics with Python*. Chapman & Hall/CRC Data Mining and Knowledge Discovery Series. CRC Press

t has information about what will happen at $t + 1$.

Isn't it cool to be able to use interrobangs‽

I think data, like humans, has also some *personality* .

their third-quarter results for 2017, beating earning and revenue estimates[3]. There are several other peaks and troughs during the year of data plotted. These are not uncommon in many financial time series, and not all may have a straightforward explanation like the one above.

Another interesting thing we can notice is that if we were to take the average of the values in the series, we can see that it is a fairly stable measure. Nonetheless, the variability of the data points changes as we move forwards in time. We shall see later on some models that will exploit these observations to analyse this type of data.

Let us see another example from a very different area: Solar dynamics. In Figure 1.2 we can see the number of sunspots per month since 1749 through 2013. The earliest study of the periodicity of sunspots was the work by Schuster[4] in 1906. Schuster is credited with coining the concept of antimatter, and as cool as that is, in this case we would like to concentrate on the periodogram analysis he pioneered to establish an approximate 11-year cycle in the solar activity.

Sunspots indicate intensive magnetic activity in the sun, and we can see in the figure the regular appearance of maximum and minimum activity. Understanding the behaviour of sunspots is important due to their link with solar activity and help us predict space weather that affects satellite communication and also provides us with awe-inspiring and spectacular auroras.

If our goal is indeed to generate predictions from the data in a time series, there are certain assumptions that can help

[3] Archer, S. (2017). Apple hits a record high after crushing earnings (AAPL). http://markets.businessinsider.com/news/stocks/apple-stock-price-record-high-after-crushing-earnings -2017-8-100222647. Accessed: 2018-05-01

An average return of approximately zero!

[4] Schuster, A. (1906). II. On the periodicities of sunspots. *Philosophical Transactions of the Royal Society of London A: Mathematical, Physical and Engineering Sciences* 206(402-412), 69–100

Sunspots are linked to solar activity, enabling us to carry out space weather predictions.

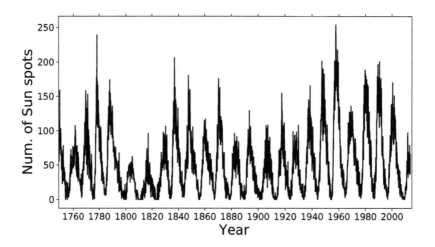

Figure 1.2: Solar activity from 1749 through 2013.

us in our quest. A typical assumption made is that there is some structure in the time series data. This structure may be somewhat obfuscated by random noise. One way to understand the structure of the time series is to think of the trend shown in the series together with any seasonal variation.

Structure = Trend + Seasonality

The trend in the Apple log returns discussed earlier on may not be very obvious. Let us take a look at the closing price of the Apple stock during the same period. In Figure 1.3 we can see the behaviour of the closing price for a year since 2017. The plot shows that there is a tendency for the prices to increase overtime. Similarly, there seem to be some periodicity in the data.

Trend, it should be said!

This brings us to the seasonality in a time series. Seasonality is understood in this case to be the presence of variations

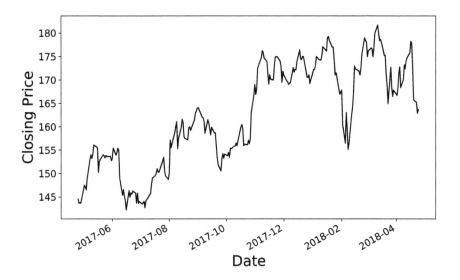

Figure 1.3: Closing prices for Apple Inc. for a year since April 2017.

observed at regular intervals in our data set. These intervals may be daily, weekly, monthly, etc. Seasonal variation may be an important source of information in our quest for predictability as it captures information that will clearly have an impact on the events you are measuring with your data. The seasonality in the sunspot activity shown in Figure 1.2 is undeniable.

Seasonality is the presence of variations at regular intervals.

1.3 Bearing with Time: Pandas Series

NOW THAT WE HAVE A better idea of what makes a time series dataset different from other types of data, let us consider how we can deal and manipulate them in a way that makes life easier for us Jackalope data scientists. I am sure that you have come across the great and useful Python module called Pandas. Its original author, Wes McKinney started developing the module to deal with **pan**el **da**ta, encountered in statistics and econometrics[5]. Indeed he started using Python to perform quantitative analysis on financial data at AQR Capital Management. Today, Pandas is a well-established open source piece of software with multiple uses and a large number of contributors.

[5] McKinney, W. (2011). pandas: a foundational python library for data analysis and statistics. Python for High Performance and Scientific Computing: O'Reilly Media, Inc

Since time is an important part of a time series, let us take a look at some data that contains time as one of its columns. We can start by loading some useful modules including Pandas and datetime:

A hint is in the name...

```
import numpy as np
import pandas as pd
from datetime import datetime
```

We can create a dictionary with some sample data:

```
data = {'date': ['2018-01-01', '2018-02-01',
    '2018-03-01', '2018-04-01',
    '2018-05-01', '2018-06-01',
    '2018-01-01', '2018-02-01',
    '2018-03-01', '2018-04-01',
    '2018-05-01', '2018-06-01'],
    'visitors': [35, 30, 82, 26,
    83, 46, 40, 57, 95, 57, 87, 42]}
```

We are creating a dataframe with two columns: Date and visitors. Each column is given as a list.

We have visitor monthly data for January through June 2018. The date is given in a format where the year comes first, followed by the month and the day. This dictionary can be readily converted into a Pandas dataframe as follows:

The date is given in the format 'YYYY-MM-DD'.

```
df = pd.DataFrame(data,
    columns=['date', 'visitors'])
```

Let us take a look at the data:

```
> df.head()

    date           visitors
0 2018-01-01         35
1 2018-02-01         30
2 2018-03-01         82
3 2018-04-01         26
4 2018-05-01         83
```

As expected, we have a dataframe with two columns.

Notice that when looking at the dataset, the rows have been given a number (starting with 0). This is an index for the dataframe. Let us take a look at the types of the columns in this dataframe:

A very Pythonic way of counting.

```
> df.dtypes

date         object
visitors     int64
dtype: object
```

The type for date is object, whereas for visitors is integer.

The visitors column is of integer type, but the date column is shown to be an object. We know that this is a date and it would be preferable to use a more relevant type. We can change the column with the to_datetime method in a Pandas dataframe:

```
df['date'] = pd.to_datetime(df['date'])
```

We can use the to_datetime method to convert Pandas columns into date objects.

Furthermore, since the date provides an order sequence for our data, we can do a couple of useful things. First we can set the index to be given by the date column, and second, we can order the dataframe by this index:

```
df.set_index('date', inplace=True)
df.sort_index(inplace=True)
```

We set an index and sort the dataframe by that index.

We have used the inplace property for both commands above. This property lets us make changes to the dataframe *in-situ*, otherwise we would have to create a new dataframe object. Let us look at the head of our dataset:

```
> df.head()


            visitors
date
2018-01-01    35
2018-01-01    40
2018-02-01    30
2018-02-01    57
2018-03-01    82
```

The inplace property lets us make changes directly to the dataframe. Otherwise, we would need to make copies of it to apply the changes.

As we can see in the code above, the rows of the dataset have been ordered by the date index. We can now apply some slicing and dicing to our dataframe. For instance, we can look at the visitors for the year 2018:

```
df['2018']
```

In this case this would correspond to all our data points.

What about if we were interested in the visitors for May, 2018? Well, that is easy:

```
> df['2018-05']

            visitors
date
2018-05-01   83
2018-05-01   87
```

Here we are filtering for the visitors in May, 2018.

Other slicing and dicing techniques used in collection objects are possible thanks to the use of the colon notation. For instance, we can request all the data from March, 2018 onwards as follows:

```
> df[datetime(2018, 3, 1):]

            visitors
date
2018-03-01      82
2018 03 01      95
2018-04-01      26
2018-04-01      57
2018-05-01      83
2018-05-01      87
2018-06-01      46
2018-06-01      42
```

The colon notation used in other collection objects in Python works for Pandas time series too.

The truncate method can help us keep all the data points before or after a given date. In this case, let us ask for the data up to March 2018:

```
> df.truncate(after='2018-03-01')


            visitors
date
2018-01-01    35

2018-01-01    40

2018-02-01    30

2018-02-01    57

2018-03-01    82

2018-03-01    95
```

We can truncate the time series with the truncate method.

Had we used the before parameter instead, we could have truncated all the data points before March, 2018 instead. We can use Pandas to provide us with useful statistics for our dataset. For example, we can count the number of datapoints per entry in the index:

```
> df.groupby('date').count()


            visitors
date
2018-01-01    2

2018-02-01    2

2018-03-01    2

2018-04-01    2

2018-05-01    2

2018-06-01    2
```

We can calculate aggregations with the help of groupby. In this case we are interested in the count.

As expected, we have two entries for each date. We can also look at statistics such as the mean and the sum of entries. In this case, we are going to use the `resample` method for a series. In effect this enables us to change the time frequency in our dataset. Let us use the `'M'` *offset alias* to tell Pandas to create monthly statistics. For the mean we have:

The `resample` method lets us change the frequency in our dataset.

```
> df.resample('M').mean()


                visitors
date
2018-01-31      37.5
2018-02-28      43.5
2018-03-31      88.5
2018-04-30      41.5
2018-05-31      85.0
2018-06-30      44.0
```

We can calculate the mean.

Similarly, for the sum we have:

```
> df.resample('M').sum()
                visitors
date
2018-01-31        75
2018-02-28        87
2018-03-31       177
2018-04-30        83
2018-05-31       170
2018-06-30        88
```

And the sum too.

An offset alias, such as 'M' used in the code above is a string that represents a common time series frequency. We can see some of these aliases in Table 1.1.

Offset aliases are listed in Table 1.1.

We can even create a plot of the dataset. In this case, we show in Figure 1.4 the monthly sum of visitors for the dataset in question.

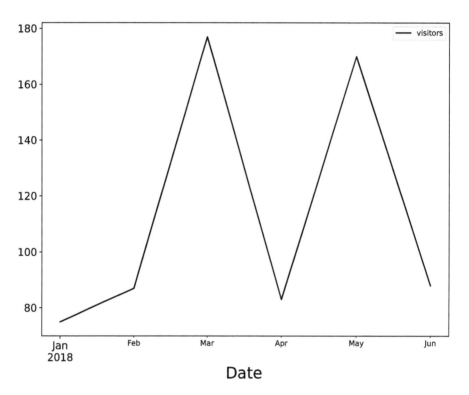

Figure 1.4: Total of monthly visitors for the data entered manually.

It is possible to obtain descriptive statistics with the use of the describe method, and we can do so per relevant group. For example, we can request the information for each date in the dataset:

Alias	Description
B	business day frequency
C	custom business day frequency
D	calendar day frequency
W	weekly frequency
M	month-end frequency
SM	semi-month-end frequency (15th and end of month)
BM	business month-end frequency
CBM	custom business month-end frequency
MS	month-start frequency
SMS	semi-month-start frequency (1st and 15th)
BMS	business month start frequency
CBMS	custom business month-start frequency
Q	quarter-end frequency
BQ	business quarter-end frequency
QS	quarter start frequency
BQS	business quarter-start frequency
A, Y	year-end frequency
BA, BY	business year-end frequency
AS, YS	year-start frequency
BAS, BYS	business year-start frequency
BH	business hour frequency
H	hourly frequency
T, min	minutely frequency
S	secondly frequency
L, ms	milliseconds
U, us	microseconds
N	nanoseconds

Table 1.1: Offset aliases used by Pandas to represent common time series frequencies.

```
df.groupby('date').describe()
```

In Table 1.2 we see the descriptive statistics for the data entered manually earlier on. For brevity we have decided not to include the count column.

date	Visitors						
	mean	std	min	25%	50%	75%	max
2018-01-01	37.5	3.53	35.0	36.25	37.5	38.75	40.0
2018-03-01	88.5	9.19	82.0	85.25	88.5	91.75	95.0
2018-04-01	41.5	21.92	26.0	33.75	41.5	49.25	57.0
2018-05-01	85.0	2.82	83.0	84.00	85.0	86.00	87.0
2018-06-01	44.0	2.82	42.0	43.00	44.0	45.00	46.0

Table 1.2: Descriptive statistics for the data entered manually. We are not including the count in this table.

Given that date and time are important components of a time series, Pandas has some neat tricks to help us deal with them. For example, it is possible to use date formats such as that shown above, i.e., 'YYYY-MM-DD'. We can also provide a date in other formats, for instance consider the following code:

We can provide a data in plain natural language, and convert it to a date type.

```
> date = pd.to_datetime("14th of October, 2016")
> print(date)


Timestamp('2016-10-14 00:00:00')
```

We have successfully transformed a date given in natural language to a time stamp. We can also do the opposite; in other words, we can obtain a string of the time stamp to tell

How cool is that?

Table 1.3: Some format directives for the strftime method.

Directive	Meaning
%a	abbreviated weekday name
%A	full weekday name
%b	abbreviated month name
%B	full month name
%c	preferred date and time representation
%d	day of the month (1 to 31)
%D	same as %m/%d/%y
%e	day of the month (1 to 31)
%m	month (1 to 12)
%M	minute
%S	second
%u	weekday as a number (Mon=1 to 7)

us the weekday, month, day, etc. We can do this thanks to the strftime method together with a format directive. Some format directives for strftime are listed in Table 1.3. Let us take a look at extracting the full weekday name (%A), the name of the month (%B) and the weekday number (%u).

strftime lets us obtain a string out of the time stamp.

```
> date.strftime('%A')


'Friday'


> date.strftime('%B')


'October'


> date.strftime('%u')
'5'
```

1.3.1   Pandas Time Series in Action

IN SOME CASES WE MAY need to create time series data from scratch. In this section we are going to explore some of the ways in which Pandas enables us to create and manipulate time series data on top of the commands we have discussed up until this point.

The first thing to take care of is the time ranges required for our data set. For example, we can ask Pandas to create a series of dates with date_range:

We can determine a time range by specifying start and end times.

```
> pd.date_range('2018-05-30', '2018-06-02')

DatetimeIndex(['2018-05-30', '2018-05-31',
               '2018-06-01', '2018-06-02'],
              dtype='datetime64[ns]', freq='D')
```

Note that the output of the command above is an index covering the time range requested with a daily frequency, as shown in the output with freq='D'.

Recall the time offset aliases shown in Table 1.1.

An alternative to the above command is to provide a start date, but instead of giving an end date, we request a number of "periods" to cover with the time series:

Alternatively, we can provide a start time and a number of periods.

```
> pd.date_range('2018-05-30', periods=4)

DatetimeIndex(['2018-05-30', '2018-05-31',
               '2018-06-01', '2018-06-02'],
              dtype='datetime64[ns]', freq='D')
```

This hints to the fact that we can provide a number of periods to cover, as well as the frequency we require. For example, we can request for four monthly periods:

```
> pd.date_range('2018-05-30', periods=4, freq='M')


DatetimeIndex(['2018-05-31', '2018-06-30',
               '2018-07-31', '2018-08-31'],
              dtype='datetime64[ns]', freq='M')
```

Here we provide a start time, a number of periods and the frequency for those periods.

As you can see, all we had to do was specify the monthly frequency with `freq='M'`.

Let us construct a more complicated dataset: For a period of four days starting on June 4, 2018; we take readings for four features called A, B, C and D. In this case we will generate the readings with a random number sampled from a standard normal distribution. Let us create some definitions:

The random number can be obtained with the method `random.randn` from numpy.

```
from numpy.random import randn
idx = pd.date_range('2018-06-04 00:00:00',
                    periods=4)
cols = ['A', 'B', 'C', 'D']
```

We will now create data for four rows and four columns with the help of randn:

`randn(m, n)` creates an array of m rows and n columns.

```
data = randn(len(idx), len(cols))
```

With this information, we now create our dataframe.

```
df = pd.DataFrame(data=data,
                  index=idx, columns=cols)
df.index.name='date'
> print(df)


                  A         B         C         D
date
2018-06-04 -0.025491  1.378149 -1.276321 -0.200059
2018-06-05  0.747168 -0.175478  0.181216 -0.601201
2018-06-06 -0.640565 -0.061296  1.495377 -0.042206
2018-06-07  1.160137 -1.909562  1.300981 -1.653624
```

Since we used random numbers to generate the data, the numbers shown here will differ from those you may obtain on your computer.

A table like the one above is useful to summarise data and it is fit for "human consumption". However, in many applications, it is much better to have a "long format" or "melted" dataset, i.e., instead of arranging the data in a rectangular format as shown above, we would like all the data readings in a single column.

In other words, it is an arrangement that a human will find easy to read and understand.

In ordet to achieve this, we need to repeat the dates and we also require a new column to hold the feature to which each reading corresponds. This can easily be done with Pandas in a single command. The first thing we need to do is reset the index.

This is because we need the date to be part of the new formatted dataset.

```
df.reset_index(inplace=True)
```

In order to melt the dataframe, we will use the melt method that takes the following parameters: A column that will become the new identifier variable with id_vars, the columns to un-pivot are specified with value_vars and finally the names for the variable and value columns with var_name and value_name, respectively:

If no value_vars is provided, all columns are used.

```
> melted = pd.melt(df, id_vars='date',
                   var_name='feature',
                   value_name='reading')
> print(melted)


       date feature   reading
0  2018-06-04       A -0.025491
1  2018-06-05       A  0.747168
2  2018-06-06       A -0.640565
3  2018-06-07       A  1.160137
4  2018-06-04       B  1.378149
5  2018-06-05       B -0.175478
...
14 2018-06-06       D -0.042206
15 2018-06-07       D -1.653624
```

The original columns have become entries in the column called "features" and the values are in the column "reading".

We can now set the index and sort the melted dataset:

```
melted.set_index('date', inplace=True)
melted.sort_index(inplace=True)
```

1.3.2   Time Series Data Manipulation

LET US TAKE A LOOK at some of the manipulations we have described above used in a more real dataset. Remember the time series for Apple Inc. returns discussed in Section 1.2?

Well, we will delve a bit more into that data. The dataset is available at[6] https://doi.org/10.6084/m9.figshare. 6339830.v1 as a comma-separated value file with the name "APPL.CSV". As usual, we need to load some libraries:

[6] Rogel-Salazar, J. (2018a, May). Apple Inc Prices Apr 2017 - Apr 2018. https://doi.org /10.6084/m9.figshare.6339830.v1

```
import numpy as np
import pandas as pd
```

We need to load the dataset with the help of Pandas; in this case, with the read_csv method:

```
appl = pd.read_csv('APPL.CSV')
appl.Date = pd.to_datetime(appl.Date,
    format='%Y-%m-%d')
```

Make sure that you pass on the correct path for the file!

In the first line of the code above, we have used the read_csv method in Pandas to load our dataset. We know that the column called "Date" should be treated as datetime and hence we use to_datetime to make that conversion. Please note that we are also giving Pandas a helping hand by telling it the format in which the date is stored, in this case as year, followed by month and day.

We are using to_datetime to ensure that dates are appropriately typed.

The dataset contains open, high, low and close (i.e., OHLC) prices for Apple Inc. stock between April 2017 and April 2018. We are going to concentrate on the "Close" column, but before we do that, we need to ensure that the dataset is indexed by the time stamps provided by the "Date" column. We can easily do that with the set_index method as follows:

```
appl.set_index('Date', inplace=True)
```

We set up the index with `set_index()`.

We can take a look at the closing prices:

```
> appl['Close'].head(3)

Date
2017-04-25    144.529999
2017-04-26    143.679993
2017-04-27    143.789993
```

We centre our attention on the use of the closing prices.

Notice that although we only requested Python to give us a look at the Close column, the printout obtained added automatically the index given by the dates. The data provided is already ordered; however, in case we are dealing with data where the index is not in the correct order, we can use `sort_index`:

```
df.sort_index(inplace=True)
```

Sorting by the index is done with `sort_index()`.

The daily closing prices can be used to calculate the return at time t for example, this can be expressed as:

$$R_t = \frac{P_t - P_{t-1}}{P_{t-1}}, \tag{1.1}$$

Effectively a percentage change.

where P_t is the price at time t and P_{t-1} is the price at the previous time period. We can apply this calculation in a very easy step in Pandas as follows:

```
appl['pct_change'] = appl.Close.pct_change()
```

We are using `pct_change()` to calculate the returns.

We can see the result of this calculation:

```
> appl['pct_change'].tail(3)


2018-04-23    -0.002896

2018-04-24    -0.013919

2018-04-25     0.004357
```

The percentage change from one day to the next is easily calculated.

Continuous compounding of returns leads to the use of log returns and as mentioned in Section 1.2 they are calculated as follows:

$$r_t = \log(1 + R_t) = \log\left(\frac{P_t}{P_{t-1}}\right) = \log(P_t) - \log(P_{t-1}). \quad (1.2)$$

Continuous compounding of returns leads to the use of log returns.

We need to calculate the logarithm of the price at each time t and then take the difference between time periods. We can certainly do this in Python, and Pandas gives us a helping hand with the diff() method:

```
appl['log_ret'] = np.log(appl.Close).diff()
```

The diff method calculates the difference from one time period to the next.

We can check the result of this operation by looking at the values in the new column we have created:

```
> appl['log_ret'].tail(3)


2018-04-23    -0.002901

2018-04-24    -0.014017

2018-04-25     0.004348
```

We are looking at the last three entries in our table.

This is the data that we show in Figure 1.1, and indeed this is the way we calculated that time series shown in the figure.

It is fairly common to have financial data series like the one we have used above, where the frequency is given by the end of day prices. However, the frequency can be different, for instance given by the minimum upward or downward price movement in the price of a security. This is known as a *tick*. Let us take a look at tick data for the Bitcoin/USD exchange rate. The dataset is available at[7] `https://doi.org/10.6084/m9.figshare.6452831.v1` as a comma-separated value file with the name `bitcoin_usd.csv`, and it contains prices for covering tick data between March 31 and April 3, 2016.

A "tick" is a measure of the minimum upward or downward movement in the price of a security.

[7] Rogel-Salazar, J. (2018b, Jun). Bitcoin/USD exchange rate Mar 31-Apr 3, 2016. https://doi.org /10.6084/m9.figshare.6452831.v1

We can read the data in the usual way. However, if we were to inspect the data, we will notice that the date is stored in a column called `time_start`, and that the format is such that the day is placed first, followed by the month and the year; the time in hours and minutes is provided. We can use this information to create a rule to parse the date:

Pro tip: Inspect your data before importing it, it will save you a few headaches!

```
parser = lambda date: pd.datetime.\
    strptime(date, '%d/%m/%Y %H:%M')
```

We can now provide extra information to Pandas to read the data and parse the dates at the same time:

```
fname = 'bitcoin_usd.csv'
bitcoin = pd.read_csv(fname,
        parse_dates=['time_start'],
        date_parser=parser,
        index_col='time_start')
```

We specify the columns to be parsed and how they shall be parsed!

Notice that we are specifying what columns need to be parsed as dates with parse_dates and how the parsing should be performed with date_parser. We also load the dataset indicating which column is the index. Let us concentrate now on the closing price and the volume:

```
ticks = bitcoin[['close', 'volume']]
```

We are effectively creating a new dataframe called ticks.

The data is roughly on a minute-by-minute frequency. We can use Pandas to resample the data at desired intervals. For instance we can request for the data to be sampled every five minutes and take the first value in the interval:

```
> ticks.resample('5Min').first()


                      close      volume
time_start
2016-03-31 00:00:00   413.27     8.953746
2016-03-31 00:05:00   413.26     0.035157
2016-03-31 00:10:00   413.51    43.640052
...
```

We can resample our data with the help of resample().

We can also ask for the mean, for example

```
> ticks.resample('5Min').mean()


                      close      volume
time_start
2016-03-31 00:00:00   413.270    2.735987
2016-03-31 00:05:00   413.264    2.211749
2016-03-31 00:10:00   414.660   37.919166
...
```

We can specify how the resampling will be performed.

In this way we could get the closing price for the day by resampling by day and requesting the last value:

```
> ticks.resample('D').last()


             close      volume
time_start
2016-03-31   416.02    0.200000

2016-04-01   417.90    52.099684

2016-04-02   420.30    0.850000

...
```

The closing for the new resampling interval can be obtained from the last value.

Now that we know how to resample the data, we can consider creating a new open, high, low and close set of prices for the resampled data. Let us do this for the five-minute bars:

```
> bars = ticks['close'].resample('5Min').ohlc()


                       open     high     low    close
time_start
2016-03-31 00:00:00    413.27   413.27   413.27   413.27

2016-03-31 00:05:00    413.26   413.28   413.25   413.28

2016-03-31 00:10:00    413.51   414.98   413.51   414.98
```

The ohlc() method lets us find the OHLC prices for our new sampled data.

Pandas will take the first and last values in the interval to be the open and close for the bar. Then it will take the max and min as the high and low, respectively. In this way, we start filtering the data. For example, imagine we are interested in the prices between 10 am and 4 pm each day:

```
> filtered = bars.between_time('10:00', '16:00')


                          open     high      low    close
time_start
2016-03-31 10:00:00     416.00   416.00   415.98   415.98
2016-03-31 10:05:00     415.98   415.98   415.97   415.97

...

2016-04-03 15:55:00     421.01   421.02   421.00   421.00
2016-04-03 16:00:00     421.01   421.01   421.01   421.01
```

Notice the use of between_time to filter the data.

We may be interested in looking at the price first thing in the morning — say 8 am:

```
> bars.open.at_time('8:00')


time_start
2016-03-31 08:00:00     416.11
2016-04-01 08:00:00     416.02
2016-04-02 08:00:00     420.69
2016-04-03 08:00:00     418.78
```

In this case we are using the at_time method.

Not only that, we can request the percentage change too by combining the methods we have already discussed:

```
> bars.open.at_time('8:00').pct_change()


time_start
2016-03-31 08:00:00          NaN
2016-04-01 08:00:00    -0.000216
2016-04-02 08:00:00     0.011225
2016-04-03 08:00:00    -0.004540
```

And the methods can be easily combined!

Please note that the first percentage change cannot be calculated as we do not have a comparison data point from the previous interval. In this case, Pandas indicates this by the use of NaN.

If we inspect the data with a bit more detail, we will see that for the last part of April 3, the frequency is such that we have some missing bars when sampling at five-minute intervals:

```
> bars.tail()

                      open   high    low  close
time_start
2016-04-03 23:35:00  420.6  420.6  420.6  420.6
2016-04-03 23:40:00    NaN    NaN    NaN    NaN
2016-04-03 23:45:00    NaN    NaN    NaN    NaN
2016-04-03 23:50:00  420.6  420.6  420.6  420.6
2016-04-03 23:55:00  421.0  421.0  420.6  420.6
```

In many cases we may find that we have some missing data in our datasets...

We can fill in missing data with the help of fillna, which takes a parameter called method. It can be either 'pad' or 'ffill' to propagate last valid observation forward; or instead either 'backfill' or 'bfill' to use the next valid observation to fill the gap. We can also limit the number of consecutive values that should be filled in with limit.

We can fill in missing data with the help of fillna().

For instance we can fill only one gap by propagating the last valid value forward:

```
> bars.fillna(method='ffill', limit=1)


...

2016-04-03 23:35:00   420.60   420.60   420.60   420.60
2016-04-03 23:40:00   420.60   420.60   420.60   420.60
2016-04-03 23:45:00      NaN      NaN      NaN      NaN
2016-04-03 23:50:00   420.60   420.60   420.60   420.60
2016-04-03 23:55:00   421.00   421.00   420.60   420.60
```

Here we have filled the missing data by bringing the last value forward and limitting the operation to one time period.

Let us fill both gaps and create a new dataframe:

```
filledbars = bars.fillna(method='ffill')
```

For the volume it would make sense to consider the sum of all the securities traded in the five-minute interval:

```
volume = ticks.volume.resample('5Min').sum()
vol = volume.fillna(0.)
```

A plot of the open, high, low and close prices for the five-minute bars, together with the corresponding volume for the 3rd of April between 9 am and 11.59 pm is shown in Figure 1.5 and can be created as follows:

```
filledbars['2016-04-03'].between_time('9:00',\
    '23:59') .plot(\
    color=['gray','gray','gray','k'],
    style=['-','--','-.','-+'])

vol['2016-04-03'].between_time('9:30','23:59')\
    .plot(secondary_y=True, style='k-o')
```

The plotting commands that we know and love are available to the Pandas series and dataframes too.

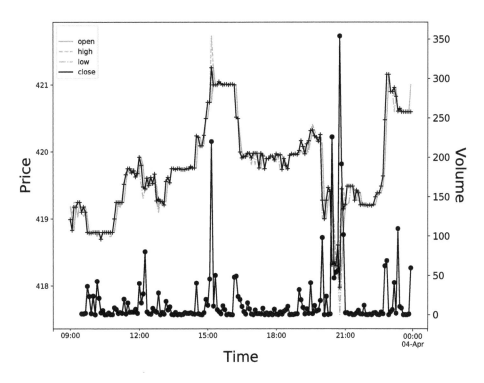

Figure 1.5: Open, high, low and close prices for the exchange rate of bitcoin/USD.

1.4   Modelling Time Series Data

WE KNOW THAT THERE IS no such a thing as a perfect model, just good enough ones. With that in mind, we can start thinking about the assumptions we can make around data in a time series. We would like to start with a simple model, and perhaps one of the first assumptions we can make is that there is no structure in the time series. In other words, we have a situation where each and every observation is in effect an independent random variate.

There is no such thing as a perfect model... just good enough ones.

A good example of this would be white noise. In this case when facing this type of signal the best we can do is simply predict the mean value of the dataset.

White noise is whose intensity is the same at all frequencies within a given band.

Let us create some white noise in Python with the help of numpy:

```
import numpy as np
import pandas as pd


white = 2*np.random.random(size=2048)-1
white = pd.Series(white)
```

In the code above, we are using the random method in numpy.random to draw samples from a uniform distribution. We would like our samples to be drawn from $Unif[a, b)$ with $a = -1$ and $b = 1$ so that we have white noise with mean zero. A plot for one such time series is shown in Figure 1.6.

Hence the use of $(b - a)(sample) + a$.

Remember that we are assuming that each observation is independent from the other. If there is correlation among the values of a given variable, we say that the variable is *autocorrelated*. For a repeatable (random) process X, let X_t be the realisation of the process at time t; also let the process have mean μ_t and variance σ_t^2. The autocorrelation $R(s, t)$ between times t and s is given by:

We are keeping it simple.

$$R(s, t) = \frac{E[(X_t - \mu_t)(X_s - \mu_s)]}{\sigma_t \sigma_s},$$ (1.3)

Autocorrelation.

where $E[\cdot]$ is the expectation value. Autocorrelation provides us with a measure of the degree of similarity

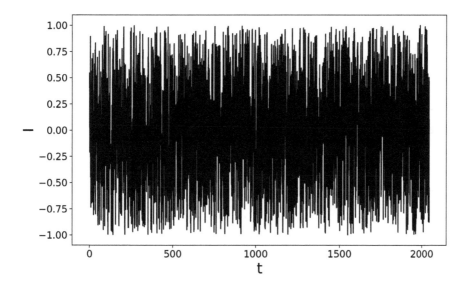

Figure 1.6: White noise with zero mean, constant variance, and zero correlation.

between the values of a time series and a lagged or shifted version of that same series. Notice that we can recover the usual correlation definition for the case where X_t and X_s are two random variables not drawn from the same process at lagged times.

Therefore, as with correlation, the values returned by an autocorrelation calculation lie between -1 and 1. It is also important to mention that autocorrelation gives us information about the existence of linear relationships. Even when the autocorrelation measure is close to zero, there may be a nonlinear relationship between the values of a variable and a lagged version of itself.

Autocorrelation values lie between -1 and 1.

Let us calculate the autocorrelation for our generated white noise:

```
> for lag in range(1,5):

    print("Autocorrelation at lag={0} is {1}".\

        format(lag,  white.autocorr(lag)))


Autocorrelation at lag=1 is 0.027756062237309434

Autocorrelation at lag=2 is 0.017698046805029784

Autocorrelation at lag=3 is -0.016764938190346888

Autocorrelation at lag=4 is -0.03636909301996918
```

Autocorrelation can be calculated with autocorr.

The values returned by autocorr are the same as those we would obtain if we calculated the correlation of the time series with a shifted version of itself. Take a look:

```
> print(white.corr(white.shift(1)))


0.027756062237309434
```

As we can see the result is the same.

Here shift(n) translates the series by n periods, in this case 1, enabling us to calculate the autocorrelation value.

Finally, predicting (or calculating) the mean value can be readily done as follows:

```
> print(white.mean())

-0.019678911755368275
```

1.4.1   Regression… (Not) a Good Idea?

WE HAVE SEEN HOW TO deal with processes that have no inherent structure, and hence the predictions we can make are quite straightforward. Let us take a step forward and consider more interesting processes. If we were to compare the time series for the closing prices of the Apple stock shown in Figure 1.3 with the white noise we generated for Figure 1.6, we can clearly see that there is indeed more structure in the price data: There are peaks and troughs and we can even notice an upward trend.

And boring ones, for that matter.

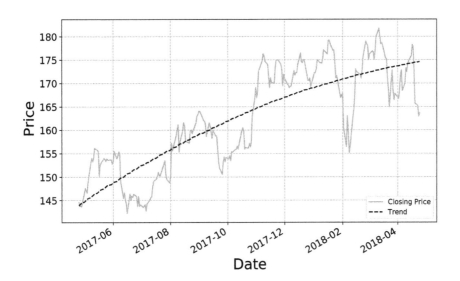

Figure 1.7: Closing prices for Apple Inc. for a year since April 2017 and a trend line provided by a multivariate regression.

We are familiar with some techniques such as multivariate regression, and it may be conceivable to apply these techniques to the data we have. At the very least, it may provide us with an idea of the trend in the time series. Ignoring seasonal variation and random noise, we can fit a polynomial model to the data as show in Figure 1.7. We can see the general trend in the set. But is this really a suitable model?

Regression may provide us with an idea of the trend.

It is hard to believe that the closing price of the Apple
stock is simply a function of the calendar date!! It is more
likely that the prices are a function of their own history,
and therefore we require methods that are able to capture
precisely this assumed dependency, and given the results
decide whether the model is fit for purpose. We will tackle
some models to achieve this in the rest of this chapter.

As well as market forces, product
announcements, etc.

1.4.2   Moving Averages and Exponential Smoothing

WE ARE INTERESTED IN FINDING a model that is able
to forecast the next value in our time series data. In the
previous section we have seen how we can make some
assumptions about the data we have and use that to our
advantage. In the example with the Apple Inc. prices, we
have been able to fit a regression model to the data, but
surely we can do better than that.

We are interested in creating a
forecast.

What about if we are able to forecast the future value based
on the past values of the time series? For example, we may
be able to take the average of the last n observations as
the forecast for the next time period. This methodology is
known as *moving averages*. For example, in the case where
$n = 3$, the smoothened value at time t, s_t, will be given by:

In moving averages, the forecast is
provided by the simple mean over
a period of time.

An alternative name for moving
averages is rolling averages.

$$s_t = \frac{x_{t-2} + x_{t-1} + x_t}{3}. \tag{1.4}$$

We can also consider giving greater importance to more
recent past values than older ones. It sounds plausible,
right? Well, this is actually what *exponential smoothing*

Exponential smoothing works by
weighting past observations.

enables us to do. The weighting is performed via constant values called *smoothing constants*. The simplest method is appropriately called *simple exponential smoothing* (SES) and it uses one smoothing constant, α.

In SES, we start by setting s_0 to x_0 and subsequent periods at time t are given by:

$$s_t = \alpha x_t + (1 - \alpha)s_{t-1}, \qquad (1.5)$$

The simple exponential smoothing method.

with $0 \leq \alpha \leq 1$. The smoothing is a function of α; we have a quick smoothing when α is close to 1, and a slow one when it is close to 0. We choose the value of α such that the mean of the squared errors (MSE) is minimised.

We can calculate moving averages and exponential smoothing on a time series with Pandas. For moving averages, we simply use the `rolling` method for Pandas dataframes. In the case of the Apple Inc. closing prices we have been investigating, we can write the following:

We can use Pandas to calculate moving averages and exponential smoothing.

```
appl['MA3']=appl['Close'].rolling(window=3).mean()
```

where we have provided the size of the moving window and indicated that the aggregation of the data will be the mean of the values.

For exponential smoothing, Pandas provides the `ewm` method. We simply pass the parameter α as follows:

EWM stands for Exponential Weighted Methods.

```
alpha=0.6
appl['EWMA']=apple['Close'].ewm(alpha=alpha).mean()
```

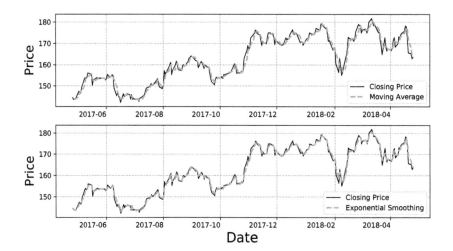

Figure 1.8: Moving averages (upper panel) and exponential smoothing (lower panel) applied to the closing prices for Apple Inc.

The method also accepts other definitions such as the centre of mass, the span or the half-life. In Table 1.4 we list the relationship between α and these alternative parameters.

Table 1.4: Parameters specifying the decay applied to an exponential smoothing calculation with ewm.

EWM parameter	Definition
Centre of Mass (*com*)	$\alpha = \frac{1}{1+com}$, for $com \geq 0$
Span	$\alpha = \frac{2}{1+span}$, for $span \geq 1$
Half-life	$\alpha = 1 - \exp\left[\frac{\log(0.5)}{halflife}\right]$, for $halflife > 0$

In Figure 1.8 we can see the result of using moving averages and exponential smoothing compared to the closing prices for Apple Inc.

1.4.3 Stationarity and Seasonality

WE HAVE BEEN CONSIDERING SOME of the assumptions we can make on our data in order to come up with models that enable us to understand the underlying phenomena and create predictions. One such common assumption is that our time series is stationary.

A stationary time series is one where its mean, variance and autocorrelation do not change over time.

In this context, we say that a process is stationary if its mean, variance and autocorrelation do not change over time. As you can imagine, stationarity can be defined in precise mathematical terms, but a practical way of remembering what we are talking about is effectively a flat-looking series, one where there is no trend and has constant variance over time and without periodic fluctuations or seasonality.

Effectively a flat-looking series.

Before we continue our discussion about stationarity, let us take a look at seasonality. This can be understood as a cycle that repeats over time, such as monthly, or yearly. This repeating cycle may interfere with the signal we intend to forecast, while at the same time may provide some insights into what is happening in our data.

Or any other time interval.

Understanding the seasonality in our data can improve our modeling as it enables us to create a clearer signal. In other words, if we are able to identify the seasonal component in our series, we may be able to extract it out leaving us with a component which we understand (the seasonal part) plus a clearer relationship between the variables at hand. When we remove the seasonal component from a time series, we end up with a so-called seasonal stationary series.

A time series with a clear seasonal component is said to be non-stationary.

There are many ways in which we can take a look at the seasonality in a time series. In this case, let us take a look at using the Fast Fourier Transform (FFT) to convert the time-dependent data into the *frequency domain*. This will enable us to analyse if any predominant frequencies exist. In other words, we can check if there is any periodicity on the data. We will not cover the intricate details of the mathematics behind the FFT, but a recommended reading is the excellent *Numerical Recipes*[8] book.

Let us take a look at the sunspot data we plotted in Figure 1.2. In that figure we have monthly observations for the sun activity. In the analysis below we will resample the data into yearly observations. The data can be found[9] at `https://doi.org/10.6084/m9.figshare.6728255.v1` as a comma-separated value file with the name "`sunspots_month.CSV`". After loading the usual modules such as Pandas, we can read the data as follows:

```
sun = pd.read_csv('sunspots_month.csv')
sun.Year = pd.to_datetime(sun.Year,
    format='%Y-%m-%d')
sun.set_index('Year', inplace=True)
```

We are specifying the format in which the dates should be parsed. We also indicate which column is the index in our dataset.

As we mentioned before, we have monthly data and we would like to take a yearly view. The first thing we are going to do is obtain a yearly average:

[8] Press, W., S. Teukolsky, W. Vetterling, and B. Flannery (2007). *Numerical Recipes 3rd Edition: The Art of Scientific Computing.* Cambridge University Press

[9] Rogel-Salazar, J. (2018d, Jul). Sunspots - Monthly Activity since 1749. https://doi.org /10.6084/m9.figshare.6728255.v1

While loading the data, we can specify the format for reading the date.

```
sun_year = sun.resample('Y').mean()
```

We are resampling the data to a yearly frequency.

Let us now load the FFT pack from `scipy`:

```
from scipy import fftpack
```

Fast Fourier transform capabilities are part of `fftpack` in scipy.

Given the signal of the yearly sunspot activity we can calculate its Fourier transform. We also calculate a normalisation constant n:

```
Y=fftpack.fft(sun_year['Value'])
n=int(len(Y)/2)
```

We calculate the FFT of the signal and a normalisation constant.

With this information we can create an array to hold the frequencies in the signal, with the period being the inverse frequency:

```
freq=np.array(range(n))/(2*n)
period=1./freq
```

With this information we can obtain the period.

We can now calculate the power spectrum of the signal as follows:

```
power=abs(Y[1:n])**2
```

And finally the power spectrum of the signal.

A plot of the power spectrum versus the period is shown in Figure 1.9 where we can see that the sunspot activity data is periodic, and that the sunspots occur with a maximum in activity approximately every 11 years. Cool!

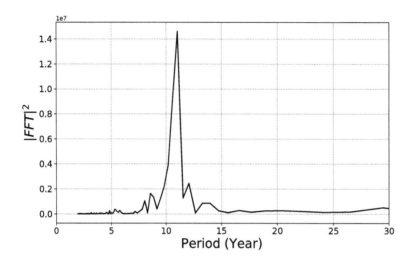

Figure 1.9: Analysis of the power spectrum of the sunspots data. We can see that a maximum in activity occurs approximately every 11 years.

1.4.4   Determining Stationarity

WE HAVE SEEN THAT THERE is seasonality in our sunspot data and so, it is a non-stationary time series. In other cases we may need to check that the mean and variance are constant and the autocorrelation is time-independent. We can do some of these checks by plotting rolling statistics to see if the moving average and/or moving variance vary with time.

Rolling statistics can help us determine stationarity.

Another method is the Dickey-Fuller test which is a statistical test for checking stationarity. In this case the null hypothesis is that the time series is nonstationary based on the results of a test statistic, and critical values for different confidence levels. If the test statistic is below the critical value, we can reject the null hypothesis and say that the series is stationary.

The Dickey-Fuller tests enables us to check for stationarity too.

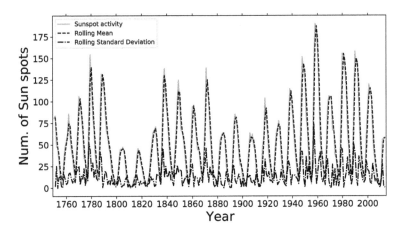

Let us see what this means for our monthly sunspot activity data. We can calculate rolling statistics for the mean and variance:

Figure 1.10: Sunspot activity and rolling statistics for the average and the standard deviation.

```
rolling_mean = sun_year['Value'].rolling(2).mean()
rolling_std = sun_year['Value'].rolling(2).std()
```

Rolling statistics for a window of 2 years.

In Figure 1.10 we can see the rolling statistics for the sunspot activity. The variation on the average is larger than that on the standard deviation, but they do not seem to be increasing or reducing with time.

Let us take a look at the Dickey-Fuller test. In this case we are going to use the adfuller method in statsmodels time series analysis module tsa.stattools:

The Dickey-Fuller test can be evaluated with the help of adfuller method in statsmodels.

```
from statsmodels.tsa.stattools import adfuller
df_test = adfuller(sun_year['Value'],autolag='AIC')
```

We can now take a look at the results of the Dickey-Fuller
test with the following function:

```python
def isstationary(df_test):
  stationary=[]
  print('Test Statistic is {0}'.format(df_test[0]))
  print('p-value is {0}'.format(df_test[1]))
  print('No. lags used = {0}'.format(df_test[2]))
  print('No. observations used = {0}'.\
      format(df_test[3]))
  for key, value in df_test[4].items():
      print('Critical Value ({0}) = {1}'.\
          format(key, value))
      if df_test[0]<=value:
          stationary.append(True)
      else:
          stationary.append(False)
  return all(stationary)
```

The Dickey-Fuller test
implementation returns 4 items
including the test statistic, the
p-value, the lags used and the
critical values.

Let us look at the results:

```
> isstationary(df_test)

Test Statistic is -2.4708472868362916
p-value is 0.12272956184228762
No. lags used = 8
No. observations used = 256
Critical Value (1%) = -3.4561550092339512
Critical Value (10%) = -2.5728222369384763
Critical Value (5%) = -2.8728972266578676
False
```

In this case we see that the Dickey-
Fuller test applied to the sunspots
data supports the null hypothesis.

As we can see, we cannot reject the null hypothesis and the yearly data for the sunspot activity is therefore non-stationary.

Extracting the trend and seasonality out of the time series data provides us with better ways to understand the process at hand. A useful technique for this is to decompose the time series into those components that are amenable to be described by a model. Given a time series Y_t, a naïve additive model decomposes the signal as follows:

$$Y_t = T_t + S_t + e_t, \tag{1.6}$$

Systematic components are those that can be modelled.

Additive decomposition.

where T_t is the trend, S_t is the seasonality and e_t corresponds to the residuals or random variation in the series. An alternative to this decomposition is the so-called multiplicative model:

$$Y_t = (T_t)(S_t)(e_t). \tag{1.7}$$

Multiplicative decomposition.

We can use `seasonal_decompose` from `statmodels` to decompose the signal using moving averages.

Since we have seen that we have a seasonality of around 11 years, we will use this information to decompose our time series:

```
import statsmodels.api as sm
dec_sunspots = sm.tsa.seasonal_decompose(sun_year,\
    model='additive', freq=11)
```

`seasonal_decompose` lets us decompose a time series into its systematic and non-systematic components.

We can use a multiplicative method by passing on the parameter `model='multiplicative'`. The result of the

decomposition is an object that has a plotting method. We
can look at the result of the decomposition by typing
dec_sunspots.plot() and the output can be seen in Figure
1.11 where we have plots for the trend, seasonality and the
residuals.

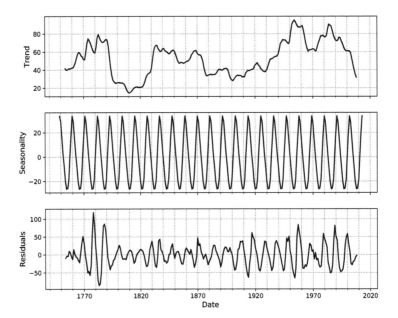

Figure 1.11: Trend, seasonality
and residual components for the
sunspot dataset.

Let us apply the Dickey-Fuller test to the bitcoin tick data
defined on page 26. Let us resample the data on 15-minute
intervals and take the average:

```
closing_bitcoin=ticks['close'].\
    resample('15Min').mean()
df_test_bitcoin = adfuller(closing_bitcoin,\
    autolag='AIC')
```

The bitcoin data is non-stationary.

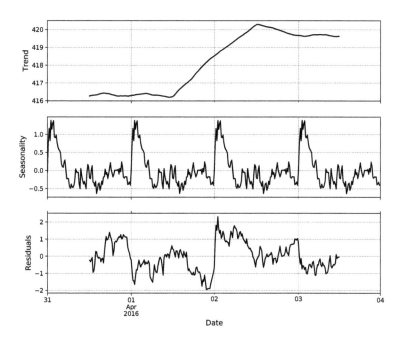

Figure 1.12: Trend, seasonality and residual components for the bitcoin dataset.

```
> isstationary(df_test_bitcoin)

Test Statistic is -1.4531293932585607

p-value is 0.5565571771135377

No. lags used = 10

No. observations used = 373

Critical Value (1%) = -3.448003816652923

Critical Value (5%) = -2.86931999731073

Critical Value (10%) = -2.5709145866785503

False
```

We can see the decomposition in Figure 1.12.

1.4.5   Autoregression to the Rescue

SO FAR, WE HAVE BEEN doing O.K. with the time series we
have seen. However, we know that simply using a linear or
polynomial fit to the data is not good enough. Furthermore,
we cannot ignore the seasonal variation and the random
noise that makes up the signal.

We have seen that using a linear or
polynomial fit is not good for time
series.

When we discussed the idea of moving averages, we
considered that a better approach was to see if the next
value in the series can be predicted as some function of its
previous values. A way to achieve this is **autoregression**. So,
we are therefore interested in building a regression model of
the current value fitted on one (or more) previous values
called *lagged values*. This sounds great, but how many
lagged values do we need?

Autoregression is exactly what it
sounds like: A regression on the
dataset itself.

Well, we can take a look at the time series and check how
much information there is in the previous values, helping
us with our prediction. We can do this with the help of the
autocorrelation function (ACF) we defined in Equation (1.3).
Similarly, we can look at the partial autocorrelation function
(PACF) which controls the values of the time series at all
shorter lags, unlike the autocorrelation.

The correlation function will test whether adjacent
observations are autocorrelated; in other words, it will help
us determine if there are correlations between observations
1 and 2, 2 and 3, ... $n - 1$ and n. Similarly, it will test at other
lags. For instance, the autocorrelation at lag 4 tests whether
observations 1 and 5, 2 and 6,... are correlated.

This is known as "lag-one
autocorrelation".

In general, we should test for autocorrelation at lags 1 to $n/4$, where n is the total number of observations in the analysis. Estimates at longer lags have been shown to be statistically unreliable[10].

We can take a look at the autocorrelation and partial autocorrelation for the sunspot dataset with the following code:

[10] Box, G. and G. Jenkins (1976). *Time series analysis: forecasting and control.* Holden-Day series in time series analysis and digital processing. Holden-Day

```
sm.graphics.tsa.plot_acf(sun_year, lags=40)
sm.graphics.tsa.plot_pacf(sun_year, lags=40)
```

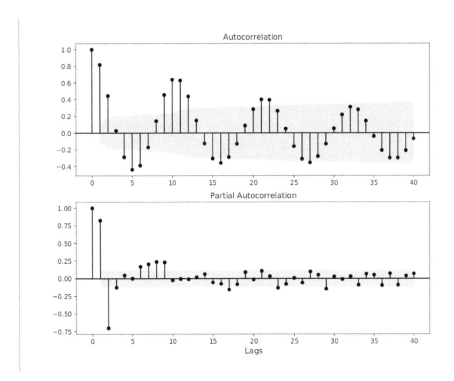

Figure 1.13 shows the result of the code above. We can see in the upper panel that the autocorrelation shows a periodic structure, reflecting the seasonality in the time series.

Figure 1.13: Autocorrelation and partial autocorrelation for the sunspot dataset.

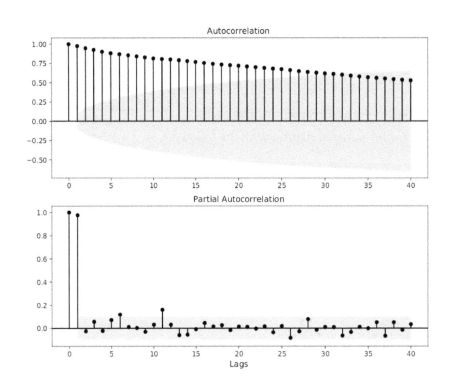

Figure 1.14: Autocorrelation and partial autocorrelation for the bitcoin dataset.

A similar computation can be carried out for the bitcoin dataset. The result can be seen in Figure 1.14. As we can see in the upper panel, the correlation fades slowly as we take longer and longer lagged values.

It stands to reason that if value 0 is correlated with value 1, and value 1 is correlated with 2, it follows that 0 must be correlated with 2. This is why we need the partial autocorrelation, as it provides us with information about the relationship between an observation with observations at prior time steps, but with the crucial difference that the intervening observations are removed.

Partial autocorrelation tells us about the relationship of observations with earlier ones, but without the intervening observations.

In the examples of the sunspot and bitcoin datasets, we can see from the lower panels of the correlograms in Figures 1.13 and 1.14 that only the most recent values are really useful in building an autoregression model.

A correlogram is a plot showing the correlation statistics.

A PACF correlogram with a large spike at one lag that decreases after a few lags usually indicates that there is a moving average term in the series. In this case, the autocorrelation function will help us determine the order of the moving average term. If instead we have a large spike at one lag followed by a damped oscillating correlogram, then we have a higher order moving average term. This is the picture we get from the lower panel of Figure 1.13 for the sunspot data.

A large spike followed by damped oscillations indicates a higher order moving average term.

In the case of the correlogram shown in the lower panel of Figure 1.14, we have a few important correlations in the first few lags that die out quite quickly. In this case we can interpret this as having a time series with an autoregressive term. We can determine the order of this autoregressive term from the spikes in the correlogram. We will discuss autoregressive models in the following section.

A spike on the first lags followed by not very important ones suggests the presence of an autoregressive term.

1.5 *Autoregressive Models*

AN AUTOREGRESSIVE (AR) MODEL IS a representation of a type of random process where the future values of the series are based on weighted combinations of past values. As such, an AR(1) is a first-order process in which the current value is based only on the immediately previous value:

$$Y_t = \beta_0 + \beta_1 Y_{t-1} + \epsilon_t. \qquad (1.8)$$

AR(1) model.

An AR(2) process,

$$Y_t = \beta_0 + \beta_1 Y_{t-1} + \beta_2 Y_{t-2} + \epsilon_t, \qquad (1.9)$$

AR(2) model.

determines the current value based on the previous two values, and so on.

It is possible to use autoregression and moving averages in combination to describe various time series. This methodology is usually called **autoregressive moving average** (ARMA) modelling. In ARMA modelling we use two expressions to describe the time series, one for the moving average and the other one for the autoregression. ARMA(p, q) denotes a model with autoregression of order p and moving average of order q.

ARMA - Autoregressive Moving Average.

A further generalisation of an ARMA model is the so-called **autoregressive integrated moving average** or ARIMA model. The AR and MA parts of the acronym follow the discussion above. The integrated (or "I") part is perhaps less clear, but effectively it means that the time series has been rendered stationary by taking differences. In other words, instead of looking at the observation Y_1 we are interested in $Y_1 - Y_0$.

ARIMA - Autoregressive Integrated Moving Average.

An ARIMA(p, d, q) model puts together all the techniques we have discussed in this chapter and is specified by three parameters: $p, d,$ and q, where:

- p: Denotes the order of the autoregression

- d: Denotes the number of difference levels

- q: Denotes the order of of moving average

The meaning of the parameters in an ARIMA(p,d,q) model.

We have some commonly used models, such as:

- ARIMA$(0,0,0)$ is simply predicting the mean of the overall time series. In other words, there is no structure!

- ARIMA$(0,1,0)$ works out the differences (not the raw values) and predicts the next one without autoregression or smoothing. This is effectively a random walk!

Some common ARIMA models.

Let us take a look at applying ARMA and ARIMA models to the sunspot dataset. For instance we can apply an ARMA$(9,0)$ model as follows:

```
arma_sun = sm.tsa.ARMA(sun_year, (9, 0)).fit()
print(arma_sun.params)

const          50.466706
ar.L1.Value     1.161912
ar.L2.Value    -0.387975
ar.L3.Value    -0.179743
ar.L4.Value     0.148018
ar.L5.Value    -0.098705
ar.L6.Value     0.036090
ar.L7.Value     0.014294
ar.L8.Value    -0.055000
ar.L9.Value     0.226996
```

The results of applying an ARMA$(9,0)$ model to the sunspot dataset.

The best model can be found by changing the parameters p and q of the model such that we minimise any of the various information criteria such as the Akaike (AIC), the Bayesian (BIC) or the Hannan-Quinn (HQIC) information criterion.

See Appendix A for more details about these information criteria.

```
print("AIC: ", arma_sun.aic)
print("BIC: ", arma_sun.bic)
print("HQIC:", arma_sun.hqic)


AIC:  2230.4154805952835
BIC:  2269.792508681132
HQIC: 2246.236568447941
```

Evaluation of the AIC, BIC and HQIC information criteria.

We can also apply an ARIMA model, in this case an ARIMA$(9,1,0)$:

```
arima_mod= ARIMA(sun_year, order=(9,1,0)).fit()
> print(arima_mod.summary())


                  ARIMA Model Results

==================================================
Dep. Variable: D.Value   No. Observations:      264
Model:  ARIMA(9, 1, 0)   Log Likelihood    -1103.368
Method:        css-mle   S.D. of innovations 15.716
...
AIC             2228.736
BIC             2268.072
HQIC            2244.542

==================================================
```

An abridged version of the summary provided by the ARIMA$(9,1,0)$ model applied to the sunspot dataset.

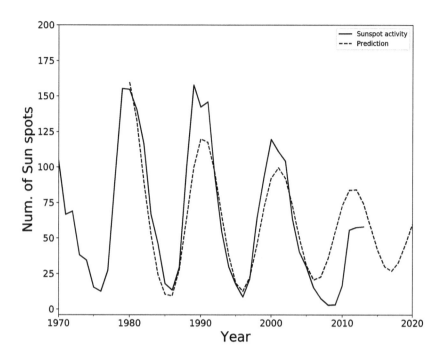

Figure 1.15: Prediction for the sunspot activity using an ARMA$(9,0)$ model.

Finally, it is important to note that in the ideal scenario we would carry out the analysis on a training dataset to develop a predictive model to be tested against a testing set. Nonetheless, let us take a look at the predictions we could draw, in this case for the ARMA model above:

```
predict_sunspots = arma_sun.predict('1980',\
    '2050', dynamic=True)
```

We can run predictions from the models with the predict method for each of them.

The result can be seen in Figure 1.15 where we can compare the actual values of the sunspot activity against the predictions made by the model for the years between 1980 and 2020. Not bad for a model that has not been curated!!

1.6   Summary

In this chapter we addressed some important aspects of dealing with time series data and no Jackalope data scientist must be without this knowledge. We have seen that time series are different from other data sets due to the time component. We saw some relevant examples such as the prices of the Apple Ltd. stock, sunspot activity since the mid-1700s and even the exchange rate of bitcoins to US dollars.

We were able to deal with these various datasets thanks to Python modules such as Pandas and statsmodels. We saw how Pandas enables us to index our dataframes with time and looked at appropriate transformations that Pandas enables us to carry out such as resampling, slicing and dicing, filtering, aggregating and plotting.

In terms of modelling time series, we covered how moving averages and exponential smoothing let us get a first approach at forecasting future values of the series based on previous observations. We discussed the concepts of seasonality and stationarity in a time series. We applied decomposition to our datasets and finally we discussed how autoregression can be used to model time series, combining the topics discussed in this chapter.

2

Speaking Naturally: Text and Natural Language Processing

THERE ARE MANY KINDS OF language: We speak with our body language, need to "mind our language" in certain situations, we learn a foreign language to ask for a *pain au chocolat* or *una cerveza* and we need language to understand a French lecture on Sheep-Aircraft. Indeed we are also using the Python programming language to create analytics workflows and train machine learning models. We speak the "language of love", and avoid being confusing by speaking in "plain language". What about *natural language*? Have you heard of it? What is it and when do we use it?

Let us take a step back: The common theme among the expressions we listed above is communication. In other words, the different expressions listed use the word *language* to emphasise the fact that we communicate with other humans in a variety of ways. Natural language is one of those forms of communication. The term refers to the use of

Presented by *le célèbre* Jean-Brian Zatapathique of course (Baa-aa, baa-aa).

There are all kinds of languages, including natural language.

Natural language has evolved naturally in humans through continued use.

any language that has evolved naturally in humans through continued use, repetition and adaptation.

English, Spanish, Japanese and Nahuatl are some examples of natural languages. In contrast, languages like Python, C++, Scala or Java, as well as Esperanto, Klingon, Elvish or Dothraki are constructed languages. As you can imagine, natural language can take different forms such as speech, writing or even singing. In any case, communicating in a natural (or constructed) language is a useful, if complex, task. You may not notice it all the time, but imagine interviewing a man who speaks entirely in anagrams. The efforts to make sense out of the conversation would bring things into focus.

These are some examples of natural languages.

Be ot or bot ne ot, tath is the nestquoi!

Now, imagine that in your intergalactic travels you encounter a rebel fleet where R2-D2 and C-3PO are on board and you have an important message for Princess Leia Organa. Naturally, you would like to communicate with them in natural language not in beep-bops. You tell them your message and they try to make sense of it, reacting rapidly with excited "Beep-bee-bee-boop-bee-doo-weep" and "You are quite clever you know... for a human being". Off they go to deliver the important information. Not bad... remember, 3PO alone is fluent in over six million forms of communication!

See what I did there!

The tasks achieved by the loyal androids to take natural language as input, and make sense out of it are referred to as *natural language processing*. Natural language processing (NLP) is an area of computer science and artificial

Natural language processing is concerned with the interactions between human language and computers.

intelligence concerned with the interactions between human (natural) languages and computers. In particular, the term refers to the programming of computers for processing and analysing large amounts of natural language data. Some typical challenges in the area go from natural language understanding to speech recognition and even language generation.

As you can imagine, in order for us to be able to parse, analyse and understand natural language with the aid of computers, we need to get hold of suitable data. A rich and readily available source of information—both for natural language and other data—is the web. In this chapter we will see how to extract data from the web using Beautiful Soup and cover some useful ways to process text data including the use of regular expressions and tokenisation. We will then use topic modelling, an unsupervised machine learning task, to start making sense of natural language.

Actually this is true not only for natural language processing.

2.1   Pages and Pages: Accessing Data from the Web

I AM SURE YOU HAVE heard the self-evident truism that *data is everywhere*. In the best of cases, it is indeed there, and it can be used immediately. Unfortunately, in more cases than not, the data that you want/need/desire is not in the appropriate format, let alone readily available to you.

Remember that seeing the information is not the same as accessing it...

A typical situation is for useful data to be displayed in webpages, but not be downloadable in a useful format. In other words, being able to see the data is not the same as accessing it. This is indeed a goal of many organisations interested in open data. Open data refers to data available to everyone and which can be freely used, re-used and redistributed, subject only, at most, to the requirement to attribute and share alike. One of the tenets of open data is that the data must be available as a whole and at no more than a reasonable reproduction cost, preferably accessed via the web in a convenient and modifiable form.

Open data is data available to everyone.

In an ideal scenario, data can be obtained with appropriate *Application Programming Interfaces* (APIs) to make requests for example via the HTTP protocol. In these cases you can use the Requests module[1] in Python for example. While the efforts of the open data movement are slowly but surely making data accessible to all, it is often the case that we still need to obtain it in a more indirect way such as scraping the contents of a webpage: We could manually copy and paste the data but that is as interesting as watching paint dry. Instead, we automate the process to do this work programmatically. There are some great modules such as Scrapy[2] or Beautiful Soup[3] to do this work. In this case we will obtain some data with the help of Beautiful Soup.

[1] Reitz, K. Requests - http for humans. http://docs.python-requests.org/en/master/

Web scraping extracts or "scrapes" data from a web page.

[2] Scrapy. https://scrapy.org
[3] Beautiful Soup. https://www.crummy.com/software/BeautifulSoup/

Given the semi-structured nature of the data encountered in the web, it is necessary for us to determine what information is relevant to be scraped and whether it requires multiple pages to be parsed. Typically, we will need to parse HTML code standard for creating webpages and web applications. The elements that describe the page are defined by *tags* using angle brackets and they may look like this: `<body>...</body>`. In this case we have a body tag

HTML stands for Hypertext Markup Language.

and the text between <body> and </body> corresponds to the visible content of the page.

Each tag has opening and closing versions; the closing tag always precedes the element with a forward slash (/). There are many other tags such as those shown in Table 2.1.

Table 2.1: Common HTML tags.

Tag	Description
html	HTML document
head	Information used by search engines and browsers.
title	The title of the document
body	The content of the web page
h1, h2,...	Headers: h1 is the main header, then h2, etc.
p	Paragraph
div	Block of content
a	Link
ol	Ordered list
ul	Unordered list
il	List item inside an ol or ul tag
table	Table
tr	Table row
th	Table header
td	Table data cell

Once we have determined the data that we are looking for, we need to:

1. Read the HTML page

2. Parse the raw HTML string into a nicer more readable format

3. Extract the information we are interested in

Beware old Jedis warning you that "These are not be the datasets you are looking for"...

Steps for web scraping the data we are interested in.

4. Process our data, i.e., clean it, make any appropriate transformations, etc.

5. Store, print, save, and take some actions with the data at hand

Let us take a look at a very small, simple HTML document:

```
<!DOCTYPE html>
  <html>
    <head>
      <title>Page Title</title>
    </head>

    <body>
      <h1>My First Heading</h1>
      <p>My first paragraph.</p>
    </body>
  </html>
```

A very simple HTML document with a title, a headline and a paragraph marked with appropriate tags.

If you save that piece of code in a text file and open it in a browser, it will look similar to the screenshot shown in Figure 2.1. We can see at the top of the page the tab with the page title, and then the main header followed by a paragraph. It is not the most exciting website, but it provides us with a flavour of what is to follow.

One of the main things we need to take into account when scraping the web for data are the terms and conditions of the site. In some cases website owners do not permit automated systems or software to extract data. The methods shown here are in no way an encouragement to abuse terms

Make sure you check the sites' terms and conditions.

My First Heading

My first paragraph.

Figure 2.1: A very simple webpage.

and conditions placed by websites. Please make sure that you:

- Respect the Terms of Service (ToS)

- Use an API if one is provided, instead of scraping data

- Respect the rules of *robots.txt*

- If ToS or robots.txt prevents you from crawling or scraping, ask a written permission to the owner of the site, prior to doing anything else

- Do not republish your crawled or scraped data or any derivative dataset without verifying the license of the data, or without obtaining written permission from the copyright holder

Robots.txt is a text file that instructs web robots (such as search engines) how to crawl pages on a website.

The other thing that you need to consider when obtaining data from webpages is the fact that the sites you are getting the data from may change from time to time. The design may be different, the position of the data in the page will move, the tags may have different metadata, there may be pagination to consider, or simply the page may vanish into thin air. You will have to be prepared to change your code accordingly if you are to obtain your data programmatically. Consider yourself forewarned.

And will definitely change!

2.1.1   Beautiful Soup in Action

NOW THAT WE HAVE A better understanding of the task
we need to accomplish, let us take a look at obtaining some
data from a website. In order to make the task reproducible,
I have created a webpage and made it available off-line.
The page can be found at[4] `https://doi.org/10.6084/`
`m9.figshare.7053392.v4` as an HTML document. For the
purposes of this book, we will work with a local copy of the
page, but you can get content live from the web too. I will
point out the way to do this as we go along.

[4] Rogel-Salazar, J. (2018c, Sep).
Iris Webpage. https://doi.org
/10.6084/m9.figshare.7053392.v4

Iris Flower Dataset

This is one of the best known datasets in data science and it is fair to say it has become a canonical example in the
training of new data scientists.

The data set contains 50 instances of 3 classes of 50 iris plants. One of the classes is linearly separable from the
other 2, and these in turn are not linearly separable from each other.

Attribute Information:

1. sepal length in cm
2. sepal width in cm
3. petal length in cm
4. petal width in cm
5. class: -- 3 values: Iris Setosa, Iris Versicolour, Iris Virginica

We have used this dataset in Chapter 3 of *Data Science and Analytics with Python* [1].

Dataset Order	Sepal length	Sepal width	Petal length	Petal width	Species
1	5.1	3.5	1.4	0.2	I. setosa
2	4.9	3	1.4	0.2	I. setosa
3	4.7	3.2	1.3	0.2	I. setosa

Figure 2.2: A preview of the Iris
HTML webpage.

Back to our *Iris Flower Dataset* webpage: If you were to
double click on the HTML document in your file system, it

will automatically be opened in your browser and will look similar to the screenshot in Figure 2.2. Our task is to extract successfully the table in the page that contains the 50 data points in the set. In order to accomplish our task, we will need to look into the source code that generates the page. The first few lines look like this:

```
<!DOCTYPE html>
<html class="client-nojs" dir="ltr" lang="en">
  <head>
  <meta http-equiv="content-type" content=
      "text/html;
      charset=windows-1252">
    <title>Iris flower data set</title>
  </head>
  <body class="qt-body">
  <h1 id="firstHeading" class="firstHeading">
<i>Iris</i> Flower Dataset
    </h1>
    <div id="bodyContent" class="mw-body-content">
    <p>This is one of the best known datasets in
    data science and it is fair to say it has
    become a canonical example in the training of
    new data scientists.</p>

      ...
```

The first few lines of the Iris HTML webpage. Notice the use of tags marking the different elements of the page.

We need to be able to read the source page and parse it so that we can make sense of its contents thanks to the tags provided. The first thing we will do is open the page. Here, I am assuming that the HTML file is saved locally in

We can now use Beautiful Soup to parse the HTML source code.

your machine with the name `iris_page.html`. We can ask Beautiful Soup to read and parse the HTML page as follows:

```
from bs4 import BeautifulSoup


fname = 'iris_page.html'
iris_soup = BeautifulSoup(open(fname), 'lxml')
```

Make sure you provide the appropriate path.

The third line above takes the HTML string to be parsed and the name of the HTML parser to use. In this case we are using `lxml` and Beautiful Soup supports the parser included in Python's standard library, `html.parser` as well as others such as `html5lib`.

In this case the string to be parsed is the HTML file.

In a more realistic situation, you may not have a local version of the HTML page. Instead you would find the page directly in the web. In this case, first you will need to do a request to the URL of the page and parse the result, as follows:

```
from urllib.request import urlopen
from bs4 import BeautifulSoup
wp='http://wikipedia.org/wiki/Iris_flower_data_set'
pageSource = urlopen(wp).read()


IrisSoup = BeautifulSoup(pageSource, 'lxml')
```

We can parse HTML source code directly from live URLs in this way.

We are using `urlopen` to request the URL of the page we are interested in and pass the result as the HTML string that Beautiful Soup will parse. Neat!

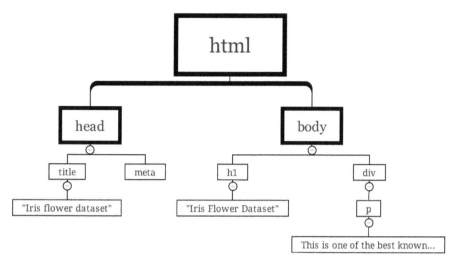

Figure 2.3: A schematic representation of HTML as a tree. We are only showing a few of the branches.

Beautiful Soup has parsed the HTML and has enabled us to make sense of the structure of the page. We can think of HTML as a tree (see Figure 2.3) with different types of objects. The objects that Beautiful Soup returns to us include:

- **Tags**: Beautiful Soup objects that correspond to the actual tags in the original HTML. Tags have attributes and methods

- **Navigable strings**: Correspond to the text within a tag

- **Comments**: A special type of navigable string to support comments in the original HTML

- **Beautiful Soup**: Represents the document as a whole. It can be searched and navigated

Beautiful Soup objects include tags, navigable strings, comments and a Beautiful Soup object.

Let us take a look at the Iris webpage soup we have in our hands. We can check the type of object in the usual manner:

Bowl?... May be better!

```
> type(iris_soup)


bs4.BeautifulSoup
```

We obtain a Beautiful Soup object when parsing our HTML file.

It is, as we can see, a Beautiful Soup object. It holds information about the original HTML document:

```
> print(iris_soup.name)


'[document]'


> print(iris_soup.title)


<title>Iris flower dataset</title>
```

The object has information about the tags in the HTML.

We can see that the name of the object is "document" and we can start looking at the different tags inside the Iris beautiful soup. In the code above, we are requesting the title of the website. Note that the output is a tag object:

```
> type(iris_soup.title)


bs4.element.Tag
```

We can refer to the tags directly by using their names.

In this case the tag is a "title" tag as we can easily verify directly in the HTML source. What about if we are interested in the actual title, i.e., the string inside the tag? Well, all we need to do is request the string of the tag as follows:

```
> print(iris_soup.title.string)


Iris flower dataset


> type(iris_soup.title.string)


bs4.element.NavigableString
```

It is possible to extract the strings inside a tag.

Et voilà! Notice the type of object that is returned by the string method for the tag: It is a navigable string. The string method returns a single string within a tag. In other words, if the tag has a single string child, then the returned value will be that string. However, if the tag has no children, or more than one child, the value returned will be None.

Remember the tree structure of the HTML code when we talk about parents and children!

In cases where the tag contains no children or more than one child, it is useful to know that you can use a text method which will return all the child strings concatenated. Let us look at an example: In our Iris dataset website, the first heading contains a string that reads "*Iris* **Flower Dataset**", with the first word in italics (see Figure 2.2). In HTML this is created with an i tag. Let us look at the contents of the heading with Beautiful Soup:

```
> iris_soup.h1.contents

[<i>Iris</i>, 'Flower\n Dataset\n ']
```

Notice that the result here is a list.

The object returned is a list with two elements. This means that the tag has effectively two children: The first one is a tag, and the second one is a string. If we were to ask for the string on this h1, we will get nothing. Instead we should be asking for the text as follows:

```
> iris_soup.h1.text


'Iris Flower \n Dataset\n'
```

The text method returns all the child strings concatenated.

Notice that the returned text has some white spaces including special characters such as the \n. We can clean these by replacing the spaces or using regular expressions for example. Beautiful Soup offers the possibility of stripping leading and trailing whitespaces with the help of the stripped_strings generator:

See Section 2.2 for more information about regular expressions.

```
> for ss in iris_soup.h1.stripped_strings:
    print(repr(ss))


'Iris'
'Flower\n Dataset'
```

Think of a generator as a function that "generates" values on the fly.

We may still have to do some cleaning on the result. For example, in the example above we still have the line feed control character \n.

Let us now take a look at other parts of our soup. For example, let us look at the first div tag:

```
firstdiv = iris_soup.div
```

We are storing the content of the div in a variable we can later use:

```
> firstdiv

<div class="mw-body-content" id="bodyContent">
<p>This is one of the best known datasets in data
science and it is fair to say it has become a
canonical example in the training of
new data scientists.</p>
<p>The data set contains 50 instances of 3 classes
of 50 iris plants. One of the classes is linearly
separable from the other 2, and these in turn are
not linearly separable from each other.</p>
</div>
```

This particular div contains two paragraphs, denoted with <p></p> tags.

We can see that there are two paragraphs inside the div. We can search the contents of the different tags with the help of methods such as find and find_all. Let us get the string of the first paragraph:

```
> paragraph = firstdiv.find('p')
> paragraph.string


'This is one of the best known datasets in data
science and it is\n fair to say it has become
a canonical example in the training of\n new
data scientists.'
```

The find method locates the first instance of the tag searched.

The find method has enabled us to search for the first instance of the p tag. In contrast, we can use the find_all method to obtain all the instances inside a list. Notice that find_all lets us search for multiple tags. For instance, if we wanted all the paragraphs and list items in the document, we can type the following:

```
> iris_soup.find_all(["p", "li"])


[<p>This is one of the best known datasets in data
science and it is fair to say it has become a
canonical example in the training of new
data scientists.</p>,
<p>The data set contains 50 instances of 3 classes
of 50 iris plants. One of the classes is linearly
separable from the other 2, and these in turn are
not linearly separable from each other.</p>,
 <li>sepal length in cm </li>,
 <li>sepal width in cm </li>,
 <li>petal length in cm </li>,
 <li>petal width in cm </li>,
 <li>class: -- 3 values:  Iris Setosa, Iris
Versicolour, Iris Virginica </li>,
 <p id="rogel1">[1] <b>Rogel-Salazar, J</b>.
(2017). <i>Data Science and Analytics with
Python</i>. Chapman &amp; Hall/CRC
Data Mining and Knowledge Discovery Series.
CRC Press. <meta content="text/html;
charset=utf-8" http-equiv="Content-Type"/></p>]
```

The find_all method locates all the instances of the tag searched and returns a list.

It is possible to use the parameter limit in combination with the find_all method to limit the number of results returned. This is particularly useful when there is a large number of entries searched.

Combining our search with filtering parameters is a great
way to hone in on the information we are looking for. We
can for example determine that we want all the paragraphs
that have a particular identifier or id:

```
> bib  = iris_soup.find_all('p', id='rogel1')
> print(bib)


<p id="rogel1">[1] <b>Rogel-Salazar, J</b>.
  (2017). <i>Data Science and Analytics with
  Python</i>. Chapman &amp; Hall/CRC
  Data Mining and Knowledge Discovery Series.
  CRC Press. <meta content="text/html;
charset=utf-8" http-equiv="Content-Type"/></p>
```

We can use parameters to search
for specific tags. In this case for
instance we are searching for a
particular id.

In this case, we are looking for all the paragraphs with
the id rogel1 and we can see that the result is one single
paragraph. Please note that the returned object is a list
of tags. If we wanted to get the text of the first (and only)
element in the list, we can do this with:

```
> my_text = bib[0].text
```

The list elements are tag objects.

As we have seen, HTML organises the contents of our
webpage. Sometimes, it is useful to define consistent style
elements for different elements of the page under a single
name. This is what a class attribute is used for in HTML.
We know that Python is an object-oriented language and
as such it enables us to create "templates" to create objects.
So what happens when we need to look for a class attribute

Remember that class is a reserved
word for both HTML and Python.

in our Beautiful Soup with Python? Well, since `class` is a
reserved word in Python we simply append an underscore
to the HTML attribute as such: `class_`.

We have enough information for the big finale of this
section: Obtaining the table of data in the Iris website.
Inspecting the source code for the page, we can see that the
tag that holds the dataset is a `table` of class
`tableizer-table`. We can use this information to find the
table and parse it:

Note that we are using the
parameter `class_` in the code
below.

```
iris_table = iris_soup.find('table',
    class_='tableizer-table')
```

From Table 2.1 we know that a well-formed HTML table
contains rows in `tr` tags, and the data cells in `td` tags. Let us
locate all the table rows to start with:

Too many tables!! I can assure
you there is no chance we may
encounter Mr. Creosote in any of
them.

```
tmp = iris_table.find_all('tr')
```

This returns a list with all the relevant tags. In particular the
first element contains the header of the table and the rest of
the elements correspond to the rows of the dataset:

```
first = tmp[0]
allRows = tmp[1:]
```

Remember how we can slice and
dice a list using the colon notation.

We can now extract the text inside each of the data cells. In
the case of the header, the tag is actually a table header, i.e.,
`th`.

```
headers = [header.text for header in\
    first.find_all('th')]
> headers


['Dataset Order',
 'Sepal length',
 'Sepal width',
 'Petal length',
 'Petal width',
 'Species']
```

We are using list comprehension to extract the relevant text from the th tags.

In the code above, we are using a Pythonic way to extract the relevant information: List comprehension. We traverse the list returned by find_all and extract the text as we go along, each entry is then stored as an element of a list.

As for the values, they are stored in td tags and we can use a similar technique as in the code above:

```
values = [[data.text for data in\
    row.find_all('td')] for row in allRows]
> values[:2]


[['1', '5.1', '3.5', '1.4', '0.2', 'I.\xa0setosa'],
 ['2', '4.9', '3', '1.4', '0.2', 'I.\xa0setosa']]
```

We use the same technique as above for the actual table contents.

Note that the information extracted is actually of string type. This is important in those cases, such as here, where some of the data is numerical, and thus we may have to carry out appropriate manipulations; for example, cleaning the nonbreakable space characters shown as \xa0.

Let us show some manipulations we can easily implement loading the data into a Pandas dataframe:

```
import pandas as pd
df = pd.DataFrame(data=values, columns=headers)
```

Et voilà! We are now in a position to use our dataset for other purposes, such as in a classification algorithm as done in Chapter 3 of *Data Science and Analytics with Python*[5]. But before we do that, let us make some minor changes in our dataset. For example, we can convert the columns containing numbers as strings into actual numbers:

[5] Rogel-Salazar, J. (2017). *Data Science and Analytics with Python.* Chapman & Hall/CRC Data Mining and Knowledge Discovery Series. CRC Press

```
cols = ['Dataset Order', 'Sepal length',
    'Sepal width', 'Petal length', 'Petal width']
df[cols] = df[cols].apply(pd.to_numeric,
    errors='coerce')
```

We can also clean the strings in the species names. You may have noticed in the code shown on page 75 that there are some strange characters in the species names. Namely, the non-breakable space encoded in latin1: \xa0. Let us clean up these spaces:

We will cover the use of regular expressions for this sort of task in Section 2.2.

```
df['Species'] = df['Species'].map(lambda x:
    x.replace('\xa0',' '))
df['Species'] = df['Species'].map(lambda x:
    x.replace('\n',''))
```

We are simply replacing the nonbreakable spaces with blanks in the first line of the code above. In the second one, we are replacing the new line character with nothing.

2.2   *Make Mine a Regular: Regular Expressions*

HAVE YOU EVER HAD THE need to determine a pattern in a piece of text, or in data in a table and either extract the regular pattern or even remove it? Sometimes, it is possible to simply scan the document in question and manually find the expression of interest. In many cases, different programs enable the use of search and replace functions and they are all the rage. However, there are times when the expression we are seeking to process is more complex to be handled with a simple search.

Welcome to the world of regular expressions! As the name implies, a regular expression is an utterance (typically in text form) that appears in a *corpus* with certain frequency or regularity. Recognising those patterns in the corpus relies on determining the characters that make up the expression, including letters, digits, punctuation and any other symbol, including special characters and even in other scripts, such as the Japanese sentence in the margin, as well as many others like Chinese, Arabic or Devanagari for example.

In Python, the re module enables us to use regular expressions. When working with Python strings which will be parsed with regular expressions, it is recommended to use raw strings. This is because in raw strings, backslashes have no special meaning as an escape character. Anyway, we mentioned above that a simple search and replace function can be used to substitute a desired pattern, let us take a look at implementing this use case with re.

I am sure you have! Particularly if, like Mr. Bounder, you need to replace the letter "C" with "K" to get the right pronunciation of some words.

A *corpus* is a large and structured set of texts upon which linguistic analysis can be performed.

このは日本語の文章.

A raw string in Python is preceded by an r as such r'This is a raw string.'

Imagine you are reading the following options from your local award-winning Viking Café:

Breakfast options:

1. Egg and baaacon - £10.0 ($12.83);

2. Egg, sausage and baaaaacon - £11.0 ($14.12);

3. Egg and beans - £12.0 ($15.40);

4. Egg, baaacon and beans - £13.0 ($16.68);

5. Beans, sausage, beans - £14.0 ($17.97);

6. Beans, baaaaacon, beans, tomato and beans - £15.0 ($19.25);

The famous Viking Café menu, sans Spam...

That new Commis Chef is at it again! Doesn't she/he know that your speciality is wonderful Spam? We need to take action immediately and change the menu before the Vikings come in. Let us fire our Python engines and read each of the lines in the corpus above. We will then use the sub method to substitute the word "beans" for "spam". We will deal with the extra bacon — the surplus letter "a" — later.

We need to replace the word "beans" with "spam".

```
import re


corpus =  r"""Breakfast options:
1. Egg and baaacon - £10.0 ($12.83);
2. Egg, sausage and baaaaacon - £11.0 ($12.83);
3. Egg and beans - £12.0 ($15.40);
4. Egg, baaacon and beans - £13.0 ($16.68);
5. Beans, sausage, beans - £14.0 ($17.97);
6. Beans, baaaaacon, beans, tomato and beans -
    £15.0 ($19.25); """
```

The string could be stored in a file. In this case we are defining a raw string: Notice the r at the start.

```
for line in corpus.splitlines():
    line = re.sub('beans','spam', line.rstrip())
    print(line)
```

The sub method enables us to make substitutions in the string.

As you would expect, after running the code, the printed new lines will have changed the word "beans" for "spam":

```
Breakfast options:
1. Egg and baaacon - £10.0 ($12.83);
2. Egg, sausage and baaaaacon - £11.0 ($12.83);
3. Egg, and spam - £12.0 ($15.40);
4. Egg, baaacon and spam - £13.0 ($16.68);
5. Beans, sausage, spam - £14.0 ($17.97);
6. Beans, baaaaacon, spam, tomato and spam - £15.0
   ($19.25)
```

The famous Viking Café menu, with wonderful Spam...

But what about lines 5 and 6 where the word "Beans" has not been changed? Well, the reason is that in those cases the capital "B" does not match the lower case "b". We shall address how to deal with this issue in the next subsection.

As well as with the misspelling of the word "bacon".

Also, note that we have not changed the text in the corpus variable; we simply took the text and made on-the-fly modifications. If we need to keep the changes, we need to make sure that the new lines are stored somewhere.

This is a nice task for you to complete now, Mr./Ms. Commis Chef!

2.2.1   Regular Expression Patterns

As you can see, looking for sequences of characters is pretty straightforward as most characters match themselves. Sounds obvious, right? However, there are some exceptions:

Exceptions include control characters such as + ? . *
^ { } $ () [ ] | \.

These characters can be matched by "escaping" them with the help of a backslash (\\). In Table 2.2 we are listing the use of these characters to match patterns in a string.

Pattern	Description
^...$	Starts and ends
*	Zero or more repetitions
+	One or more repetitions
?	Optional character
.	Any character
abc...	Letters
123...	Digits
\d	Any digit
\D	Any non-digit character
[abc]	Only a, b, or c
[^abc]	Not a, b, nor c
[a-z]	Characters a to z
[0-9]	Numbers 0 to 9
\w	Any alphanumeric character
\W	Any non-alphanumeric character
{m}	m repetitions
{m,n}	m to n repetitions
\s	Any whitespace
\S	Any non-whitespace character
[...]	Character sets
(...)	Capture group
(:?...)	Non-capture group
(a(bc))	Capture sub-group
(.*)	Capture all
(123|abc)	Matches 123 or abc

Table 2.2: Regular expression patterns. We use ellipses (...) to denote sequences of characters.

The re module we encountered previously supports two different ways to find patterns using regular expressions: match and search. The first one matches only at the

We can use match or search with the re module.

beginning of a string, whereas the second one searches for a match anywhere in the string. If you are interested in using a single regular expression multiple times, you may want to use the `compile` method to be used with `match` and `search`.

We can use `compile` in cases where we need to use an expression multiple times.

OK, so we are ready to start matching some patterns in our Viking Café menu. We can match lines beginning with a number using an expression such as:

```
'^1',  '^2', ..., '^6'
```

The caret symbol (^) matches a pattern at the beginning of a string.

What about if we are interested in a more general expression that captures a line starting with any number? From Table 2.2 we can see that the pattern \d matches any digit!

```
'^\d'
```

\d matches any single digit.

So we can actually write the following to print all the lines that start with a number:

```
numlines = re.compile('^\d')
for line in corpus.splitlines():
    result = numlines.search(line)
    if result:
        print(line)
```

This piece of code prints lines in the corpus that begin with a number.

Try it out and convince yourself that the outcome is as expected. Note that this only works for strings that begin with the pattern provided.

We can also search for lines ending in a particular pattern. In this case, we need to use the dollar sign ($). For example, if we wanted to print only the lines that finish with a closing parenthesis, we will have to write the following regular expression:

```
endparenthesis = re.compile('\)$')
```

The dollar sign ($) matches a pattern at the end of a string.

Note that we need to "escape" the closing parenthesis, i.e., \), to match expressions containing that character. The same behaviour applies to any of the other control characters we have described above.

Remember the task we were trying to accomplish in the last section? We were interested in replacing all the "beans" for "spam", but capitalised words were not replaced. One way (among many) to deal with this is the use of character sets such that we search for the word "bean" spelled either with "B" or with "b". We can do that with the following expression '[Bb]eans'

The square brackets represent character sets, the pattern [123] matches a single 1, 2 or 3 and nothing else. It is possible to match sequential characters: [0-9] will match a single digit between 0 and 9.

```
> for line in corpus.splitlines():
    line = re.sub('[Bb]eans','spam', line.rstrip())
    print(line)


Breakfast options:
1. Egg and baaacon - £10.0 ($12.83);
2. Egg, sausage and baaaaacon - £11.0 ($12.83);
3. Egg and spam - £12.0 ($15.40);
4. Egg, baaacon and spam - £13.0 ($16.68);
5. spam, sausage, spam - £14.0 ($17.97);
6. spam, baaaaacon, spam, tomato and spam - £15.0
    ($19.25)
```

In this case we are using [Bb]eans to match the words "beans" or "Beans".

What about if we wanted to match all the words that started with the letter "b", either capital or lower case? We can achieve this with the help of \w which matches any alphanumeric character. In order to ensure that we capture words of any length, we can use the + character that will match one or more repetitions. This leaves us with the following expression:

The pattern \w matches any alphanumeric character.

Whereas the + matches one or more repetitions of a character.

```
bwords = re.compile("[Bb]\w+")
```

Let us use this compile regular expression with another great method in the re module: findall which will return a list with all the matches for the pattern provided:

```
> bwords.findall(corpus)

['Breakfast', 'baaacon', 'baaaaacon',
'beans', 'baaacon', 'beans',
'Beans', 'beans', 'Beans',
'baaaaacon', 'beans', 'beans']
```

We find all the matches for words starting with "B" or "b".

Not bad, eh? We can use the repetition to capture all those misspelled "bacons":

```
> re.findall('ba+\w+', corpus)

['baaacon', 'baaaaacon', 'baaacon', 'baaaaacon']
```

Here we look for all the words that have a "b" followed by any number of letters "a".

In this case we are searching for all the words that have the letter "b" followed by any number of letters "a", and any number of other characters. We can also specify the number of repetitions as follows:

```
re.findall('ba{3,5}con', corpus)
```

In this case we are looking for repetitions of the letter "a" between 3 and 5 times followed by the letters "con".

For the next pattern, let us get the prices in sterling from the menu. We are interested in the figures after the pound sterling symbol (£), so we will use the parentheses to capture the group (see Table 2.2).

The use of parentheses lets us specify a group in the pattern that we are interested in extracting.

```
> re.findall('£(\d+\.0)', corpus)

['10.0', '11.0', '12.0', '13.0', '14.0', '15.0']
```

Here we are looking for any number of digits (\d+) followed by a dot (\.) and a zero. Notice that we enclose the expression in parentheses to capture only the information required, leaving out the pound symbol. For the prices in dollars, we need to make sure to escape the dollar sign and the parentheses:

We use \. to specify a dot in the pattern. On its own, a dot is a wildcard that represents any character.

```
> re.findall('\(\$(\d+\.\d+)\)', corpus)

['12.83', '12.83', '15.40', '16.68', '17.97',
'19.25']
```

We need to escape both the dollar sign ($) and the parentheses.

Finally, let us use the capture sub-group to get both prices at the same time:

```
prices = re.compile('(£(\d+\.0) \(\$(\d+\.\d+)\))')
captures = prices.findall(corpus)
```

The result will be list with tuples containing a match for the entire expression (e.g., '£10.0 ($12.83)'), a match for the first sub-group (e.g., '10.0') and a match for the second sub-group (e.g., '12.83'). We can then use the resulting list for our own purposes, for example:

We can use the sub-group pattern (a(bc)) to capture multiple groups of interest.

```
> for capture in captures:
    print('{0} in pounds and {1} in dollars'.
        format(capture[1], capture[2]))


10.0 in pounds and 12.83 in dollars
11.0 in pounds and 12.83 in dollars
12.0 in pounds and 15.40 in dollars
13.0 in pounds and 16.68 in dollars
14.0 in pounds and 17.97 in dollars
15.0 in pounds and 19.25 in dollars
```

The Commis Chef can now use her/his newly acquired knowledge of regular expressions to fix the menu:

```
fix_bacon = re.compile('ba+con')
fix_spam = re.compile('[Bb]eans')
new_corpus = ''
for line in corpus.splitlines():
    line = fix_bacon.sub('bacon', line)
    line = fix_spam.sub('spam', line)
    new_corpus += line
```

This is one way the Commis Chef can fix the menu!

First we create regular expressions to find the misspelled words with multiple letters "a", then one to find the words "beans" and "Beans". We then parse each line making appropriate replacements and saving the new fixed lines in a new corpus.

```
> print(new_corpus)

Breakfast options:
1. Egg and bacon - £10.0 ($12.83);
2. Egg, sausage and bacon - £11.0 ($12.83);
3. Egg and spam - £12.0 ($15.40);
4. Egg, bacon and spam - £13.0 ($16.68);
5. spam, sausage, spam - £14.0 ($17.97);
6. spam, bacon, spam, tomato and spam - £15.0
    ($19.25)
```

Et voilà!

It is not quite perfect yet, as we have some instances of "spam" that should really be capitalised, but getting there.

Check out re's documentation for further information[6], as there are many more things you can do with regular expressions. Python also has other tricks under its sleeve. For example, there are some flags that you can set:

[6] re - Regular expression operations. https://docs.python.org/3.6/library/re.html

- re.IGNORECASE: case insensitive pattern matching

- re.DOTALL: Make the special character . match any character including newline (\n)

- re.MULTILINE: make ^ and $ match at the beginning/end of the string and of each line

Some flags you can set to be used with your regular expressions.

Do not be discouraged by how cryptic some of the regular expressions seem to be. The vast majority of us will probably not become master regex ninja Jackalopes, but with the help of a cheat sheet like Table 2.2 and an online tester such as https://pythex.org or https://regex101.com, we can all find the perfect match.

There are some interesting attempts to make readable and maintainable regular expressions such as `cursive_re` for Python 3.6 and up[7]. For instance, matching the prices in sterling from our Viking Café menu can be achieved as follows with `cursive_re`:

[7] Cursive Re. https://github.com/Bogdanp/cursive_re

```
import cursive_re as cre
pound = cre.text('£')
pndnum = pound + cre.group(cre.one_or_more(
    cre.any_of(cre.in_range('0','9'))) +
    cre.text('.0'))
```

In the second line above, `text` matches the given string exactly, escaping any special characters. The `any_of` function matches any of the given characters and in this case they are characters in the range from 0 to 9. Since we want one or more of these digits, we use the `one_or_more` function. Finally, the `group` function lets us define the group whose contents we want to retrieve. We can see the result of these commands by casting the result as a string:

Cursive Re provides a number of functions that attempt to make regular expressions easier to read and maintain.

```
> str(pndnum)

'\\£([0-9]+\\.0)'
```

We can compile the expression into a real regular expression and use it as normal:

```
> testing = cre.compile(pndnum)

> testing.findall(corpus)


['10.0', '11.0', '12.0', '13.0', '14.0', '15.0']
```

2.3 Processing Text with Unicode

WHEN DEALING WITH TEXT DATA, it is unavoidable to consider the characters that we use to represent words. We rarely think about this, but ever since we start learning how to read and write, we are encoding information particular to the natural language we use in our everyday lives. You are able to read these lines of text because you are familiar with the Latin alphabet with 26 characters that is used in English, but that is not the whole story. *Si leyeras estas líneas en Español necesitarías 27 caracteres, más vocales acentuadas como: á, é, í, ó, ú, & ü.* Other languages have their own letters and they all need to be encoded so that they can be represented by your computer.

If you were reading these lines in Spanish you would need 27 characters plus accented vowels.

For many decades, computers were able to represent characters based on the American Standard Code for Information Interchange standard, better known as ASCII, first proposed in the early 1960s[8]. ASCII defines 256 characters using 8 bits to encode characters including the usual printable ones in a Latin alphabet including accented vowels and other characters such as ç, ß and ñ (among others), plus some control characters such as carriage return, line feed, etc.

[8] Russell, A. (2014). *Open Standards and the Digital Age.* Cambridge Studies in the Emerg. Cambridge University Press

All this is well and good, but what happens with languages that do not use the Latin alphabet such as Japanese, Chinese, or Greek? ASCII would not be able to accommodate these scripts and thus we need a new character set. Welcome to Unicode!

Languages with non-Latin scripts are not supported in ASCII.

Unicode does not have every imaginable character in it, but at least in version 11.0 there are $137,375$ characters including 146 different scripts and even emojis[9]. This all makes sense and you would think that this is the end of the story, right? Well, you will be surprised to see the "*It's... not*". There are different ways to implement Unicode such as the Unicode Transformation Format (UTF), and the Universal Coded Character Set (UCS).

[9] Unicode 11.0.
http://www.unicode.org/versions/Unicode11.0.0/

No need to run in from the sea to tell you this.

Let us take for instance UTF encoding. If we chose to use 8 bits to do the encoding we would end up with UTF-8, which offers great compatibility with ASCII. Alternatively, we can use 16 bits and end up with UTF-16. There are other mappings out there, including UTF-32, UTF-7, etc. As you can imagine, dealing with encodings can be a bit tricky.

Some common encodings include UTF-8 and UTF-16.

In Python 3, all text is Unicode[10], but it is important to remember that encoded Unicode is represented by binary data. This is one of the main differences with Python 2.7. Python 3 has one text type, i.e, `str` which holds Unicode data, and there are two byte types `bytes` and `bytearray`. Let us take a look at some of this. For example, let us define a string in Python and look at its type:

[10] van Rossum, G. (2009). Text Vs. Data Instead of Unicode Vs. 8-bit. https://docs.python.org/release/3.0.1/whatsnew/3.0.html

```
> type('Hello world!')


str
```

A string is indeed a string.

It is indeed an object of `str` type, or a string. What about if we want to define a `bytes` literal? Well, we can simply prefix the string with a b:

```
> type(b'Hello world!')


bytes
```

We can define a `bytes` literal with the b prefix.

Let us try to define a byte object containing non-ASCII characters:

```
> type(b'こんにちは世界！')

SyntaxError: bytes can only contain ASCII literal
characters.
```

In this case, we are printing "Hello world!" in Japanese!

This error tells us that we will need to transform our string with non-ASCII characters into a bytes object first, and we will need to provide an encoding to do this:

```
> sekai = 'こんにちは世界！'

> bytes(sekai, 'utf-8')


b'\x81\x93\xe3\x82\x93\xe3\x81\xab\xe3\x81\xa1\xe3
\x81\xaf\xe4\xb8\x96\xe7\x95\x8c\xef\xbc\x81'
```

When casting as a `bytes` literal we need to specify the desired encoding.

There is no easy way to determine what type of encoding is used in byte strings. In Section 2.1.1 we learnt how to scrape a website, and in reality we need to check what encoding is used for the strings we are getting from the web. That is true of any other processing we need to carry out with strings.

After the operation above is executed, we have a `bytes` object encoded in UTF-8. Another, and probably better, way to do this is to use the `encode` method for strings:

```
> sekai.encode()

b'\x81\x93\xe3\x82\x93\xe3\x81\xab\xe3\x81\xa1\xe3
\x81\xaf\xe4\xb8\x96\xe7\x95\x8c\xef\xbc\x81'
```

As you can see, we have obtained the same result as before, please note that by default Python 3 uses UTF-8 for encoding. Should we need to use a different encoding, we simply pass it to the method. For example, we can encode our string in UTF-16 as follows:

```
> sekai.encode('utf-16')

 b'\xff\xfeS0\x930k0a0o0\x16NLu\x01\xff'
```

As you can imagine, it is possible to do the reverse operation and decode bytes objects too:

```
> japan = b'\xe6\x97\xa5\xe6\x9c\xac'
> japan.decode()

'日本'
```

It is best practice to specify the encoding when reading files, but it may not be that easy to tell what encoding has been used.

A better way to deal with the encoding is to use the `encode` method.

You can specify other encodings too.

We can decode a bytes literal too.

Please remember that you will need to provide the correct encoding (UTF-8, UTF-16, etc.) to the decoding method; otherwise, you will get a Unicode error at best or a miss-encoding at worst!

Providing the correct encoding is important.

Since we are dealing with characters, and all text in Python 3 is Unicode, it makes sense that the regular expression patterns that we discussed in Section 2.2 also hold for non-Latin characters:

The use of regular expressions patterns can be applied to Unicode too.

```
> thirtyseven='さんじゅなだ''
> re.sub('だ'', 'な'', thirtyseven)

'さんじゅなな'
```

It is also possible to use the \uFFFF Unicode notation, enabling us to use character ranges and all the fun that comes with regular expressions:

This is a hexadecimal representation for the Unicode character.

```
> re.sub('\u3060', '\u306a', thirtyseven)

'さんじゅなな'
```

You can check the Unicode code points in sites such as www.utf8-chartable.de or www.key-shortcut.com for example.

Check Unicode tables in sites such as www.utf8-chartable.de or www.key-shortcut.com.

In Section 2.1.1 we read an HTML page and we encountered some interesting non-breakable spaces shown as \xa0. It turns out that these are non-breakable spaces encoded in Latin1 or ISO−8859 − 1. We dealt with this issue with a replacement in Pandas. An alternative may be to use a regular expression to remove all non-US-ASCII characters, i.e., characters outside the \u0000-\u007F.

```
> test_text='abc\xa0\u3060\u306a\u3060\xa0de!'
> print(test_text)


abc だなだ de!

> only_ascii = re.compile(r'[^\u0000-\u007f]')
> only_ascii.sub('', test_text)


'abcde!'
```

Here we are removing characters outside the range of US-ASCII characters.

Notice that when printing the string there are some blank spaces between the Latin and Japanese characters. In this case, we are using an exclusion in a character set to remove all non-US-ASCII characters. It is a drastic measure, but I am sure you get the point.

Remember that [^abc] means not a, b nor c.

As you can imagine, it is not unusual to to come across encoding problems when opening files in Python 3, and there are some modules that may help with these issues. Say you are interested in opening a CSV file to be loaded into a Pandas dataframe. If the stars align and the creator of your CSV is magnanimous, they may have saved the file using UTF-8. If so you may get away with reading the file as follows:

Python 3 uses UTF-8 as default. You may need to specify the file encoding to ensure appropriate handling for other encodings.

```
import pandas as pd
df = pd.read_csv('myfile.csv')
```

As we mentioned before, it is not easy to tell what encoding was used to create a file and in principle you should pass a parameter to Pandas telling it what encoding the file has been saved with, so a more complete version of the snippet above would be:

In Pandas you can provide an encoding parameter.

```
import pandas as pd

df = pd.read_csv('myfile.csv', encoding='utf-8')
```

What happens when you do not know what encoding was used to save the file? Well, you can ask, but it is very unlikely that the file creator would know or tell you... In those cases, modules such as chardet[11] can help you detect the character encoding in your file. The detect function in the module returns a dictionary containing the auto-detected character encoding and a confidence level from 0 to 1.

[11] Chardet.
https://chardet.readthedocs.io

```
> import chardet
> chardet.detect(b'I.\xa0setosa')

{'encoding': 'ISO-8859-1', 'confidence': 0.73'}
```

In this case, the string is detected to be encoded in ISO$-8859-1$.

The example above tells us that the likely encoding for the string passed to the detect function is ISO$-8859-1$ (with a confidence level of 0.73). Let us take a look at an example implementation for a file:

```
import chardet
import pandas as pd


def find_encoding(fname):
    r_file = open(fname, 'rb').read()
    result = chardet.detect(r_file)
    charenc = result['encoding']
    return charenc



my_encoding = find_encoding('myfile.csv')
df=pd.read_csv('myfile.csv', encoding=my_encoding)
```

Use this snippet to detect file encodings with chardet.

Finally, what about writing a file with the correct encoding? Well, if you are using Pandas, it is quite straightforward as you simply pass a parameter with the desired encoding as follows:

Or nothing, as the default is UTF-8.

```
> df.to_csv('newfile.csv', encoding='utf-8')
```

Otherwise, you need to ensure the encoding of the strings as you write them down:

```
sekai = "こんにちは世界！"

with open('sekai.txt', 'wb') as f:
    f.write(sekai.encode())
```

Do not forget to encode your strings when writing to a file, and tell your users!

2.4   Tokenising Text

WE HAVE BEEN DEALING WITH text in full, and most of
our discussion has been about obtaining and pre-processing
it. We started this chapter talking about the importance
of natural language and how to make sense of it with the
aid of computers. One of the first tasks that will enable us
to do this is to split up our text into meaningful units, or
tokens. This is called *tokenisation* and it is a typical first step
in natural language processing.

In this context, a token is a meaningful unit of text.

In languages like English or Spanish, simple tokenisation
can be used by separating the tokens by whitespaces.
Unfortunately, for languages such as Chinese or Japanese,
where whitespaces are not used between words, the
tokenisation tasks becomes more involved. The tokenisation
process may also require to discard some tokens such as
punctuation, numbers, or some common words. We will
cover more of this later on in this section.

A common tokenisation technique involves separating tokens by whitespaces.

We can readily split a string of text as follows:

```
> sentences = "I know, I know! Nobody expects the
    Spanish Inquisition. In fact, those who do
    expect -"
> sentences.split()

['I', 'know,', 'I', 'know!', 'Nobody', 'expects',
'the', 'Spanish', 'Inquisition.', 'In', 'fact,',
'those', 'who', 'do', 'expect', '-']
```

We can separate tokens with the split *method for strings.*

We could in principle also define a string of characters on which to split the sentence. For example, if we wanted to split on the comma, we can do the following:

```
> sentences.split(',')


['I know',
 ' I know! Nobody expects the Spanish Inquisition.
   In fact',
 ' those who do expect -']
```

We can also specify other separators for splitting.

You may notice that in the first example, the punctuation marks are joined to the words, and in the second one there are some whitespaces at the beginning of the second and third elements in the list. We can use regular expressions to split on the desired marks, in this case for instance on comma, exclamation mark, dot, hyphen and whitespaces:

```
> import re
> re.split('[,!\.\-\s]+',sentences)


['I', 'know', 'I', 'know', 'Nobody', 'expects',
'the', 'Spanish', 'Inquisition', 'In', 'fact',
'those', 'who', 'do', 'expect', '']
```

We can even use a regular expression to specify the separator!

There are other ways to start our processing of natural language and a package that comes to mind in this context is the Natural Language Toolkit, or NLTK for short. Word tokenisation can be done with the word_tokenize function:

Do check out what NLTK has to offer!

```
> import nltk
> nltk.word_tokenize(sentences)

['I', 'know', ',', 'I', 'know', '!', 'Nobody',
'expects', 'the', 'Spanish', 'Inquisition', '.',
'In', 'fact', ',', 'those', 'who', 'do', 'expect',
'-']
```

Word tokenisation can be easily done with NLTK's word_tokenize.

Furthermore, we can use NLTK to tokenise at a sentence level:

```
> nltk.sent_tokenize(sentences)

['I know, I know!',
 'Nobody expects the Spanish Inquisition.',
 'In fact, those who do expect -']
```

Whereas sentence tokenisation is handled with sent_tokenize.

As we can see, in this case we end up with a list with three sentences. Not bad!

We can now start to normalise the text so that we can match tokens despite some differences such as the use of capital letters (cat, Cat and CAT can be assumed to refer to the same friendly Über-being.) or inflections (cat, cat's, cats and cats' all come from the same common base *cat*). It is possible to use the lower method to deal with the use of capital letters:

We can normalise the text so that we can match tokens that may be different in form but not in meaning

```
> words = nltk.word_tokenize(sentences.lower())
```

We can take a look at the result of the tokenisation:

```
> print(words)

['i', 'know', ',', 'i', 'know', '!', 'nobody',
'expects', 'the', 'spanish', 'inquisition', '.',
'in', 'fact', ',', 'those', 'who', 'do', 'expect',
'-']
```

In this case, we have changed all the text into lowercase.

To deal with inflections, we can use *stemming* or *lemmatisation*. The former refers to the process of severing word endings, whereas the latter relies on a more systematic analysis to obtain the so-called *lemma*, or dictionary form, of a word. NLTK comes with a couple of stemmers, such as the Porter stemmer:

Lemmatisation and stemming can help us normalise the text too.

```
> porter = nltk.PorterStemmer()
> [porter.stem(word) for word in words]

['i', 'know', ',', 'i', 'know', '!', 'nobodi',
'expect', 'the', 'spanish', 'inquisit','.', 'in',
'fact', ',', 'those', 'who', 'do', 'expect', '-']
```

An example of stemming text with PorterStemmer.

Lemmatisation can be done with WordNetLemmatizer:

```
> lemmatiser = nltk.WordNetLemmatizer()
> [lemmatiser.lemmatize(word) for word in words]

['i', 'know', ',', 'i', 'know', '!', 'nobody',
'expects', 'the', 'spanish', 'inquisition', '.',
'in', 'fact', ',', 'those', 'who', 'do', 'expect',
'-']
```

Lemmatising can be done with WordNetLemmatizer.

Another useful thing that comes with NLTK is the regexp_tokenize function with similar functionality to re.findall, but efficient for the tokenisation task. It becomes particularly useful in the tokenisation of utterances in social media such as tweets. For example, lets take the following made-up tweet:

> @norwegian_blue This parrot is no more!!! :(#sad
> https://jrogel.com

Tokenisation can also be done with the help of regular expression.

If we use the tokeniser straight out of the box, we end up with some tokenisations that are no longer meaningful in the context of a tweet:

```
> tweet='@norwegian_blue This parrot is no more!!!
    :( #sad... https://jrogel.com'
> nltk.word_tokenize(tweet)

['@', 'norwegian_blue', 'This', 'parrot', 'is',
'no', 'more', '!', '!', '!', ':', '(', '#', 'sad',
'...', 'https', ':', '//jrogel.com']
```

Using the tokeniser straight out of the box results in a bad tokenisation.

It may be preferable to parse the text so as to render a meaningful tokenisation. We can use regular expressions to do this, and in particular, we can use the regexp_tokenize function that comes with NLTK offering consistency with other NLTK functions. Also it may provide some efficiencies when parsing for the desired pattern. It is important to note that the order of the arguments in the regexp_tokenize function is as follows: First the string to be parsed and then the regular expression. We shall put together a sequence of regular expressions that break our strings in the chosen manner.

re functions take their arguments in the reverse order.

Let us then define a regular expression pattern that enables a more meaningful tokenisation for our example tweet above:

```
pattern = r'''(?x) # A verbose regex
    [\$£]?\d+[\.:%]?\d*%?
    |(?:[A-Z]\.)+
    |(?:https?://)?(?:\w+\.)(?:\w{2,})+(?:[\w/]+)?
    |[@\#]?\w+(?:[-']\w+)*
    |\.\.\.
    |[!?]+
    |:[()]'''
```

Looks complex, but we shall unravel the regexp line-by-line below.

The first line in our regular expression starts with (?x) which lets the parser know that we are defining a verbose regular expression. This lets us create a more readable pattern and even include comments with #. The next line, [\$£]?\d+[\.:%]?\d*%? captures decimal numbers, percentages and currency figures (in this case dollars $, or pounds £). We then use (?:[A-Z]\.)+ to obtain abbreviations where characters are separated by dots. The fourth line captures URLs and the next one deals with @ mentions and hashtags (#). We capture ellipses with \.\.\. and multiple exclamation and question marks with [!?]+. Finally, we capture a couple of ASCII emoticons such as :) and :(with :[()].

A lot of useful information here. Make sure you check out the regular expression patterns in Table 2.2.

We can now try our new shiny pattern on the example tweet we have used before:

```
> nltk.regexp_tokenize(tweet, pattern)


['@norwegian_blue', 'This', 'parrot', 'is', 'no',
'more', '!!', ':(', '#sad', '...',
'https://jrogel.com']
```

This is a much better tokenisation of the sample Tweet!!

This has broken down the tweet in a more meaningful way, where we can distinguish hashtags (#sad) , user mentions (@norwegian_blue), and even emoticons. This sort of task is so common that NLTK has a tweet tokeniser that can be used out of the box:

```
> from nltk.tokenize.casual import TweetTokenizer
> TweetTokenizer().tokenize(tweet)


['@norwegian_blue', 'This', 'parrot', 'is', 'no',
'more', '!', '!', ':(', '#sad', '...',
'https://jrogel.com']
```

Check out the TweetTokenizer that comes with NLTK.

You can see some differences in the results compared to those from our own pattern. The flexibility offered by using either pattern depends on our particular use case.

2.5   Word Tagging

NOW THAT WE ARE ABLE to tokenize a corpus and break it down into its (meaningful) components, we can turn our attention to the categorisation of those units. For instance, we can try to distinguish between verbs, adjectives and nouns and start making sense of the utterances in the corpus.

Categorising the words into the parts they play in the speech is imaginatively called *Part-Of-Speech tagging*, or POS tagging. NLTK lets us carry out POS tagging with the post_tag function. Lets take a look using the corpus sentences we defined in Page 96. For the purposes of this example, we will concentrate on the second sentence, i.e., *"Nobody expects the Spanish Inquisition"*:

Part-Of-Speech tagging categorised the words into the parts they play in a sentence.

```
s = nltk.sent_tokenize(sentences)
s1 = nltk.word_tokenize(s[1])
> nltk.pos_tag(s1)

[('Nobody', 'NN'),
 ('expects', 'VBZ'),
 ('the', 'DT'),
 ('Spanish', 'JJ'),
 ('Inquisition', 'NNP'),
 ('.', '.')]
```

A POS tagged sentence with NLTK.

We can see that "Nobody" is a noun (NN), "expects" is a verb in the present tense (VBZ), "the" is a determiner (DT), "Spanish" is an adjective (JJ) and "Inquisition" is a proper noun (NNP).

You can look at the definitions of the tags using nltk.help.upenn_tagset() and pass the tag as an argument.

We can put all this together and analyse a larger corpus than the ones we have been dealing with so far. Let us take a look at one of the first speeches made by Barack Obama back in 2009. We will carry out the following steps:

1. Visit The American Presidency Project website

   https://www.presidency.ucsb.edu

2. Scrape the speech from the "Address Before a Joint Session of the Congress" from February 24th, 2009[12]

   [12] Address Before a Joint Session of the Congress. Barack Obama. 44th President of the United States: 2009-2017. https://www.presidency.ucsb.edu/node/286218

3. Save the speech to a local plain text file

4. Parse the sentences of the speech

5. Run some POS and determine the top named entities in the speech

It sounds like something we can definitely do. So let us get started by reading the speech page and loading it into Beautiful Soup:

Yes, we can!

```
wp='https://www.presidency.ucsb.edu/node/286218'
pageSource = urlopen(wp).read()
pa2009 = BeautifulSoup(pageSource, 'lxml')
```

We can now find the place where the actual speech is located. In this case, it is in a div with class field-docs-content inside another div with class main-container container, yes... two containers... We are interested in all the paragraphs and therefore we use the find_all method to obtain them:

Remember that if the page source changes, this code will need to be adapted accordingly.

```
maincontainer = pa2009.find('div',
    class_='main-container container')
content = maincontainer.find('div',
    class_='field-docs-content')
content_p = content.find_all('p')
```

Refer to Section 2.1 for the use of Beautiful Soup.

Now that we have the paragraphs, we can get the text and start cleaning it. For example, we need to get rid of heading and trailing spaces, as well as joining the paragraphs in a single string:

```
paragraphs = [p.get_text().strip() for p in
    content_p]
speech = ' \n'.join(paragraphs)
```

We are concatenating all the paragraphs, leaving a new line in between them.

We can now use this string to write the text to a file:

```
with open('obama2009.txt', 'wb') as f:
    f.write(speech.encode())
```

It is possible now to separate each of the sentences in the speech:

We use sentence tokenisation to separate each of the sentences in the speech.

```
sentences = nltk.sent_tokenize(speech)
```

and obtain the word tokens that can be POS tagged:

```
tokenized_sentences = [nltk.word_tokenize(sentence)
    for sentence in sentences]
tagged_sentences = [nltk.pos_tag(sentence) for
    sentence in tokenized_sentences]
```

Finally we tokenise each of the sentences and POS tag the tokens we have obtained.

So far so good! We now have tagged sentences and we could take a look at those to obtain the nouns mentioned in the speech. However, we are interested in more than simply getting all the nouns. We would like to get those named entities that are the subject of the sentences, in other words the protagonists of the speech. To that end, we will use a technique called *chunking*, which is a process to extract phrases from unstructured text. In this way, a phrase such as "United States" becomes a single entity instead of ending up with two separate words "United" and "States".

As it is the case with POS tagging, there are standard chunk tags that can be obtained, such as Noun Phrases (NP), Verb Phrases (VP) and Named Entities (NE) for example. In NLTK we can use the ne_chunk_sents which uses a maximum entropy (MaxEnt) classifier using data from the ACE (Automatic Content Extraction)[13] corpus. The ACE corpus has been manually annotated for named entities. The named entity chunker uses the following features to predict NEs, among others:

- Capital letters, no numbers in the word

- Word length

- First and last three letters of the word

- POS tag

- Dictionary words

- POS tags of the preceding and following words

Let us determine the named entities in the tagged sentences from Obama's speech:

```
chunked_sentences = nltk.ne_chunk_sents(
    tagged_sentences, binary=True)
```

In this case, binary=True lets NLTK know that we want to use the binary named entity chunker. The result is a

Chunking lets us extract phrases from unstructured text, and in this case obtain named entities.

[13] ACE 2004 Multilingual Training Corpus. https://catalog.ldc.upenn.edu/LDC2005T09

These are some of the features that determine a named entity in NLTK.

We are using NLTK's ne_chunk_sents to chunk the sentences.

generator with `Tree` objects. In this context, a tree is a hierarchical grouping of syntactical elements that make up a natural language utterance.

A `Tree` consists of a node value which is typically a string label and a Python iterable object comprising the node's children which in turn can also be `Tree` objects themselves. Let us look at an example with the sentence shown in Figure 2.4.

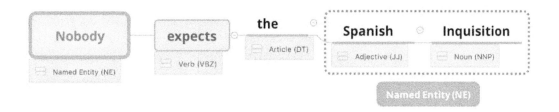

The sentence has two named entities, i.e., "Nobody" and "Spanish Inquisition", one verb in the present tense ("expects") and a definite article ("the"). We can recreate that `Tree` in NLTK as follows:

Figure 2.4: A chunked sentence with two named entities.

```
from nltk.tree import Tree
ne1 = Tree('NE', [('Nobody', 'NN')])
ne2 = Tree('NE', [('Spanish', 'JJ'),
    ('Inquisition', 'NNP')])
s = Tree('S', [ne1, ('expects', 'VBZ'),
    ('the', 'DT'), ne2])
```

The Tree structure of the chunked sentence shown in Figure 2.4.

In this case, we can see that the first named entity is a tree labelled `NE` and the token is appropriately tagged as a noun

(NN). With this knowledge, let us write a function that parses the Tree recurrently and gets the entity names in a chunked sentence:

```
def get_entity_names(tree):
    entity_names = []
    if hasattr(tree, 'label') and tree.label:
        if tree.label() == 'NE':
            entity_names.append(' '.join([child[0]
                for child in tree]))
        else:
            for child in tree:
                entity_names.extend(
                    get_entity_names(child))
    return entity_names
```

A function to extract named entities from a given Tree.

We can finally apply our function to the speech we are analysing:

```
entity_names = []
for tree in chunked_sentences:
    entity_names.extend(get_entity_names(tree))


> entity_names[-5:]


['South Carolina', 'American', 'God',
'United States', 'America']
```

We extract the named entities from the speech using the function above.

Let us finish this section by creating a dataframe with the data obtained and determine the top 10 named entities by frequency of mentions in the speech made by Obama in 2009 before a Joint Session of the Congress:

```
from collections import Counter

import pandas as pd


data_names = Counter(entity_names)

df = pd.DataFrame(list(data_names.items()),

    columns=['Entity Name', 'Freq'])

df.set_index('Entity Name', inplace=True)
```

The named entities can be loaded into a Pandas dataframe and be analysed.

We can see the top 10 named entities in the speech in Figure 2.5.

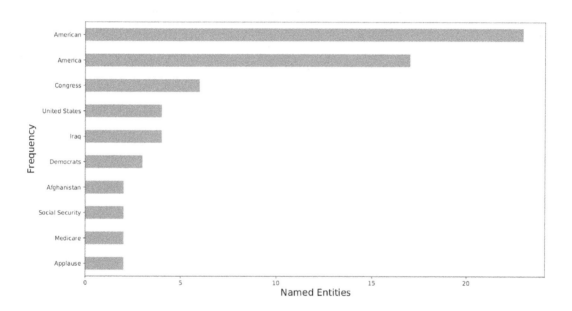

Figure 2.5: Top 10 named entities in the 2009 speech made by Barack Obama before a Joint Session of the Congress.

2.6   *What Are You Talking About?: Topic Modelling*

UNDERSTANDING THE DIFFERENT THEMES OR topics that a piece of text is about constitutes another important and useful application of natural language processing. The identification of topics from the word patterns present in a corpus is known as topic modelling and is an unsupervised task. In contrast to topic modelling, we have rule-based text mining approaches based on the use of keyword searching.

But, what is a topic? In this context, we are interested in looking for repeating patterns of terms that co-occur in a given corpus. This means that the end result of topic modelling is a set of words that can be used to describe the theme or themes in the corpus. Please note that the algorithm does not provide a closed, definitive topic. Instead, we require a human to provide the label. Also, since topic modelling is an unsupervised task, the other important task in the process requires the identification of the likely number of topics in the corpus.

2.6.1   Latent Dirichlet Allocation

ONE OF THE MOST POPULAR algorithms employed in topic modelling is the Latent Dirichlet Allocation algorithm (LDA). It enables us to explain existing observations based on latent, or unobserved, groups of variables that account for similarities in the original data.

One of the first descriptions and uses of LDA was in the area of population genetics by Pritchard, Stephens and Donnelly[14]. In their paper, the authors address the problem of assigning individuals to K populations (with K potentially being unknown). In this case, instead of different pieces of text, we have individual genotypes, and instead of

[14] Pritchard, J. K., Stephens, M., and Donnelly, P. (2000). Inference of population structure using multilocus genotype data. *Genetics* 155(2), 945–956

looking at the frequency of words in each text, we are interested in the allele frequencies in the populations. The distribution on these frequencies is assumed to have a Dirichlet distribution which has the property that the frequencies add up to 1.

In short, the Latent Dirichlet Allocation algorithm takes information from latent variables taking samples over a probability simplex representing probabilities over K distinct categories, and the aim is to allocate each observation to one of the categories.

Think of a simplex as a set of numbers that add up to 1.

A more formal description of the LDA algorithm was done by Blei, Ng and Jordan[15] in 2003. In that paper, LDA is presented in the context of topic modelling where each piece of text is seen as a mixture over an underlying set of topics. Here, we will provide an intuitive explanation of the main concepts behind the algorithm.

[15] Blei, D. M., Ng, A. Y., and Jordan, M. I. (2003). Latent Dirichlet Allocation. *Journal of Machine Learning Research 3*, 993–1022

Let us start by considering a collection of documents we are interested in analysing. Each individual document talks about particular subjects and we can safely assume that each document contains a mixture of different topics. One topic may contain the words "quantum", "atom", "energy" and "tunnelling", whereas another may have words such as "data", "statistics", "python" and "analytics".

Any given document is thought of containing a mixture of different topics.

Topics are therefore abstract entities that we cannot directly see. Nonetheless, the appearance of the words mentioned in our example lets us infer that documents that contain the first set of words are about *"quantum physics"*, whereas those containing the second are about *"data science"*, for example.

Nonetheless, we can try to identify a dominant topic in each document.

This all sounds very encouraging; however, it is not possible to infer the topics exactly. There may be some documents about doing research in quantum physics using Python to analyse data! In any event, we may be able to work backwards and still be able to say something about the latent topics in our corpora.

We can, for instance, assume that we know which topic created each and every word in the collection, and then we see a word w_n in document $\mathbf{w}$ whose topic of origin is unknown to us. Furthermore, we have a corpus made out of M documents denoted $D = \{\mathbf{w}_1, \mathbf{w}_2, \ldots, \mathbf{w}_M\}$. Our task is to decide if word w_n comes from topic z_n.

A document here is a sequence of N words denoted by $\mathbf{w} = (w_1, w_2, \ldots, w_N)$.

Some avenues we may be able to pursue to answer the question include the frequency with which word w_n appears in documents about topic z_n. Also, we may want to consider if topic z_n is prevalent in the rest of document $\mathbf{w}$. At this point, it may be convenient to remind ourselves of the powerful Bayes' theorem:

The powerful Bayes' theorem strikes again!

$$P(A|B) = \frac{P(A)P(B|A)}{P(B)}, \qquad (2.1)$$

where $P(A|B)$ is the conditional probability of event A taking place given B. We provided a derivation of this expression in Chapter 6 of *Data Science and Analytics with Python*[16].

[16] Rogel-Salazar, J. (2017). *Data Science and Analytics with Python*. Chapman & Hall/CRC Data Mining and Knowledge Discovery Series. CRC Press

In this case, we know the frequency of the word w_n in topic z_n as well as the total number of words in that topic. Also we have a prior of the number of words in document $\mathbf{w}$ that come from topic z_n. We can use Bayes' theorem to determine the probability of having topic z_n given the word w_n in document **w**.

In LDA for each document **w** in corpus D we require the following constructs:

- The sequence of N that makes up a document follows a Poisson distribution, and

  This requirement on N can be relaxed.

- θ follows a Dirichlet distribution denoted $\text{Dir}(\alpha)$

  α will become one of our parameters.

For each of the N words we choose a topic z_n that follows a multinomial distribution with parameter θ, and then we choose a word w_n from the multinomial probability conditions on the topic z_n, i.e., $p(w_n|z_n, \beta)$.

Another parameter in our model is β.

What does this all mean? Well, remember that we started up assuming that the words in a document come from a specific topic, and vice versa. Let us then get all the words and allocate them to random topics to test if our initial assumption holds. Effectively we use the words in the documents to assess the words in the topics, and then we use the words in the topics to assess the words in the documents. If the words fit in the topic distribution, then we can go home. However, if they do not, then we change the topic the word is in. This is done iteratively until not many words need to be changed.

This is in effect the iterative work we require in the algorithm to determine the topic distribution in our corpus.

In the expressions above, you may have noticed two hyperparameters in our model, namely α and β. The first one is related to the document-topic density, in other words the number of topics per document; whereas the second one tells us something about the topic-word density. That is the

The higher the value of α, the higher the number of topics in a document. The higher the value of β, the higher the number of words per topic.

number of words per topic. The other parameter that needs to be given as an input is the number of topics!

As stated by Blei et al[17], the inferential problem in LDA is computing the posterior distribution of the latent variables given a document:

[17] Blei, D. M., Ng, A. Y., and Jordan, M. I. (2003). Latent Dirichlet Allocation. *Journal of Machine Learning Research 3*, 993–1022

$$p(\theta, \mathbf{z} | \mathbf{w}, \alpha, \beta) = \frac{p(\theta, \mathbf{z}, \mathbf{w} | \alpha, \beta)}{p(\mathbf{w} | \alpha, \beta)} \qquad (2.2)$$

It is possible to represent the LDA model as a probabilistic graphical model as shown in Figure 2.6. The parameters α and β are sampled once and are defined at a corpus level. The variables θ are sampled once per document, whereas w and z are sampled once for each word in each document.

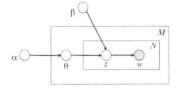

Figure 2.6: Graphical model representation of LDA.

From the discussion above, it is clear that we need to break down our documents into the constituent words and the information presented earlier on in this chapter is therefore quite useful. In particular, we will need to create a vocabulary of all the known words and measure their presence in our corpus. This is usually referred to as a *bag of words*, where information about the word order or even the sentence structure is disregarded, and we are only concerned with whether individual words are present or not in a document. If we look at individual words, we have a *unigram* analysis; in case we are interested in pairs of words appearing together we are analysing *bigrams* and as you can imagine this can be extended to *n-grams*.

We need to determine the vocabulary in our corpus and we do this with a bag of words approach.

For probabilistic models, it is common to use the log-likelihood of a held-out test for evaluation. We should be familiar with the idea of partitioning our dataset into training and testing sets, and in this case we would have $\mathbf{w}_d$ unseen documents and for our purposes of evaluation we can ignore the topic-distributions as they correspond to the training set. The *perplexity* measure is defined in terms of the log-likelihood as:

$$Perplexity(\mathbf{w}_d) = \exp\left(-\frac{\sum_d \log p(\mathbf{w}_d|\mathbf{z},\alpha)}{\text{count of tokens}}\right). \qquad (2.3)$$

The perplexity measure can help us determine the performance of our model.

The perplexity is a decreasing function of the log-likelihood of the unseen documents, and the lower the perplexity, the better the model.

2.6.2   LDA in Action

IT IS NOW TIME TO take a look at LDA in action. There are several options we have with Python including the excellent gensim[18] package, or spaCy[19]. In this case we are going to concentrate on our good old friend Scikit-learn.

In Chapter 6 of *Data Science and Analytics with Python*[20], we encountered a dataset containing a number of tweets used in the context of explaining the naïve Bayes classifier algorithm. We will be using the same corpus here. The data contains two sets: A training dataset with labelled tweets, and a testing dataset without labels. For the purposes of the discussions in this chapter, we will not be using the given labels in the training dataset. Remember that topic modelling is an unsupervised task! The data can be

[18] Řehůřek, R. and P. Sojka (2010, May). Software Framework for Topic Modelling with Large Corpora. In *Proceedings of the LREC 2010 Workshop on New Challenges for NLP Frameworks*, Valletta, Malta, pp. 45–50. ELRA. http://is.muni.cz/publication/884893/en
[19] spaCy. https://spacy.io
[20] Rogel-Salazar, J. (2017). *Data Science and Analytics with Python*. Chapman & Hall/CRC Data Mining and Knowledge Discovery Series. CRC Press

obtained at `https://doi.org/10.6084/`
`m9.figshare.2062551.v1`[21].

[21] Rogel-Salazar, J. (2016, Jan). Data Science Tweets. https://doi.org/10.6084/ m9.figshare.2062551.v1

Let us first read the data into Python:

```
import pandas as pd


tweets = 'Train_QuantumTunnel_Tweets.csv'
tweets = pd.read_csv(tweets, encoding='utf-8')
```

The location of your file may be different!

As we are interested in the words that appear in our tweets, we are bound to lose some information such as URLs and even @-mentions and hashtags. We will process our data to capture this information with the following function:

```
def mentions_hashtags_urls(tw):
    mnt = re.compile(''@\w+(?:[-']\w+)*|'')
    hash = re.compile(''#\w+(?:[-]\w+)*'')
    urls = re.compile(''http\S+'')
    mention = '' ''.join(mnt.findall(tw))
    hashtag = '' ''.join(hash.findall(tw))
    link = '' ''.join(urls.findall(tw))


    return mention, hashtag, link
```

This function lets us capture @-mentions, hashtags and URLs.

This compiles a regular expression to capture @-mentions, hashtags and URLs. and returns a concatenated version of each of these items. We can now map this function from the "Tweets" column in our dataset to three new columns as follows:

Remember that `findall` returns a list.

```
tweets['Mentions'], tweets['Hashtags'],\
    tweets['URLs'] = zip(*tweets['Tweet'].\
        map(mentions_hashtags_urls))
```

Here we use the power of zip to populate three columns in our dataframe! Cool, right?

We are not going to do much else here with this information, but you can take a look at the results and perhaps use them to improve the vocabulary in our bag of words. Here is some of that information though:

```
tweets[['Mentions', 'URLs', 'Hashtags']].tail(3)


Mentions        URLs                        Hashtags
@R_Trotta

                https://t.co/no4Usx6djV     #maths
                http://t.co/fW7pSgTWGj
```

These three columns can help inform our topics. We will not use them in the rest of our analysis though.

We are ready to start the tokenisation of our corpus and for that we need to bring up some useful packages and functions. First we will be using the TweetTokenizer we encountered in Section 2.4. We can also decide to use a lemmatiser or a stemmer for the pre-processing part. In this case, we will use a stemmer which we hope will help with some differences in spelling for example between American and British English:

You write *tokenize*, I write *tokenise*. Let's call the whole thing off.

```
import nltk
from nltk.tokenize.casual import TweetTokenizer


porter = nltk.PorterStemmer()
```

We may also want to get rid of the most common words in our bag, either in the language of the corpus such as "a", "the" "this", "that", ..., or words that we specifically would like to remove. For that we will use `stopwords` from NLTK:

In this case, the language is English.

```
from nltk.corpus import stopwords
import string


stop_words = stopwords.words('english')
stop_words.extend([''i've''])
```

Notice that we can even extend the list of words adding those which are of no interest to us. NLTK supports other languages including Spanish, German, Italian, etc. Another thing we will need to take care of is punctuation. For that matter we will use the `punctuation` method of `string` when processing our documents.

Stop words for other languages are available. We will also eliminate punctuation in our documents.

In a bag of words analysis we need to consider that for a computer, capital and lowercase letters are not the same. So "President" and "president" would count as two different words in their eyes. We can deal with this issue by transforming all capital letters into lowercase as part of the pre-processing we need to carry out.

I know... anthropomorphising computers is not very useful but then again...

Here are the steps we will be taking:

- Transform the text into lowercase characters

- Remove @-mentions

- Remove character sequences that contain numbers

- Remove URLs

- Tokenise each document with `TweetTokenizer`

- Remove stop words (English)

- Stem the tokens

- Remove punctuation

- Finally we join back the tokens in a processed string

Let us take a look:

```
def tw_preprocess(tw):
    tw = tw.lower()
    tw = re.sub('@\w+(?:[-']\w+)*', '', tw)
    tw = re.sub(r'\S*\d\S*', '', tw)
    tw = re.sub('http\S+', '', tw)
    tw = re.sub('[#|']', '', tw)
    tokens = TweetTokenizer().tokenize(tw)
    tokens = [t for t in tokens if t not in
              stop_words]
    tokens = [porter.stem(t) for t in tokens]
    tokens = [t for t in tokens if t not in
              string.punctuation]
    tokens = ' '.join(tokens)
    return tokens
```

We will use this function to process our corpus. It will later be employed on unseen tweets too.

OK, it is now time to process our corpus:

```
tweets['Processed_Tweet'] = tweets['Tweet'].\
    apply(tw_preprocess)
```

Let us preview the result:

```
> tweets["Processed_Tweet"].tail()


                            perhap peopl level
yay connect automat eduroam univers michigan great
true mean would cinema arriv late also paid ent...
            report card famou mathematician math
      princeton guid linear model logist regress r
```

Remember that we have stemmed our words.

We are in a position to vectorise our documents; in other words, we would like to create a (sparse) matrix containing the words that make up each of the documents in our corpus. We can do this in Scikit-learn with the help of CountVectorizer:

```
from sklearn.feature_extraction.text import \
    CountVectorizer


no_features = 1000
vectoriser = CountVectorizer(
    min_df=2,
    max_features=no_features)
```

CountVectorizer creates a matrix of token counts from the words contained in our corpus.

We are defining a matrix of token counts where we require at least 2 occurrences of the token (mid_df=2) and consider a vocabulary of 1000 features ordered by term frequency across the corpus (max_features). We can define other parameters such as the use of stop_words to remove stop words, or define regular expressions to extract tokens with token_pattern.

We have already taken care of stop words above.

Now that we have instantiated our vectoriser, let us learn
the vocabulary and return the term-document matrix for
our corpus:

```
tw_vectorised = vectoriser.\
    fit_transform(tweets['Processed_Tweet'])
tw_vectorised_names = vectoriser.\
    get_feature_names()
```

We use get_feature_names to
obtain a human readable version
of the tokens used in our model.

We can get the actual tokens that have been used in the
construction of the matrix with the help of the
get_feature_names method. Let us look at the first few
entries:

```
> print(tw_vectorised_names[:5])

['actual', 'ai', 'algorithm', 'alien', 'amaz']
```

See the result of
get_feature_names here.

The term-document matrix we have now obtained can be
used to feed to the Latent Dirichlet Allocation algorithm.
Scikit-learn has an implementation of the LDA algorithm in
sklearn.decomposition. We will now instantiate an object
to be used in our modelling:

Scikit-learn provides
LatenDirichletAllocation to
implement LDA.

```
from sklearn.decomposition import\
    LatenDirichletAllocation
```

Remember that the number of topics is an input parameter.
However, we do not know a priori how many topics there
are. So, we are going to carry out a grid search on the

number of topics. The implementation offers two learning methods: A batch variational Bayes method, and an online one. The latter uses a mini-batch of training data to update the topics incrementally. The learning rate for the online method is controlled by the learning decay and learning offset parameters.

Number of components in the language of Scikit-learn.

Our grid search will be done over both the number of topics and the learning decay. We will look at having between 3 and 7 topics in the corpus and learning decay equal to 0.6, 0.8 and 1.0.

We will carry out a grid search over two parameters: The number of topics and the learning decay.

```
n_components = range(3, 8)
search_params = {''n_components'': n_components,
    ''learning_decay'': [0.6,  0.8, 1.0]}
```

Let us instantiate our LDA model:

```
lda = LatentDirichletAllocation(
    max_iter=10,
    learning_method=''online'',
    random_state=0,
    evaluate_every=-1,
    learning_offset=50.0)
```

Our model needs to be instantiated before we are able to use it. This is true for other Scikit-learn models too.

We have a model with 10 as the maximum number of iterations, using the online Bayesian method with a random number generator seeded with 0. We can evaluate the perplexity at a number of iterations. If the evaluate_every parameter is 0 or negative, we do not evaluate the perplexity in training at all. Finally, a positive learning offset down-weights early iterations of the online learning method.

Let us search the parameters; in this case, we are requesting a 15-fold cross-validation and iid=True means that we want to get the average score across folds, weighted by the number of samples in each test set.

In this case we are performing a grid search with a 15-fold cross validation.

```
from sklearn.model_selection import GridSearchCV


model = GridSearchCV(lda,
    param_grid=search_params,
    cv=15,
    iid=True)
```

Training the model may take some time, and in the end we are interested in the best estimator found:

The best model out of the grid search is returned with the best_estimator_ method.

```
model.fit(tw_vectorised)
best_lda_model = model.best_estimator_
```

The best model obtained has the following parameters:

```
> print(''Best Model's Params: '',
    model.best_params_)


Best Model's Params: {'learning_decay': 1.0,
    'n_components': 3}
```

The chosen parameters for the best estimator can easily be obtained.

As you can see, we seem to have 3 topics in the corpus. The model's score and perplexity are:

```
> print(''Best Log Likelihood Score: '',
    model.best_score_)


Best Log Likelihood Score:   -936.9353366306428


> print(''Model Perplexity: '',
    best_lda_model.perplexity(tw_vectorised))


Model Perplexity:   730.704993701156
```

Please remember that there is an element of randomisation in the process and you may not get exactly the same scores and results shown here.

With the model trained, we can now create our document-topic matrix and extract the dominant topic for each document:

Once we have the model, we can create our document-topic matrix.

```
lda_output=best_lda_model.transform(tw_vectorised)
```

The output of the LDA model can be added to our original dataframe:

```
topicnames = ['Topic' + str(i) for i in
    range(best_lda_model.n_components)]


tweets = pd.concat([tweets,
    pd.DataFrame(
        np.round(lda_output, 2),
        columns=topicnames)], axis=1)
```

The output of the model can be added to our original dataframe.

Finally, we can obtain the dominant topic for each of the documents:

```
dominant_topic = np.argmax(

    df_document_topic[topicnames].values, axis=1)


tweets['Dominant_Topic'] = dominant_topic
```

The dominant topic is the one with the highest score.

We can take a look at some of the results obtained:

```
> tweets[['Tweet', 'Dominant_Topic']].head(4)


Tweet                      Dominant_Topic
Oh... It is even worse...        0
RStudio OS X Mavericks...        2
A Hubble glitch has pr...        0
@kwbroman Good questio...        1
```

And the results are in!

The first and second tweets correspond to topic 0, the second one to topic 2 and the fourth one to topic 1. We can take a look at the distribution of the tweets among the three topics:

```
df_topic_distribution = (
    tweets['Dominant_Topic'].\
        value_counts().reset_index(
            name="Num Documents"))
df_topic_distribution.columns = ['Topic Num',
    'Num Documents']
```

We can take a look at the distribution of topics.

This leaves us with the following distribution:

```
> print(df_topic_distribution)


  Topic Num  Num Documents

       1           125

       2           107

       0            92
```

Once again, your results may be different from these ones.

Topic modelling tells us the most likely dominant topic for each of the documents in our corpus. Nonetheless, we must remember that the method is an unsupervised task and therefore it cannot provide us with a label for each of the topics. That falls to the human in the middle. In other words, we may take a look at the words that are contained in each of the topics and we can try to make sense out of them. With that in mind, let us create a function that is able to extract the top n_words from each of the topics:

We can take a look at the words that make up each topic to provide a label.

```
def topic_words(model, feature_names, n_words=10):
    for idx, topic in enumerate(model.components_):
        print('Topic '.format(idx))
        print(' '.join([feature_names[i]
            for i in topic.\
                argsort()[: -n_words - 1: -1]]))
```

This function extracts the top n_words in each topic for us to assess.

The function above will provide by default the top 10 words in each of the topics found in the training of our algorithm. For our purposes, let us take a look at the top five words in our topics:

```
> topic_words(best_lda_model, tw_vectorised_names,
    n_words=5)


Topic 0
rugbi via xma think use
Topic 1
new physic statist star time
Topic 2
data xkcd great scienc make
```

Et voilà!

From the information above we can see that Topic 0 is a general topic including tweets about rugby; Topic 1 can be safely labelled as physics and science; and Topic 2 as data science and machine learning.

I can say it is a general topic given the familiarity with the documents. It may not be that obvious in other corpora!

Our last step is to use these new labels on unseen tweets. Fortunately in this case we do have a testing dataset. Let us take a look:

```
testtweets = 'Test_QuantumTunnel_Tweets.csv'
testtweets = pd.read_csv(testtweets,
    encoding='utf-8')
```

We need to perform the same processing done to our documents, and this can easily be carried out by applying the tw_preprocess function defined above to our test tweets:

We need to apply the same processing to unseen documents for scoring.

```
testtweets['Processed_Tweet'] = \
    testtweets['Tweet'].apply(tw_preprocess)
```

We will need to apply the vectoriser transformation to our new documents and then the model itself so that we can get the dominant topic. All this can be done with the following function:

```
def determine_topic(x, vec, model):
    mytext = [x]
    vec_transf = vec.transform(mytext)
    topic_prob_scores = model.transform(vec_transf)
    topic = np.argmax(topic_prob_scores)


    return topic
```

This function lets us score unseen documents with the trained model obtained.

All is left to do is to apply this function to our dataset:

```
testtweets['Topic']=testtweets['Processed_Tweet'].\
    apply(determine_topic, vec=vectoriser,
        model=best_lda_model)
```

Together with the processed tweets, the results can easily be saved if we wanted to. For now, we can take a look at some of the predictions made:

```
> testtweets[['Tweet', 'Topic']].tail(3)


                               Tweet   Topic
knitr in a knutshell tutorial htt...       2
Up all night to get data, a music...       0
A survival guide to Data Science ...       2
```

And there we have it, topic modelling completed!

And there you have it, LDA is served!

2.7   *Summary*

THIS CHAPTER HAS A LOT of very useful information to
deal with unstructured data such as text. We started our
discussion by defining what natural language is, and how
natural language processing is concerned with
programming computers to process and analyse large
amounts of natural language data. That sounds like
something a good Jackalope data scientist should master,
right?

We saw how to use Python to access data directly from the
web, and in particular we saw the use of Beautiful Soup to
scrape data from webpages. This required an understanding
of HTML and the way information is organised in terms
of tags. Beautiful Soup enabled us to scrape data from a
page containing the Iris Dataset and we got to grips with
using tags, navigable strings, comments and Beautiful Soup
objects in general.

We also covered the use of regular expressions to capture
specific patterns in a piece of text that is of interest to us.
We discussed some regular expression patterns and
familiarised ourselves with the re module in Python. This
led our discussions to the processing of text in Unicode and
we addressed some of the ways in which Python deals with
encoding issues. We even played with writing in Japanese
and processed the characters appropriately.

As part of the process of understanding text, we discussed
tokenisation and used NLTK as a way to extract meaningful

tokens out of our text. We did this with the help of available methods as well as creating our own, based for example on regular expressions. NLTK was also used in the context of stemming and lemmatising our tokens.

We saw how it is possible to use part-of-speech (POS) tagging on our tokens so as to be able to distinguish between important elements in a natural language, e.g., verbs, adjectives, nouns, clauses, etc. We used POS tagging in a US presidential speech to extract named entities mentioned.

Finally, we discussed topic modelling as an unsupervised learning task to identify the possible themes or topics that are addressed in a set of documents. The Latent Dirichlet Allocation algorithm, or LDA, was our main discussion point and we applied it to a corpus of tweets we had used before in the context of the naïve Bayes classifier. C-3PO watch your step, here we come!

3

Getting Social: Graph Theory and Social Network Analysis

NETWORK ANALYSIS ENCOMPASSES THE STUDY of relations between interconnected entities. It is based on the use of graphs to represent those entities (called nodes or vertices) and their connections (called edges, arcs or lines). These graphs can be layered with attributes and can also be rendered as diagrams.

Graph in the mathematical sense; not to be confused with a plot or a chart.

Network analysis has a large number of applications, from statistical physics to biology and from communications to finance. In particular, their application to undestanding social structures has gained prominence in behavioural organisational settings as well as psychology, political science and sociology.

Applications of network analysis can be quite wide.

As you can imagine networks can be varied, and the field tends to be rather multidisciplinary. In this chapter we will introduce network analysis for social relationships.

However, the tools and methods we will cover can readily be applied to a variety of other areas. Once you start looking through the lens of a graph analysis, you may start seeing networks everywhere.

3.1   Socialising Among Friends and Foes

AN INTEGRAL PART OF BEING human is our ability to identify a variety of structures and patterns. That is also certainly true when it comes down to social relationships between individuals, organisations, teams, countries, etc. Think about your own social relationships, there are people with whom you have a strong social bond such as your close family and friends. You may even have met friends of friends, some of whom have become closer to you over time. Others may not and in some situations they may even have become your nemeses.

You may want to hug your friends (please do!), and through the Holy Hand Grenade of Antioch towards thy foe! (please don't!).

The purpose of social network analysis (or SNA for short) is to understand the relationships between actors with a tie. The actors in the network are referred to as nodes or vertices and the ties are usually called edges (undirected), arcs (directed) or lines. In a social network, the nodes are usually people and the edges represent a social connection between them. The focus of analysis is not necessarily at the individual level, instead we are interested in the connections that are embedded in the network. In other words, we would like to understand what information passes through the network.

Here, we will refer to *nodes* and *edges*.

It is easy to see that relationship between actors in the network carries some meaning. Going back to thinking about your own social relationships, the meaning may represent the level of affection, membership, or communication, etc. These ties can have a direction. Consider for example the relationship "love" where the feeling may sadly not be reciprocated. In those cases, we have a *directed* graph. However, in a situation where the tie means "shared interests" the relationship is directionless and we therefore have an *undirected* graph.

Directed graphs have edges with direction, represented with an arrow.

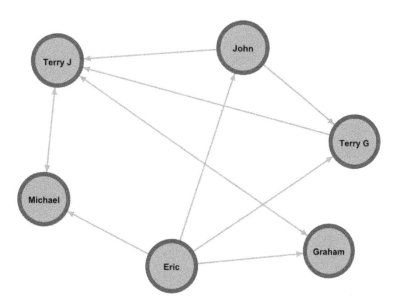

Figure 3.1: An example of a social network with directed edges.

In the network shown in Figure 3.1, we can see a directed network where the arrows indicate the direction of the relationship. We can see that Michael and Terry J have a mutual relationship, as well as Terry J and Graham. John has two outgoing relationships (with Terry J and Terry G) and one incoming relationship with Eric.

We know it is directed as the edges are represented with arrows.

Sometimes it is useful to concentrate our exploration of a network on a specific node. Within a social network context, we refer to those subsets as *ego networks*. The ego network for Terry G in our example can be seen in Figure 3.2. As you can see, this enables us to focus only on the edges that connect the node of interest with the rest of the network.

Ego networks concentrate on a specific node in the network.

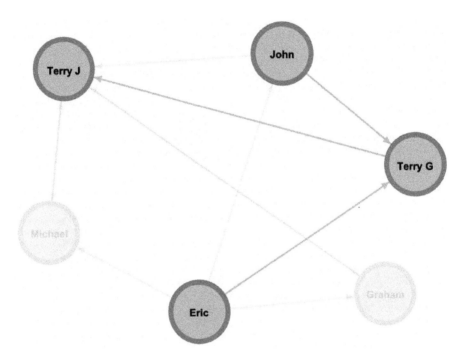

Figure 3.2: The ego network for Terry G. Only the related nodes are highlighted and the rest are dimmed down for clarity.

The ties that connect the nodes in the network can tell us things regarding how strongly (or weakly) the actors interact. We can identify clusters in the network exhibiting characteristics such as **homophily**, that is the tendency of individuals to associate and bond with similar actors, or **transitivity**, i.e., when there is a tie from node i to node j, and also from node j to node k the relationship is transitive if there is also a tie from i to k (see Figure 3.3). We can

Homophily → "Birds of a feather flock together".

Transitivity → "Friends of my friends are my friends".

also distinguish **cliques** which are densely, fully connected components in the network.

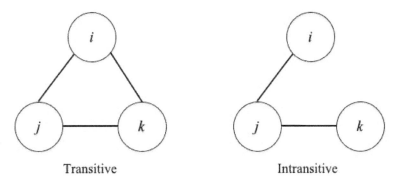

Transitive   Intransitive

Figure 3.3: Transitivity in a network.

All these relationships can be uncovered, studied and understood using the tools developed by the branch of mathematics known as graph theory. It has a long and distinguished history starting in the 18th century with the Swiss mathematician Leonhard Euler solving a pass time puzzle that entertained people in the old Prussian city of Königsberg, now Kaliningrad, Russia. The layout of the city connected four land masses divided by the Pregel river by seven bridges. The puzzle challenged the walker to find a way through the city crossing each bridge only once.

Graph theory is at the heart of social network analysis.

Leaving behind the geographical position of the land masses and the bridges, Euler's solution consisted instead of concentrating on the connections[1]. The result can be represented with a graph. See our depiction in Figure 3.4. Euler's approach laid the foundations of network theory as we know it today.

[1] Euler, L. (1736). Solutio problematis ad geometriam situs pertinentis. *Comment. Acad. Sci. U. Petrop. 8*, 128–140

The nodes in Figure 3.4 represent the land masses and the edges are the bridges. When looking at the problem in this

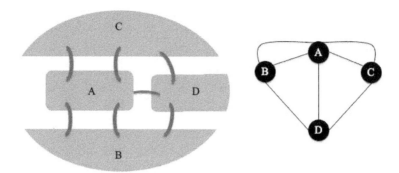

Figure 3.4: A schematic
geographical representation
of the seven bridges of Königsberg
and a network highlighting the
connectivity of the four land
masses in question.

way and according to the puzzle rules, you can see that
when you arrive to any particular node via an edge you
will need to leave it via a different line (unless it is the final
destination!). This means that any node that is neither the
starting, nor the ending position requires to have an even
number of lines, in other words, for every bridge used to
enter, there needs to be one bridge to leave.

You can follow this discussion
with the network shown in Figure
3.4.

This means that to be able to have a walking journey that
crosses every edge once, at most two nodes can have odd
number of edges. As we can see from the graph in Figure
3.4, all nodes have an odd number of edges and as such the
puzzle has no solution. Voilà!

Either two nodes, or none at all!

Graph theory is therefore the study of relationships: Given a
set of edges and nodes, which can be references to people,
computer networks, companies, atoms, etc., it is possible to
quantify and understand a variety of dynamic systems. If
the nodes were cities and the edges refer to routes
connecting those cities, we end up with a classical problem
known as the *travelling salesman problem* where given a finite
number of cities, along with the cost of travel between each

The travelling salesman problem
is a classic algorithm problem in
computer science.

pair of cities, the task is to find the cheapest way of visiting all of the places and returning home (i.e., the starting point).

The problem can be posed in a variety of ways. A great example is the puzzle game invented in the late 1850s by the mathematician William R. Hamilton known as the Icosian game[2] where the aim is to find a Hamiltonian cycle, in other words, a graph that visits each node only once, along the edges of a dodecahedron. The travelling salesman problem is a computationally difficult problem, and a large number of heuristics and exact methods are known to tackle it; in some instances, a solution can be found for tens of thousands of cities.

Ever since Euler's incursion in the field, mathematicians, physicists, biologists, chemists, engineers and social scientists have found uses for graphs. Given our interest in social analysis, perhaps it is illustrative to explore some of these applications. A great place to start is the game that the characters in Frigyes Karinthy's short story *Chains*[3] create: Find the chain that connects two individuals through at most five acquaintances. This is the beginning of the **small-world** experiments that gave us the notion of the *six degrees of separation*.

During the 1960s the experimental psychologist Stanley Milgram devised a series of experiments to prove the existence of short paths (the eponymous six degrees) among social connections[4]. The main aim was to test the notion that the world has shrunk in an ever interconnected world. Today the experiment may seem a bit rudimentary given the

[2] Ball, W.W.R. and Coxeter, H.S.M. (1987). *Mathematical Recreations and Essays*. Dover Recreational Math Series. Dover Publications

Actually it is an NP-Hard problem.

[3] Karinthy, F. (1929). Chains in Everything is Different. Online at http://bit.ly/karinthy_chains. Translated from Hungarian and annotated by Adam Makkai. Edited by E Jankó

[4] Milgram, S. (1967). The small world problem. *Psych. Today* 1(1), 60–67

social media tools we have at our disposal, but back in the 1960s the mere idea of interconnectedness was put to the test. In one of the experiments for example, Milgram arranged for 96 packages to be sent randomly to chosen people living in Omaha, Nebraska. Each package contained instructions for each recipient telling them to get the package back to a friend of his who lived in Boston, Massachusetts. The name of the ultimate recipient was provided, along with his address and his occupation (a stockbroker).

They were randomly chosen from a telephone directory!

The task requested that each recipient of a package send it to a person they knew on a first-name basis and who they felt would be socially closer to the ultimate addressee. These new recipients were in turn asked to do the same until, of course, the package was hopefully received by the stockbroker in Boston. The lucky Bostonian received 18 of the 96 original packages, and the mean number of the connections from start to end turned out to be around 5.9, leading to the famous 6 degrees everyone, including ourselves, is talking about.

18 of the 96 packages reached their destination with a mean number of connections equal to 5.9.

The imagination of a lot of us has been captured by this "small world" phenomenon, but the real surprise is the easiness with which, using local information, it is possible to navigate a large social network. So much so, that similar challenges have kept film trivia boffins entertained with calculating the so-called *Bacon number* where the aim is to find the shortest path that connects any given actor to Mr. Kevin Bacon in terms of having worked together.

The Bacon number connects any given actor to Mr. Kevin Bacon.

The Bacon number is in fact an application of the *Erdös number* used and abused by mathematicians to describe the distance of academic collaboration with the prolific Hungarian mathematician Paul Erdös. The measurement is the authorship of papers that connect mathematicians: Erdös himself has number 0; those mathematicians who co-authored a paper with him have an Erdös number of 1, co-authors who have penned a paper with a scientist whose Erdös number is n have an Erdös number equal to $n + 1$. The calculation is given by the so-called shortest path algorithm which aims to find a path between two nodes such that the sum of the weights of the edges is minimal.

The Erdös number connects any given mathematician to Paul Erdös.

There is even a combined Erdös-Bacon number which is the sum of someone's Erdös number with their Bacon number. Some of my favourite nodes in the network that intersects thespians with scientists include Mayim Bialik of *The Big Bang Theory* fame and Natalie Portman (aka *Star Wars*'s Queen Amidala among other characters) both have an Erdös number of 5 and a Bacon number of 2 (as of 2018), leaving them with an Erdös-Bacon number of 7. Carl Sagan and Stephen Hawking both have an Erdös-Bacon number equal to 6 (Bacon= 4, Erdös= 2).

The sitcom by the way, not the event that created the Universe.

The work of Duncan Watts and Steve Strogatz on small-world networks[5] has become so influential that these networks are often referred to as Watts-Strogatz networks. It is important to mention that the wide preference is to use the term specifically to describe graphs with a small mean geodesic path length and significant local clustering. We will come to explain some of these terms in the next section.

[5] Watts, D. and Strogatz, S. (1998). Collective dynamics of small-world networks. *Nature* 393(1), 440–442

These days, the opportunities to analyse social media data are open to a lot of us, from using Twitter data[6] to help better define the term digital humanities, all the way through to finding what combinations of flavours make some dishes taste great[7].

Some applications could be as complex as understanding the symptoms experienced by cancer patients undergoing chemotherapy[8]; or simply visualising the relationships between philosophers over centuries[9]. We need to be mindful, of course, of the data privacy issues that may arise when sourcing information from various social media platforms and other sources of information. This is not just important in the analysis of social networks, but indeed more general to any data science work we are involved with. Be a good Jackalope data scientist!

[6] Grandjean, M. (2016). A social network analysis of Twitter: Mapping the digital humanities community. *Cogent Arts and Humanities 3*, 1–14

[7] Simas, T. et al. (2017). Food-Bridging: A new network construction to unveil the principles of cooking. *Frontiers in ICT 4*, 14

[8] Papachristou, N. et al. (2019). Network Analysis of the Multidimensional Symptom Experience of Oncology. *Scientific Reports 9*(1), 2258

[9] Noichl, M. (2017). Relationships between Philosophers, 600 b.c - 160 b.c. https://homepage.univie.ac.at/noichlm94/full/Greeks/index.html. Accessed: 2019-02-18

3.2   *Let's Make a Connection: Graphs and Networks*

Now that we have a better idea of the applications and usefulness of networks, it is time to provide some of the notions that underpin the framework that enables us to understand the connections (edges) between the actors (nodes) in a given network. That framework is largely built around graph theory, a branch of mathematics interested in the properties of graphs. As we saw in the previous section, the basic idea of graphs was introduced by Euler and in this section we will address some important aspects we need to understand to work with graphs, but we will not cover graph theory in its full glorious interconnectedness.

Graph theory is a branch of mathematics interested in the properties of graphs.

Up until now we have defined a graph in a loose way. Let us correct that and define a graph G as an object that consists of a collection of nodes or vertices V, and arcs or edges E, that connect pairs of vertices and can be expressed as $G = (V, E)$. We will refer to an arc as a directed connection between two nodes. If we consider two nodes v_1 and v_2 in G, an arc will be denoted as the ordered pair (v_1, v_2). If the connection is undirected, we will refer to it as an edge and will be denoted as $(v_1 : v_2)$. Notice that the order in this case is irrelevant.

$G = (V, E)$ denotes the graph G with nodes V and edges E.

The neighbours of a node v_i are denoted as $N(v_i)$ and are all the nodes immediately connected to v_i. A walk in graph G is a sequence that traverses the graph from neighbour to neighbour. The length $|s|$ of the walk is the number of lines it contains. A walk is closed if the starting and ending points are one and the same node. There are other kinds of walks:

A walk is a sequence that traverses a graph from neighbour to neighbour.

- A **trail** is a walk where no lines (i.e., arcs or edges) are repeated. This was the aim in Euler's Königsberg puzzle: We cannot use the same bridge again.

- A **path** is a walk where no nodes are repeated. Using the Königsberg arrangement, this would be a case where we cannot visit the same land mass more than once.

There are other kinds of walks, such as trails, paths, cycles and chains.

- A **cycle** is a closed walk where all the nodes are different. In contrast, an *acyclic graph* does not contain any cycles.

- A **chain** or **semi-walk** is a walk where the direction of the lines is not considered.

The distance of shortest length between two nodes is denoted as $d(v_i, v_j)$. We can take a look at the largest (maximum) distance between any two vertices in the graph, i.e., $\max_{v_i, v_j \in V} d(v_i, v_j)$. This is the diameter of the graph and is denoted as $diam(G)$. On the other hand, the shortest paths are called **geodesic** paths.

The diameter of a graph is the path of maximum length.

Remember: No repeated nodes.

Consider the graph in Figure 3.5, the distance from node 1 to 2 is $d(1,2) = 1$ and the distance from node 1 to 4 is $d(1,4) = 4$.

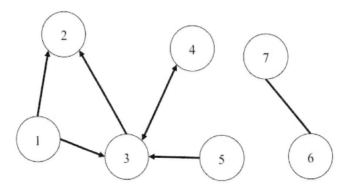

Figure 3.5: An example graph with seven nodes, and two sub-graphs.

If the nodes are not connected, then $d(v_i, v_j) = \infty$. This means that the graph is disconnected, and thus the vertices v_i and v_j live in separate parts of the graph, such as nodes 1 and 7 in Figure 3.5, where we can clearly see the disconnection too. If the relationship in the graph was communication between actors, this situation would mean that there is no way for any messages to be passed between nodes $1, 2, 3, 4, 5$ and $6, 7$ in our example graph.

A disconnected graph has paths with distances equal to infinity (∞).

We say that node v_j is **reachable** from node v_i if and only if (iff) there is a walk starting at v_i and ending at v_j. We have a **weakly connected** node iff there is a semi-walk between nodes v_i and v_j. Iff both nodes are reachable, then we have a **strongly connected** pair of nodes. In our example graph, node 4 is reachable from node 1 (as are nodes 2 and 3); node 5 is weakly connected to 1. Nodes 3 and 4 are strongly connected. Notice that nodes 6 and 7 are also strongly connected, as we are assuming that the lack of arrows in the line indicates bidirectionality and therefore the relationship is undirected.

As we can see, it is possible to characterise the connectedness of our graphs.

We have seen a typical depiction of a network showing the connections among neighbours and, if appropriate, the direction of those connections. It is possible to represent a graph with the help of an **adjacency matrix**, i.e., a square matrix whose elements indicate whether a pair of vertices are connected or not. In an undirected graph, the matrix is symmetric, and typically we will show a 0 if the nodes are not connected and a 1 if they are. Values different from 1 are possible, and this would indicate the strength or weight of the connection.. The adjacency matrix for the graph in Figure 3.5 is given by:

An adjacency matrix indicates whether two nodes are connected or not.

$$
\begin{array}{c c}
& \begin{array}{c c c c c c c} 1 & 2 & 3 & 4 & 5 & 6 & 7 \end{array} \\
\begin{array}{c} 1 \\ 2 \\ 3 \\ 4 \\ 5 \\ 6 \\ 7 \end{array} &
\begin{bmatrix}
0 & 1 & 1 & 0 & 0 & 0 & 0 \\
0 & 0 & 0 & 0 & 0 & 0 & 0 \\
0 & 1 & 0 & 1 & 0 & 0 & 0 \\
0 & 0 & 1 & 0 & 0 & 0 & 0 \\
0 & 0 & 1 & 0 & 0 & 0 & 0 \\
0 & 0 & 0 & 0 & 0 & 0 & 1 \\
0 & 0 & 0 & 0 & 0 & 1 & 0
\end{bmatrix}
\end{array} .
\qquad (3.1)
$$

This is the adjacency matrix for the graph in Figure 3.5.

Notice that only the entries for nodes 3 and 4, and 6 and 7 are symmetric. For the rest, we need to read the matrix row-by-row to find the connections.

You may have noticed that there is a large number of zero entries in the adjacency matrix. Computationally speaking, it may be possible to store this information in a sparse matrix. An alternative way to store the information contained in the adjacency matrix is via an **edge list** where each entry is given by a pair of vertices that are connected. The edge list for our example graph is given by:

$$G = [[1,2], [1,3], [3,2], [3,4], [4,3], [5,3], [6,7], [7,6]]. \quad (3.2)$$

> If the graph is weighted, the entry is a triplet: The first two elements being the nodes and the third one is the weight.

Finally, a way that combines the connectivity format of an adjacency matrix with the briefness of an edge list is the **adjacency list**. In this case, for each node in the graph we store a list that contains the nodes adjacent to it. If the graph is weighted, we can add the weight to the connected node too. The adjacency list for our example graph is as follows:

> An adjacency list combines the connectivity format of an adjacency matrix, with the briefness of an edge list.

$$
\begin{aligned}
G \quad = \quad & [[1 \rightarrow [2,3]], \qquad\qquad (3.3) \\
& [3 \rightarrow [2,4]], \\
& [4 \rightarrow [3]], [5 \rightarrow [3]], \\
& [6 \rightarrow [7]], [7 \rightarrow [6]]].
\end{aligned}
$$

It is possible to define a **partition** of nodes V as the set of subsets of nodes $\mathbf{C} = \{C_i\}$ such that the union of C_i is equal to V and for subsets $C_i \cap C_j = \emptyset$ (with $i \neq j$). In other words, the subsets do not overlap and when looking at them together as a whole they regenerate the original set V. We can also define an **equivalence** relation R on V iff it is reflexive ($\forall v \in V : vRv$), symmetric ($\forall u, v \in V : uRv \rightarrow vRu$) and transitive ($\forall u, v, z \in V : uRz \land zRu \rightarrow uRv$). Each equivalence relation determines a partion into equivalence classes $[v] = \{u : vRu\}$; and each partition determines an equivalence relation. Weak and strong connectivities as defined above are equivalence relations, defining weak and strong components.

Each equivalence relation determines a partition into equivalence classes, and vice versa.

3.2.1   Taking the Measure: Degree, Centrality and More

WE ARE NOW WELL CONNECTED with the idea of a graph and we have defined a number of attributes related to it. In this section we will define characteristics of the nodes themselves as well as characterising the relationship between the nodes in a graph.

Pun definitely intended!

Let us start by defining the **degree** of a node v, $deg(v)$, as the number of edges that are connected to node v. In Figure 3.5 the degree of nodes 1 and 3 are $deg(1) = 2$ and $deg(3) = 4$, respectively.

The degree of a node is the number of edges that are connected to it. The in- and outdegrees are only applicable to directed graphs.

The **outdegree** is only applicable for directed graphs and $outdeg(v)$ is the number of arcs outgoing from node v. Similarly, the **indegree**, $indeg(v)$ is the number of arcs incoming to node v. In our example graph above, for node 1 we have that $outdeg(1) = 2$, and $indeg(1) = 0$; whereas for node 3, the measures are $outdeg(3) = 1$, and $indeg(3) = 3$.

The centrality of the nodes is another important attribute that gives us information about the most prominent actors in a network. Centrality in this case refers to how well connected a node is to the rest of the network. We can think of highly connected nodes as power centers, or information hubs. As such a higher centrality is judged to be an important asset for a node. We already know how to calculate the **degree centrality** of a node: It is simply the degree measures we defined earlier on.

In other words, how *central* the node is.

There are other types of centrality, such as the so-called **betweenness**, which is useful in measuring the influence that a particular node has over a network. We can think of this measure as a way to finding bridges between different components of a graph. Betweenness centrality is calculated by the shortest (weighted) path between every pair of nodes and is given by:

Betweenness tells us about the influence of nodes over the graph, thinking of them as bridges over the network.

$$g(v) = \sum_{a \neq v \neq b} \frac{\sigma_{ab}(v)}{\sigma_{ab}}, \qquad (3.4)$$

where σ_{ab} is the number of geodesic paths from node a to node b and $\sigma_{ab}(v)$ is the number of those paths that pass through node v.

There are cases where we may be interested in finding out which nodes are able to spread information more efficiently through the network. In those cases, the centrality measure we are interested in is called **closeness**. The closeness centrality of a node is proportional to the inverse of the average distance from the node to the rest of the network. In this way, a node with high closeness centrality has the

Closeness centrality tells us about the nodes that are able to spread information more efficiently in the network.

shortest distances to all the other nodes. This can be
expressed as follows:

$$C(v) = \frac{N}{\sum_x d(v, x)},$$

(3.5)

where $d(v, x)$ is the distance between nodes v and x, and N
is the number of nodes in the graph. Closeness centrality is
sensitive to the size of the graph. As you intuitively know, it
is harder to keep a close relationship with every single one
of the members in a network, and as the network grows in
size this gets harder and harder. Multiplying by the number
of nodes provides a form of correction for this situation.

Closeness centrality is sensitive to
the size of the network.

In some cases, instead of asking how efficient the
communication between nodes may be, we may be
interested in finding out how well-connected the actors in
our network are. This can be seen as an extension to the
degree centrality we discussed earlier on. The indegree
centrality scores a point for every link a node receives;
however, in a more general case, not all nodes are equivalent
and there may be some that are more relevant / powerful /
important than others. This is effectively a case of being
endorsed by influential nodes. This can be measured by the
eigenvector centrality which tells us that a node is
important if it is linked to other important nodes.

This is the equivalent of "having
friends in high places".

Eigenvector centrality tells us
that a node is important if it is
connected to other important
nodes.

A node receiving many connections does not necessarily
have a high eigenvector centrality score (the actor can have a
lot of friends, but none are in high places); furthermore, a
node with a high eigenvector centrality score is not
necessarily highly linked (the actor has a few but very

important friends). To calculate the eigenvector centrality, we take advantage of the matrix representation of the graph and calculate its eigenvectors. First of all, we need to calculate a measure that is proportional to the sum of the scores of all nodes connected to a given node, i.e.:

Hence the name!

$$x_i = \frac{1}{\lambda} \sum_{j \in M(i)} x_j, \qquad (3.6)$$

where the sum is over all $j \in M(i)$ such that the nodes j are connected to the node in question (i). Another way to calculate this is using the adjacency matrix A and we let $\mathbf{x}$ be the vector that has the centrality scores enabling us to write the following eigenvector equation:

$$A\mathbf{x} = \lambda \mathbf{x}, \qquad (3.7)$$

Surely you can recognise this as an eigenvector equation.

where λ is called the eigenvalue. Our task is to find λ, and in general there may be multiple non-trivial solutions to the problem. We need to use an extra tool from our Jackalope data scientist belt: If we require that all the entries in the eigenvector are non-negative, thanks to the Perron-Frobenius theorem[10], there is only one eigenvalue that satisfies this requirement! This corresponds to the largest eigenvalue and that is good enough for ranking our nodes in terms of this centrality measure.

[10] Bapat, R., R. Bapat, T. Raghavan, C. U. Press, T. S, G. Rota, B. Doran, P. Flajolet, M. Ismail, T. Lam, et al. (1997). *Nonnegative Matrices and Applications*. Encyclopedia of Mathematics and its Applications. Cambridge University Press

The **PageRank** algorithm, famously used by Google Search to rank webpages, is a variant of eigenvector centrality. It is used to determine the importance of a webpage considering the number of links it gets, the link propensity of other pages and the centrality of those pages.

PageRank is a variant of eigenvector centrality.

We can calculate the PageRank centrality of a node as follows:

$$x_i = \alpha \sum_k \frac{a_{k,i}}{outdeg(k)} x_k + \beta, \qquad (3.8)$$

where α and β are constants, $outdeg(k)$ is the outdegree of node k, and $a_{k,i}$ is the (k, i) entry in the adjacency matrix for the graph. We can write this equation in matrix form as $x = \alpha x D^{-1} A + \beta$, with D^{-1} being a diagonal matrix with k-th diagonal element equal to $1/outdeg(k)$. We can solve for x as $x = \beta(I - \alpha D^{-1} A)^{-1}$. We call α the damping factor, and its value should be chosen between 0 and $1/\rho(D^{-1}A)$, where $\rho(D^{-1}A)$ is the largest eigenvalue of $D^{-1}A$. It must be said that for large networks, it is more efficient to compute the PageRank via power iteration, as it does not have to deal with matrix decomposition and it works very well with sparse matrices.

Note that if the outdegree of k is null, we require that $outdeg(k) = 1$ in this calculation.

See more about power iteration in Appendix B.

3.2.2   Connecting the Dots: Network Properties

WE HAVE DESCRIBED A FEW attributes that characterise the individual nodes in a graph, and although they are important, the power comes from the collective properties that the nodes provide to the whole network, as they show the structure in the relationships between the actors. The emerging properties of the network as a whole provide us with a view of the aggregate effects individual nodes have on the whole.

We are interested in understanding the aggregate effects individual nodes have on the whole network.

For instance, looking at the different centrality measures discussed in the previous subsection, we can take a look a the **centralisation** of the overall graph. In other words,

Centralisation is an important characteristic of a network as a whole.

we can measure how even the scores of the nodes are. If they are evenly distributed we can talk about distributed networks, where every node is as central as any other. If the scores are not even, we refer to centralised networks, where one node is maximally central, and the rest are not.

This brings us to the concept of the **density** of the network. It is a measure of how the network nodes are connected to each other. In the case where all the nodes are connected to one another, we have a complete graph and the density is equal to one. Formally speaking, the density $D(G)$ of graph G is defined by the number of existing edges, m, in the graph, compared to the total number of all possible edges:

The density measures how nodes are connected to one another.

$$D(G) = \frac{2m}{n(n-1)}. \qquad (3.9)$$

The total number of possible edges is given by $n(n-1)/2$.

The value of $D(G)$ ranges between 0 and 1. In many real situations, the density of a graph is low. Think of a typical network in social media: A user will be connected to a few other users, while the actual network contains many, many more.

Now that we know about network density, it is straightforward to talk about **cliques** or **clusters** in the network. We are interested in knowing how much the nodes tend to form dense subgraphs, i.e., cliques or clusters. In a way, this is related to figuring out if two people are friends given that each person is friends with a common third party. We call this the **local clustering coefficient**, and it is given

Cliques are densely, fully connected components in the network.

by the following expression:

$$C_i = \frac{2T(i)}{deg(i)\,(deg(i)-1)}.$$ (3.10)

The local clustering coefficient.

In other words, this is the ratio of the pairs of friends of v_i who are friends among themselves, $T(i)$, and the total number of pairs of v_i's friends. $T(i)$ is given by the number of closed triangles with node v_i as one of the vertices, whereas the total number of pairs of v_i's friends is given by:

$$\frac{deg(i)}{2}\,(deg(i)-1).$$ (3.11)

In turn, the clustering in the network can be measured by the average **clustering coefficient**:

$$C = \frac{1}{n}\sum C_i,$$ (3.12)

The average clustering coefficient.

where n is the number of nodes in the graph.

A closely related measure to the clustering coefficient is the transitivity of the network. The average transitivity of a network is defined over the number of triangles in the graph:

We introduced the concept of transitivity on page 134.

$$Transitivity = \frac{3(\text{num. of triangles})}{(\text{num. of connected triples})},$$ (3.13)

where a connected triple is any trio of nodes i,j,k that forms an open triangle, for example with connections between i and j, and i and k. Notice that a closed triangle can be thought of as being composed of three open triangles. Transitivity measures the fraction of open triangles that are actually closed.

Hence the factor of 3 in the formula.

We are interested in the clustering coefficient and the transitivity of a graph as they can be used to check for structural holes in the network. In other words, these measures show missing links between neighbours of a node. They give us information about the efficiency of information diffusion in the network, as well as how robust it may be to disruptions.

We may also be interested in identifying the **giant component** of a network. This is the largest strongly connected subgraph in a large network such that its size is a constant fraction of the entire graph as the latter grows in size. If N_1 is the size of a connected component K in a network with N nodes, then K is a giant component if:

> The giant component is the largest strongly connected graph in a network.

$$\lim_{N \to \infty} \frac{N_1}{N} = c > 0, \tag{3.14}$$

with c being a constant.

Once we are able to detect cliques and giant components, it is natural to ask if the network exhibits clusters that are not densely connected to others, but which are densely connected within themselves. We can think of these situations as having different "communities" within the network. **Community detection** is a hot research topic as it is an NP-complete problem and in many cases the full exploration of the entire network is required. The task in community detection is to find a subgraph S of $G(V, E)$ where the nodes $V_S \in V$ share some similarity.

> NP-complete means that we can verify the answer *quickly*, but sadly there is no known way to find a solution quickly.

One way we can start detecting groupings in a network is by finding sub-graphs which keep nodes connected as we traverse the graph. In other words, we need to find a k-component of the graph. We define a k-component as a maximal subgraph with, at least, connectivity k. Put in a different way, if we wanted to break that subgraph into more components, we would need to remove at least k nodes from it. The algorithm from Moody and White[11] can help us with this task. Note that there is a hierarchical nature to the structure of k-components in that the subgraphs are nested from a connectivity point of view: A given network can have a number of 2-components, which in turn can have one or more 3-components, and so on.

[11] Moody, J. and White, D. (2003). Social cohesion and embeddedness: A hierarchical conception of social groups. *Am. Soc. Rev. 68*(1), 103–128

In terms of community detection, an algorithm usually employed for this purpose is the Girvan-Newman algorithm.[12] It aims to find the communities in a network by iteratively removing edges from the initial graph; as such, the remaining connected components are deemed to be the communities. The algorithm extends the definition of betweenness to the edges of the network, with **edge betweenness** being the number of geodesic paths between pairs of nodes that pass through a given edge. The idea is that separate communities are connected via edges with high edge betweenness. If we remove these edges, the community structure is unraveled.

[12] Girvan, M. and Newman, M.E.J (2002). Community structure in social and biological networks. *Proc. Natl. Acad. Sci. USA 99*, 7821–7826

There are a number of algorithms attempting to find community structures in networks[13] from graph partitioning and hierarchical clustering through to optimisation and generative model techniques. Unfortunately, we do not have the remit to cover these methods at length, but we can highlight the **Louvain**

[13] Fortunato, S. (2010). Community detection in graphs. *Phys. Rep. 486*(3-5), 75–174

method[14] used to detect communities in large network settings based on a greedy optimisation approach. At the heart of both the Girvan-Newman and Louvain methods lies the concept of **modularity** as a way to quantify how cohesive the communities in a network are.

[14] Vincent D Blondel, Guillaume, J.-L., Lambiotte, R., and Lefebvre, E. (2008, Oct.). Fast unfolding of communities in large networks. *J. Stat. Mech-Theory E* 2008(10), P10008

We can define modularity in terms of the adjacency matrix of the graph, A and the sum of the edge weights attached to a node i given by $k_i = \sum_j A_{ij}$:

$$Q = \frac{1}{2m} \sum_{i,j} \left[A_{ij} - \frac{k_i k_j}{2m} \right] \delta(c_i, c_j). \qquad (3.15)$$

Each term in the sum contributes to the overall modularity measure by comparing nodes being in the same community c_i. The Kronecker delta function $\delta(c_i, c_j)$ is equal to 1 if $i = j$; if not, the nodes are not in the same community and $\delta(c_i, c_j) = 0$. The total edge weight in the entire network is given by $m = \frac{1}{2} \sum_{i,j} A_{ij}$.

In other words, if both nodes are in the same community we multiply the contribution by 1, otherwise by 0.

Let us try to get a better understanding of each contribution to the expression above: We know that k_i is the total of the edge weight attached to i. We can consider a situation where node i assigns this edge weight randomly to other nodes in a way that is proportional to their own edge weight values. In that case, $\frac{k_j}{2m}$ is the average fraction of node i's edge weight that would be assigned to node j. Put in a different way, each contribution tells us how strongly nodes i and j are connected in the actual graph, in contrast to the case where the nodes are connected in a random network.

A dissection of the modularity terms in Equation (3.15).

The Louvain method proceeds in two steps. In the first step, we start up by assigning each node to its own community. We calculate the change in the modularity score defined above caused by removing each and every node from its current community, and placing them in the community of one of their neighbours. If the changes are negative, we keep the node in the current community, but if the changes are positive we assign the node to the community that generated the highest change.

In a network with N nodes, we start with N communities.

The second step makes use of the newly created communities from the first step. These communities are effectively the nodes of a new network. In this new network, the edge weight is given by the total of all the edge weights between the new nodes. There are also self-loops whose weights are given by the edge weights within each community. We then simply do repeated iterations of these two steps until there is no improvement in the modularity measure and the communities are therefore said to be stable.

Iterations over the two steps in the Louvain algorithm return the communities in the network.

The Louvain algorithm is fast compared to other methods and provides a hierarchical community structure that can shed light to the networks under scrutiny. However, due to the merging of communities that happens during the second step detailed above, detecting small groupings in a large network results in poor resolution. It is important therefore to be aware that for sufficiently large networks, the algorithm may not return the expected communities. The other issue that we need to take into account is the fact that determining a global maximum may not be possible,

Be aware that the Louvain algorithm may result in poor resolution of the communities in the network.

resulting in a degeneracy where several solutions with
maximum modularity scores are possible.

3.3   Social Networks with Python: NetworkX

WE ARE GOING TO USE NetworkX to analyse networks, but
before we do that let us get acquainted with the module.
NetworkX is a Python module that enables us to carry out
computational network modelling tasks. It is effectively a
memory graph database with some good rendering
capabilities that let us draw the graphs we analyse.
Although it is not ideal for truly large-scale applications, it
is a good package that a Jackalope data scientist can use for
analysing networks (social or otherwise).

NetworkX is a Python module for analysing network/graph data.

It is possible to represent various network types with
NetworkX including directed and undirected graphs, as
well as multigraphs. Furthermore, the nodes in our graphs
can be any hashable object, and the edges can contain
arbitrary data. The package comes with a variety of useful
algorithms, and it is easy to use.

Think metadata!

3.3.1   NetworkX: A Quick Intro

LET US START BY IMPORTING the NetworkX module,
alongside some other useful ones:

```
import networkx as nx
import numpy as np
import matplotlib.pyplot as plt
```

A canonical abbreviation for NetworkX is nx.

We need to instantiate a graph object to which we can add
nodes:

```
g = nx.Graph()
g.add_node('A')
```

We need to instantiate a graph
object with Graph().

The nodes can also be added from a given list. In this case
we will need to use the add_nodes_from method:

```
g.add_nodes_from(['B', 'C'])
```

Adding nodes and edges to the
object is straightforward.

From our discussion in Section 3.2 we know that apart from
nodes, we also need edges. These can be added as follows:

```
g.add_edge('A', 'B')
```

In this case we are adding an edge between nodes A and B.
We can also add edges from a list of tuples:

```
g.add_edges_from([('C', 'D'),
    ('E', 'F')])
```

Edges can be added by specifying
the two nodes connected.

Note that in this case we are adding edges between nodes
C and D on the one hand, and E and F on the other one.
NetworkX is smart enough to figure out that although the
nodes have not been defined, they get created as required.

Finally, we can also add weighted edges. In this case we
require a tuple with three entries, the first two entries
correspond to the nodes to be connected, and the third entry
is the weight:

```
g.add_weighted_edges_from([(1, 'E', 2),
    ('C', 2, 3.5)])
```

Weighted edges are defined with a third value in the tuple.

Notice that the nodes can also be numbers, not just strings. In the example above, we are creating an edge between nodes 1 and E with a weight of 2, and an edge between nodes C and 2 with a weight of 3.5.

We can take a look at the nodes:

```
> g.nodes()

NodeView(('A', 'B', 'C', 'D', 'E', 'F', 1, 2))
```

We can look at the nodes in a network with the nodes() method.

and edges:

```
> g.edges(data=True)

EdgeDataView([('A', 'B', {}),
('C', 'D', {}),
('C', 2, {'weight': 3.5}),
('E', 'F', {}),
('E', 1, {'weight': 2})])
```

To see the metadata we can add data=True to both the nodes or edges methods.

of our graph g. We are requesting information about the edges by passing the parameter data=True, otherwise (the default) we will simply get a list of existing edges.

We can render the network with the draw_network method as follows:

```
nx.draw_networkx(g,
    node_color='black',
    font_color='white',
    node_size=800)
```

We can plot the network with
draw_network.

Here we are requesting that the nodes are coloured in black
and that the font is white with a size of 800 pt. The result
can be seen in Figure 3.6. Remember that the position of the
nodes is not important, and indeed the rendering may look
different in your screen.

The position of the nodes is not
important (until it is! ... for ease of
visualisation!)

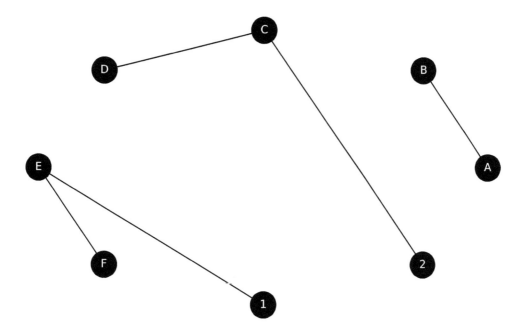

Figure 3.6: A simple graph
depicting eight nodes and five
edges.

We know that it is possible to represent a graph with the
help of an adjacency matrix. For the undirected graph
shown in Figure 3.6 the adjacency matrix is symmetric and

it can be expressed as:

$$
\begin{array}{c|cccccccc}
 & \mathbf{A} & \mathbf{B} & \mathbf{C} & \mathbf{D} & \mathbf{E} & \mathbf{F} & \mathbf{1} & \mathbf{2} \\
\hline
\mathbf{A} & 0 & 1 & 0 & 0 & 0 & 0 & 0 & 0 \\
\mathbf{B} & 1 & 0 & 0 & 0 & 0 & 0 & 0 & 0 \\
\mathbf{C} & 0 & 0 & 0 & 1 & 0 & 0 & 0 & 3.5 \\
\mathbf{D} & 0 & 0 & 1 & 0 & 0 & 0 & 0 & 0 \\
\mathbf{E} & 0 & 0 & 0 & 0 & 0 & 1 & 2 & 0 \\
\mathbf{F} & 0 & 0 & 0 & 0 & 1 & 0 & 0 & 0 \\
\mathbf{1} & 0 & 0 & 0 & 0 & 2 & 0 & 0 & 0 \\
\mathbf{2} & 0 & 0 & 3.5 & 0 & 0 & 0 & 0 & 0
\end{array}
. \tag{3.16}
$$

Notice that the weighted edges we created above are shown in the corresponding elements of the matrix. We can see the adjacency matrix for our graph in NetworkX as follows:

```
adj_matrix = nx.adj_matrix(g)
> print(adj_matrix.todense())

[[0.  1.  0.  0.  0.  0.  0.  0. ]
 [1.  0.  0.  0.  0.  0.  0.  0. ]
 [0.  0.  0.  1.  0.  0.  0.  3.5]
 [0.  0.  1.  0.  0.  0.  0.  0. ]
 [0.  0.  0.  0.  0.  1.  2.  0. ]
 [0.  0.  0.  0.  1.  0.  0.  0. ]
 [0.  0.  0.  0.  2.  0.  0.  0. ]
 [0.  0.  3.5 0.  0.  0.  0.  0. ]]
```

We can see the adjacency matrix with the adj_matrix method.

We need to use the todense() method as the matrix is stored as a sparse matrix. It is easy to see why this is the case, particularly when we consider the number of zero entries in matrix (3.16). An alternative representation for the matrix is as an edge list:

```
> edge_list = nx.to_edgelist(g)
> print(edge_list)


[('A', 'B', ), ('C', 'D', ),
('C', 2, 'weight': 3.5), ('E', 'F', ),
('E', 1, 'weight': 2)]
```

The edgelist methods shows us the edge list of our network.

Finally, it is possible to define the graph as an adjacency list. This is actually a dictionary object where the keys are nodes in the graph and the values are themselves dictionaries. The latter contain the nodes to which the key node is connected, and the values can store the weight of the edge (if required). The adjacency list for our graph is:

```
> for n in g.adjacency():
     print(n)


('A', {'B': {}})
('B', {'A': {}})
('C', {'D': {}, 2: {'weight': 3.5}})
('D', {'C': {}})
('E', {'F': {}, 1: {'weight': 2}})
('F', {'E': {}})
(1, {'E': {'weight': 2}})
(2, {'C': {'weight': 3.5}})
```

The adjacency list can be obtained with the adjacency method.

As it is the case in many applications, we usually require to read and write our data in a more expedient manner. NetworkX is no exception, and it is possible to read and write graph data in a variety of commonly used formats such as the ones described above, i.e., edge lists or adjacency lists, as well as others such as GML, GraphML, pickle, LEDA, JSON, etc.

NetworkX supports formats such as GML, GraphML, pickle, LEDA, JSON, etc.

3.4   Social Network Analysis in Action

IN THIS SECTION, WE WILL take a look at using the concepts and techniques described earlier in the chapter and start us to answer questions we may have about specific networks at hand. First, we will take a look at a classic example of social network analysis given by the Zachary karate club network. We will look at some social dynamics shaping the network. Second, we will analyse the interactions of Jedis, Siths, Droids and Princesses with a *Star Wars* network. Punch it!

We will analyse data for Zachary's karate club, and *Star Wars*!

3.4.1   Karate Kids: Conflict and Fission in a Network

THE ART OF EMPTY-HAND FIGHTING, karate, is a relatively recent martial art originated on the island of Okinawa, but influenced by ancient Chinese martial arts known as kung-fu. Today, karate is a wide-spread sport, with karatekas all over the world and plenty of dōjōs from which to choose.

空手 is read as karate. 空 (kara) means "empty" and 手 (te) means "hand". *Karaoke*, meaning "empty orchestra" shares the same first word with karate!

Konishi Yasuhiro, an early karate sensei, is quoted to say that "Karate aims to build character, improve human behaviour, and cultivate modesty; it does not, however, guarantee it." And indeed this is something that can be corroborated with some karate clubs out there. A case in point is a now famous karate club studied over three years by Wayne W. Zachary[15] in the 1970s to analyse conflict and fission in small groups.

[15] Zachary, W. W. (1977). An information flow model for conflict and fission in small groups. *J. Anthropol. Res.* 33(4), 452–473

The club was based at a university, and tensions between the club president, John A., and a part-time instructor, Mr. Hi, had been brewing for some time due to the setting of fees. Over time, the club became divided over these issues with the eventual separation of the club into two: One that supported Mr. Hi's teachings, and another one that followed John A. and the club officers.

The club was eventually split into two factions.

Zachary collected information about the original club and the dataset obtained is now known as "Zachary's karate club" network. The groups that emerged from the fission of the karate club were factions not necessarily recognised by the club members. Instead, the friendship network among members gave rise to them during a moment of conflict.

The dataset called `karate.gml` can be obtained at `https://doi.org/10.6084/m9.figshare.7985174.v1`[16] and we will use it in the rest of this section. It contains 34 nodes representing individuals within the karate club. The edges in the network are given by interactions between two individuals outside the activities of the club such as actual lessons or meetings.

[16] Rogel-Salazar, J. (2019c, Apr). Zachary's karate club. https://doi.org/10.6084/m9.figshare.7985174.v1

Let us take a look at the data in the network. We can read the GML directly with NetworkX as follows:

GML - Graph Modelling Language.

```
import networkx as nx


fname = 'karate.gml'

K = nx.read_gml(fname)
```

Remember to refer to the correct path for the file!

We can plot the network with the `draw_networkx` method. In this case, we will colour the nodes black, with white labels and a size of 800. By default, the method uses a force-directed layout to position the nodes and in this case we make this explicit:

```
nx.draw_networkx(K, node_color='black',
    font_color='white',
    node_size=800,
    pos=nx.spring_layout(K))
limits = plt.axis('off')
plt.show()
```

In a force-directed layout the edges are roughly of equal length, and crossings are reduced by assigning forces to the edges similar to spring-like forces based on Hooke's law.

We can see the connections among members in the network depicted in Figure 3.7. Node number 1 is Mr. Hi (the instructor) and node 34 is John A. (the administrator). Let us see some basic statistics of the network:

```
> print(nx.info(K))


Name:
Type: Graph
Number of nodes: 34
Number of edges: 78
Average degree:   4.5882
```

General information about the network is obtained with `info`.

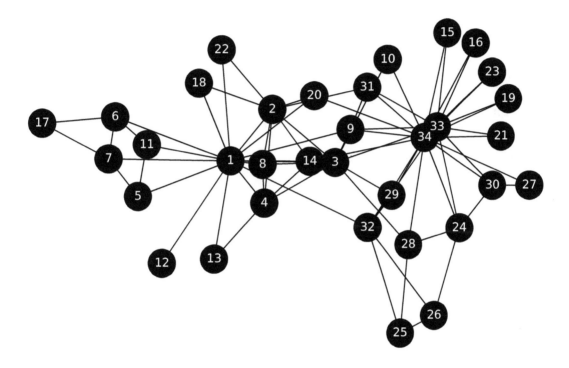

Figure 3.7: Zachary's karate club: 34 individuals at the verge of a club split. Edges correspond to friendship relationships among club members.

We can see that the average degree of the network (4.5882) falls within the small world networks discussed earlier on in the chapter. We can request the degree of Mr. Hi and John A. with the help of the degree method for the network object:

```
> K.degree(['1', '34'])


DegreeView('1': 16, '34': 17)
```

Degree information for individual nodes from a list.

More information can be obtained with the info method:

```
> print(nx.info(K, '1'))


Node 1 has the following properties:

Degree: 16

Neighbors: 2 3 4 5 6 7 8 9 11 12 13 14 18 20 22 32


> print(nx.info(K, '34'))


Node 34 has the following properties:

Degree: 17

Neighbors: 9 10 14 15 16 19 20 21 23 24 27 28 29
30 31 32 33
```

The info method can provide further information about specify nodes.

Decisions in the club structure were made by consensus during club meetings. This meant that having a majority in a meeting would result in decisions being swayed in favour of one faction over the other. If Mr. Hi called for a meeting, it would be advantageous for him if his supporters received the information, but not the opposers. This effectively

Information transmission in Zachary's karate club network was important in the decision-making process, and eventual split.

means that the connections between individuals enable the flow of communication among parties. Those individuals that were undecided about giving support to one group over the other one become key players. They are able to pass on the information more readily than others.

According to the information provided by Zachary, once the unity of the club was unsustainable, two groups formed and the membership for each of them is listed in the paper. Nodes 1 − 9, 11 − 14, 17, 18, 20 and 22 became Mr. Hi's club and the rest remained with John A. Let us add this information as metadata to our network. First we create a dictionary called club holding the membership for each node:

We know what actors in the network moved to each of the two groups after the split.

```
mr_hi = [*range(1, 10), *range(11, 15),
    17, 18, 20, 22]


club = {}
for m in range(1, 35):
    if m in mr_hi:
        club[str(m)] = ''Mr. Hi''
    else:
        club[str(m)] = ''John A.''
```

We can encode this metadata in our network with the help of a dictionary.

We can now add this dictionary as an attribute to the nodes in the network:

```
nx.set_node_attributes(K, club, 'club')
```

And add the dictionary as an attribute to our network.

Let us check the information we just added:

```
> nodes = K.nodes(data=True)
> print(list(nodes)[:3])


[('1', 'club': 'Mr. Hi'), ('2', 'club': 'Mr. Hi'),
('3', 'club': 'Mr. Hi')]
```

Remember that data=True provides us with metadata of both nodes and edges.

We know that the degree centrality of a node tells us the number of connections to that node. We saw above that Mr. Hi and John A. have the largest degrees, but what about the rest of the nodes? We can answer this question very easily:

```
kdeg = K.degree()
```

The degree of the nodes is obtained with the degree method.

The result is a dictionary that we can query at will. For instance, we can check the degree of node 9:

```
> kdeg['9']


5
```

We can query the dictionary as usual.

Node 9 is an interesting one as mentioned by Zachary. Individual 9 backed (weakly) John A. but ended up joining Mr. Hi's club after the split. The explanation provided was that the person was only three weeks away from a black belt test and staying with Mr. Hi ensured that the test could be taken.

Node 9 in the karate network is an interesting one. Read on!

We can plot a network encoding the degree of nodes, their size, and colouring them according to the final affiliation of the new clubs. Let us start by defining the color map we will use:

```
import itertools

nodes = K.nodes(data=True)

clubs = set(nx.get_node_attributes(K,\
    'club').values())

mapping = dict(zip(sorted(clubs),\
    itertools.count()))

colors = list(mapping[n[1]['club']] for n\
    in nodes)
```

In order to add colour or size attributes to the nodes, we need to create appropriate mappings.

The third line in the code above creates a set (unique values) of the clubs in the node attributes. We use this to create a mapping between the unique clubs and a count to serve as an index. Finally, we use the mapping to create a list that will be used to assign the colour index to each of the nodes.

Let us now create the plot:

```
nx.draw_networkx(K, node_color=colors,
    node_size=[200*val for (node, val) in kdeg])

limits = plt.axis('off')

plt.show()
```

Notice that we need to pass a value for each of the node sizes. In this case, the values are given by the degree centrality of the node in question.

It is possible to customise the plot defining the colour map, font colour, position, etc. The result can be seen in Figure 3.8. The size of the nodes corresponds to their degree, and the colour indicates the affiliation to the groups formed after the split, with the darker grey nodes being Mr. Hi's group and the light grey ones are John A.'s supporters.

The largest nodes seem to be nodes 1, 34 and 33. We can corroborate this with the information that we calculated

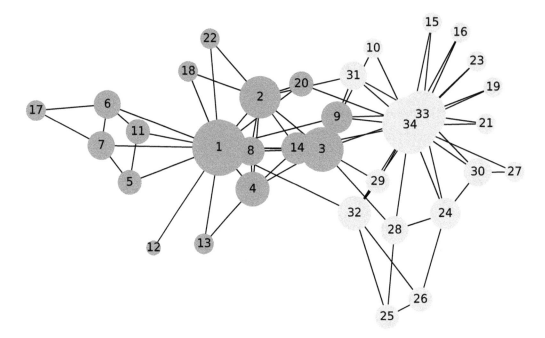

Figure 3.8: Degree measure of the Zachary karate club network. The size of the nodes denotes the degree and the color corresponds to the groups formed after the split of the club. The darker grey nodes are Mr. Hi's group and the light grey ones are John A's supporters.

before. In order to make it easier to grab this information, let us create a function that lists the top *n* nodes given a centrality measure (as a dictionary):

```
def get_top_nodes(cdict, num=5):
    top_nodes = {}
    for i in range(num):
        top_nodes = dict(
            sorted(cdict.items(), key=lambda x: x[1],
                reverse=True)[:num]
        )
    return top_nodes
```

We will use this function in the rest of this chapter. Remember it well!

As we can see from the result below, the nodes with the largest degree in descending order are 34 with degree 17, 1 with degree 16, node 33 with 12, followed by nodes 3 with 10, and 2 with 9:

```
> get_top_nodes(dict(kdeg))

{'34': 17, '1': 16, '33': 12, '3': 10, '2': 9}
```

Not surprising to see 34 and 1 in the top nodes... right?

The total number of connections is a good start, but what about if we weight this measure by the maximum possible degree in a simple graph $n - 1$, where n is the number of nodes in the network. We can calculate this in NetworkX with the degree_centrality function:

```
degree_centrality = nx.degree_centrality(K)
nx.set_node_attributes(K,\
  degree_centrality, 'dc')
```

Calculate the degree centrality with degree_centrality. Simple, right?

We can use this normalised measure to look at a histogram of the degree centrality for the karate club. We can obtain the frequencies by sorting the values of the measure and use the Counter from the collections module:

```
deg_values = sorted(set(degree_centrality.\
  values()))

from collections import Counter

value_counts = Counter(degree_centrality.values())
deg_hist = [value_counts[x] for x in deg_values]
```

Counting the number of nodes with a particular degree centrality is straightforward.

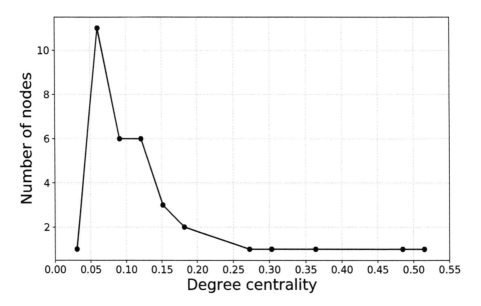

Figure 3.9: Frequencies of the degree centrality measure for the karate club network.

In Figure 3.9 we can see the result of the calculations above. There are only a few nodes with degree centralities higher than 0.4. The bulk of the nodes in our network has lower scores for this measure. Let us create a plot of the network using the size as the degree centrality:

```
nx.draw_networkx(K, node_color=colors,
    node_size=[3000 * v for v in
        nx.get_node_attributes(K, 'dc').values()])
```

We have left out the commands to avoid showing the axis and the plot itself.

We can see in Figure 3.10 how the degree centrality keeps the information about the network. We perhaps have learnt nothing new. However, the normalised version provides us with an easier way to make comparisons between the nodes than the degree directly.

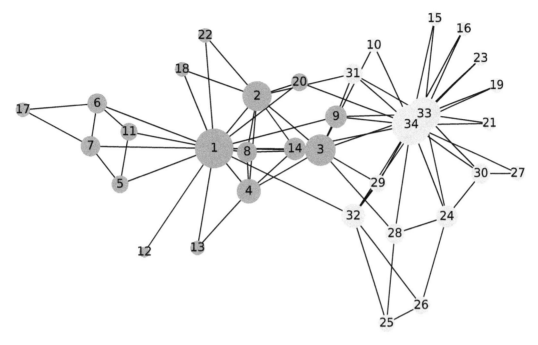

Figure 3.10: Degree centrality measure of Zachary's karate club. The size of the nodes denotes the degree centrality. We can see the importance of not only nodes 1, 34, 33, but also 2 and 3.

We know that the betweenness, tells us about the influence of particular nodes over the network. Let us calculate the betweenness for our karate club. This can be done with the betweenness_centrality function as follows:

```
betweenness_centrality = \
    nx.betweenness_centrality(K)
nx.set_node_attributes(K,
    betweenness_centrality, 'bc')
```

Calculate the betweenness with betweenness_centrality.

We mentioned before that betweenness can be seen as a measure of nodes serving as a bridge between different components of a graph. Let us have a look at these "bridges" by getting the top 5 nodes by betweenness.

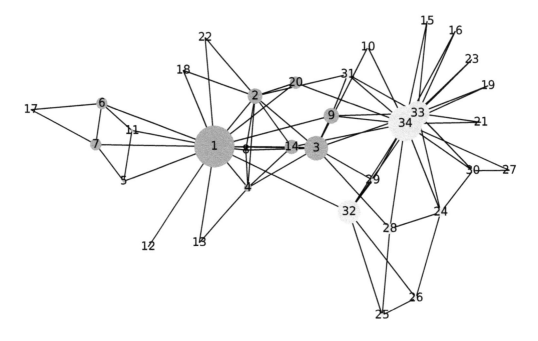

Figure 3.11: Betweenness of Zachary's karate club network. The size of the nodes denotes the betweenness. We can see the importance of nodes 1, 34, as well as 33 and 3. Node 32 is a bridge in the network.

```
> get_top_nodes(betweenness_centrality)

{'1': 0.43763528138528146,
  '34': 0.30407497594997596,
  '33': 0.145247113997114,
  '3': 0.14365680615680618,
  '32': 0.13827561327561325}
```

Remember the function get_top_nodes we defined above?

Mr. Hi (1) and John A. (34) are indeed prominent in the network. We can see the presence of nodes 33 and 3 as before, but a new comer has appeared in the top 5: Node 32. We can see the relative importance of the betweenness measure in Figure 3.11. The code for this plot is as follows:

```
nx.draw_networkx(K, node_color=colors,
  node_size=[4000 * v for v in
    nx.get_node_attributes(K, 'bc').values()])
```

We know that the flow of information in the network was an important way to ensure that the decision taken during meetings favoured the faction with a majority. A way to assess which nodes are able to spread information more efficiently is given by the closeness. We can calculate the closeness as follows:

```
closeness_centrality = nx.closeness_centrality(K)
nx.set_node_attributes(K,
  closeness_centrality, 'cc')
```

The closeness_centrality lets us calculate the closeness of the nodes in the network.

The "closest" nodes in the karate club network are as follows:

```
> get_top_nodes(closeness_centrality)

{'1': 0.5689655172413793,
 '3': 0.559322033898305,
 '34': 0.55,
 '32': 0.5409836065573771,
 '9': 0.515625}
```

We finally see node 9 appear as an important, close, node in the network!

Things are getting interesting. We can still see Mr. Hi (1) and John A. (34) as important nodes. Nothing surprising there, or indeed by having node 3 in the top "closest" nodes. We again have node 32 appearing, and now we finally see node 9 in there. It is through these nodes that information about meetings would have flowed.

The closeness measure of the nodes is very similar and showing this measure as the size of the nodes results in a plot that does not showcase the importance of certain nodes. Instead, we will show this measure as the colour of the nodes. This requires us to draw the network's parts separately as follows:

```
pos = nx.spring_layout(K)

ec = nx.draw_networkx_edges(K, pos=pos)

nc = nx.draw_networkx_nodes(K, pos=pos,
    node_color=[v for v in
      nx.get_node_attributes(K, 'cc').values()],
    node_size=[1200 * v for v in
      nx.get_node_attributes(K, 'cc').values()])
lb = nx.draw_networkx_labels(K,pos =pos)
```

We can use separate methods to render the network in the way we want. Using draw_networkx_edges for the edges, draw_networkx_nodes for the nodes and draw_networkx_labels for the labels. Notice that all have the same position attribute.

We are drawing separately the edges, nodes and labels all with the same position layout. Note that we are encoding the closeness measure both in the size of the node and in its colour. Figure 3.12 shows the result of the commands above. You can see that the size alone would not tell us much about the closeness; however, the colour lets us obtain the information desired.

We can now turn our attention to what nodes are best connected within the network. We have seen that the eigenvector centrality provides a view of the nodes that are endorsed by influential actors. We can calculate the eigenvector centrality as follows:

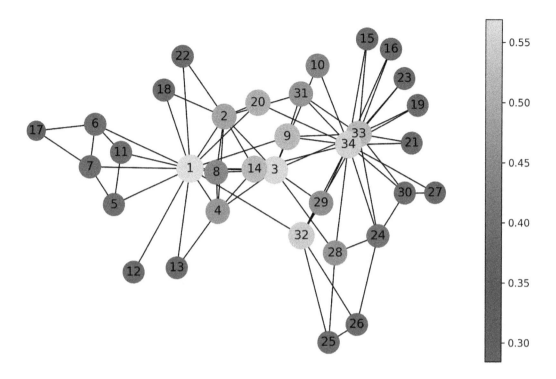

Figure 3.12: Closeness of Zachary's karate club network. The size of the nodes denotes the closeness. We can see the importance of the nodes we already know about: 1, 34, 33 and 3. Node 9 is a close node in the network too.

```
eigenvector_centrality = \
   nx.eigenvector_centrality(K)
nx.set_node_attributes(K, eigenvector_centrality,
   'ec')
```

The best connected nodes in our network are:

```
get_top_nodes(eigenvector_centrality)

{'34': 0.373371213013235,
  '1': 0.3554834941851943,
  '3': 0.31718938996844476,
  '33': 0.3086510477336959,
  '2': 0.2659538704545025}
```

Get the eigenvector centrality with eigenvector_centrality. Getting the gist of it, right?

We see John A. be an influencer, with a higher eigenvector centrality than Mr. Hi. Once again, node 2 makes an appearance, together with nodes 3 and 33. The eigenvector centrality network can be seen in Figure 3.13.

```
nx.draw_networkx(K, node_color=colors,
   node_size=[2400 * v for v in
     nx.get_node_attributes(K, 'ec').values()])
```

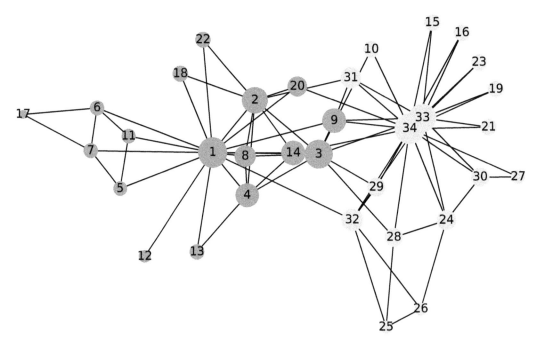

Figure 3.13: Eigenvector centrality of Zachary's karate club network. The size of the nodes denotes the eigenvector centrality of the network.

Once we have taken a look at the eigenvector centrality, the next logical step is to calculate the PageRank. As you can imagine, there is a handy function in NetworkX to let us do this: pagerank.

```
pagerank_centrality = nx.pagerank(K,\
nx.set_node_attributes(K,\
  pagerank_centrality, 'pr')
```

The PageRank can be calculated with pagerank.

The top five nodes per PageRank are as follows:

```
> get_top_nodes(pagerank_centrality)

{'34': 0.10345460652842152,
 '1': 0.09923208031303203,
 '33': 0.07330616298815512,
 '3': 0.05919704684187155,
 '2': 0.0543403155825792}
```

The ranking of the nodes with PageRank returns the usual karate kids.

We can see the usual karate kids: In this case though, nodes 33 and 3 have swapped places in the ranking. We can get a plot of the network as we have done in the previous cases:

```
nx.draw_networkx(K, node_color=colors,
  node_size=[5000 * v for v in
    nx.get_node_attributes(K, 'pr').values()],
    pos=pos)
```

We can see the result in Figure 3.14, where, as usual, we have encoded the PageRank centrality score in the size of the node. We can see the prestige of nodes 34, 1, 33, 3 and 2. We can start thinking of the factions that were created during the conflict and look at those nodes that are central to the network. We will keep Mr. Hi and John A. in the network for obvious reasons. However, we can consider what happens when we remove some of the nodes whose

We can consider what happens to the graph when we remove certain nodes.

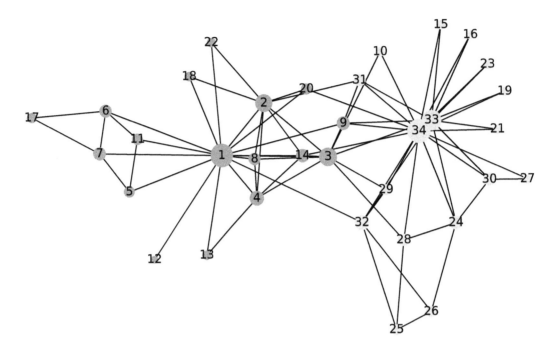

Figure 3.14: PageRank of Zachary's karate club network. The size of the nodes denotes the PageRank scores of the network.

centrality measures indicate importance, i.e., nodes 2, 3, 9 and 32 for example.

```
k = K.copy()
k.remove_nodes_from(['2', '3', '32', '9'])
```

The result of this removal can be seen in Figure 3.15. It is clear that a number of connections have disappeared in this reduced network and these individuals can be thought of as being important for the cohesion of the network.

The clustering coefficient for the nodes in the karate network can be obtained with the clustering function. Notice that the result is a dictionary where the keys are the individual nodes and the values are the clustering coefficients:

We can remove nodes with remove_nodes_from and provide a list with the nodes we want expunged.

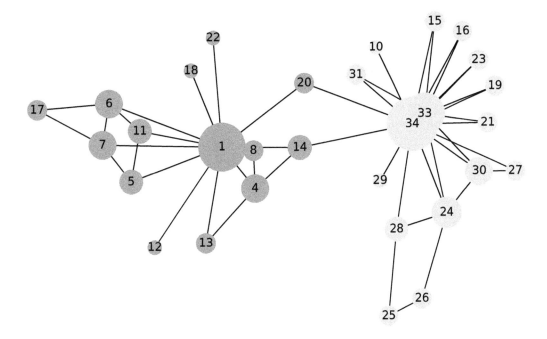

Figure 3.15: Reduced network for Zachary's karate club. We have removed nodes 2, 3, 9 and 32 that are important for the cohesion of the network. The size of the nodes denotes the degree centrality of the nodes.

```
> ccoeff = nx.clustering(K)

> print(ccoeff['1'])


0.15
```

The average clustering coefficient is given by the average_clustering function:

```
> avg_ccoeff = nx.average_clustering(K)

> print(avg_ccoeff)


0.5706384782076823
```

Calculate the clustering coefficient of the network with average_clustering.

Now that we started looking at removing nodes and at the clustering of the network, we can consider calculating the *k*-components of the karate club. The k_components function enables us to do this in NetworkX.

Remember that a *k*-component is a maximal subgraph with, at least, connectivity *k*.

```
components = nx.k_components(K)
```

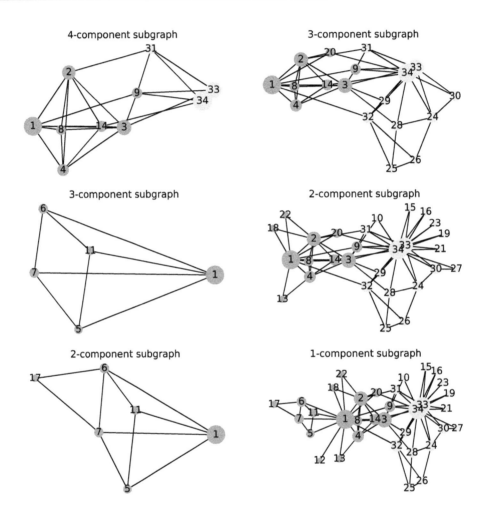

Figure 3.16: *k*-components of Zachary's karate club network.

The result is a dictionary with connectivity level *k* as key and a list of sets of nodes that form a *k*-component of level *k*. For instance, the network has one single 4 level component and is given by:

```
> print(components[4])

[{'1', '14', '2', '3',
 '31', '33', '34', '4', '8', '9'}]
```

We can see the different k-components of Zachary's karate club network in Figure 3.16.

It is also possible to answer the question regarding the fully connected components in the network, in other words the cliques. As you can imagine, NetworkX provides a way to find the cliques: `find_cliques`.

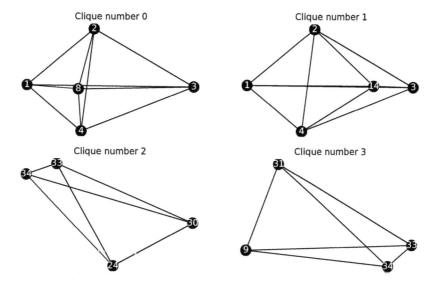

Figure 3.17: Some of the cliques in Zachary's karate club network.

```
cl = nx.find_cliques(K)
```

The result is an iterator over maximal cliques, providing a list of nodes in the network. You can verify that there are 36 cliques and we show 4 of these in Figure 3.17.

There are several ways to detect communities in the network. One simple way is to look at hierarchical clustering which we discussed in Chapter 7 of *Data Science and Analytics with Python*[17] where we learnt how to construct dendrograms. Let us use the shortest path lengths between the nodes in our network:

[17] Rogel-Salazar, J. (2017). *Data Science and Analytics with Python*. Chapman & Hall/CRC Data Mining and Knowledge Discovery Series. CRC Press

```
path_length = nx.all_pairs_shortest_path_length(K)
```

We will now use this information to get a distance measure between the nodes and build a dendrogram:

```
n = len(K.nodes())
distances = np.zeros((n, n))

from scipy.cluster import hierarchy
from scipy.spatial import distance

for u, p in path_length:
    for v, d in p.items():
        distances[int(u) - 1][int(v) - 1] = d
sd = distance.squareform(distances)
h = hierarchy.average(sd)
```

We are using scipy to calculate hierarchical clustering in our network.

The resulting dendrogram can be seen in Figure 3.18 where we can see a hierarchy of 2 and then 4 clusters, or communities.

We discussed in this chapter how the Girvan-Newman algorithm discovers communities in a network. NetworkX provides us with a function to do just this: `girvan_newman()` in `community`.

The `girvan_newman()` function in `community` from `networkx.algorithms` does what it says on the tin.

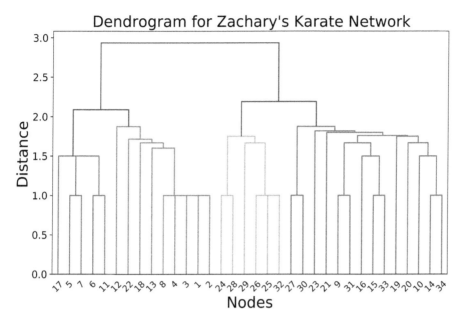

Figure 3.18: Hierarchical clustering over Zachary's karate club network.

```
from networkx.algorithms import community


comp = community.girvan_newman(K)

communities = tuple(sorted(c) for c in next(comp))
```

The function returns an iterator over tuples, and each tuple is a sequence of communities.

The algorithm has found 2 communities in the network:

```
> len(communities)


2
```

Let us add this information to the metadata of our network.

First let us create two subgraphs, one for each community:

```
c_1 = K.subgraph(communities[0])

c_2 = K.subgraph(communities[1])
```

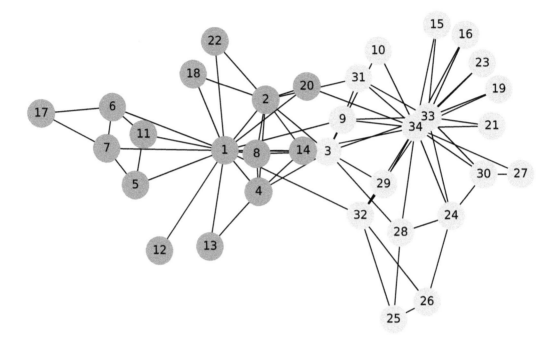

We can now use the nodes in each community to add a new attribute to our network:

Figure 3.19: Communities discovered by the Girvan-Newman algorithm on Zachary's karate club network. Notice that nodes 3 and 9 have been assigned to John A.'s faction.

```
comm = {}

for c in c_1:

  comm[str(c)] = 'community 1'


for c in c_2:

  comm[str(c)] = 'community 2'


nx.set_node_attributes(K, comm, 'comm')
```

This calculation could be reduced to a single for loop. See next section for this.

In Figure 3.19 we can see the plot of the network with the nodes coloured by the community to which they were assigned by the algorithm. We can see that the network looks roughly the same as that in Figure 3.8. However, if you closely inspect the nodes you will see that nodes 3 and 9 have been assigned to John A.'s faction and not to Mr. Hi. We knew about node 9 and his black belt test, perhaps node 3 had similar reasons to join one group over the other.

Girvan-Newman has found that two nodes would naturally switch sides. This confirms explanations provided by Zachary.

Finally, let us see what the Louvain algorithm has to say about the communities in Zachary's karate network. At the time of writing, the Louvain algorithm is not part of NetworkX. Instead, you can install the package with pip in your command line as follows:

Currently the Louvain algorithm needs to be installed separately.

```
> pip install python-louvain
```

Information about the implementation can be obtained in the following GitHub repository: https://github.com/taynaud/python-louvain/. You will notice that the module is actually called community and we aim to find the best partition:

best_partition calculates the partition that maximises the modularity using the Louvain algorithm.

```
import community

louvain = community.best_partition(K)
```

The result is a dictionary where the keys are the nodes and the values correspond to the community to which the nodes have been assigned. We can take a look at the communities discovered in Figure 3.20.

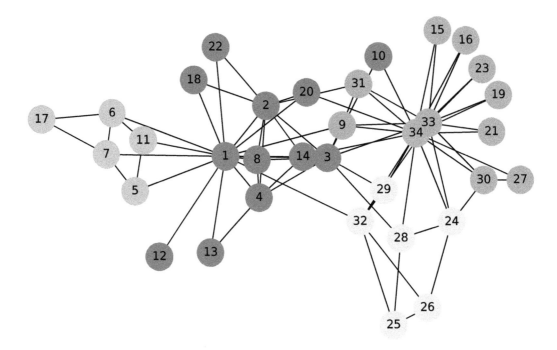

Figure 3.20: Communities discovered by the Louvain algorithm on Zachary's karate club network. We have four communities denoted by different shades of grey.

We can take a look at what nodes have been assigned to each of the four communities that the algorithm has discovered. Let us navigate the dictionary and filter the nodes per community:

```
for i in set(louvain.values()):
 print('Community '.format(i))
 members = [n for n in louvain.keys()\
   if louvain[n] == i]
 print(members)
```

The result is returned as a dictionary.

For completeness, let us show the result of the code above. We can see how each community contains non-overlapping nodes:

```
Community 0
['1', '2', '3', '4', '8', '10', '12', '13', '14',
'18', '20', '22']
Community 1
['5', '6', '7', '11', '17']
Community 2
['9', '15', '16', '19', '21', '23', '27', '30',
'31', '33', '34']
Community 3
['24', '25', '26', '28', '29', '32']
```

In this case, we have four communities. Notice that we start counting in a Pythonic style — from 0.

Let us finish this section by mentioning that the karate club network we have been playing with is also part of NetworkX and you can load it as follows:

```
G = nx.karate_club_graph()
```

You will be glad to know that Zachary's karate club network is included in NetworkX.

Please note that in this graph the nodes have been labelled in a Pythonic style starting from 0: Hi is node 0 and John A. is node 33.

3.4.2 *In a Galaxy Far, Far Away: Central Characters in a Network*

FROM ANCIENT JAPAN TO GALAXIES far, far away..., it is widely known that George Lucas is a fan of Akira Kurosawa's work and the influence of films such as *The Hidden Fortress* from 1958 is patent in the story of *Star Wars*, from the spiritual elements of the Force to the use of swords

From ancient Japan to galaxies far, far away.

in battle and the armour of Lord Vader himself. Much has been written about these influences, and in this case we are interested in finding out more about the interactions among our favourite characters in this space opera.

The first step in the process is to get hold of the data that we will use to analyse our characters. In this case, we will be using data from the work that Evelina Gabasova[18] has done in a series of blog posts. The nodes in the network represent our beloved characters. The connections between them represent interactions between the characters in the form of dialogue in the films scenes. The data can be obtained directly from Gabasova's reference above. For completeness, a GML format file with the network can be obtained at `https://doi.org/10.6084/ m9.figshare.7993292.v1`[19] with the same information as the original JSON files provided by Gabasova.

[18] Gabasova, E. (2016). *Star Wars* social network. https://doi.org/10.5281/ zenodo.1411479

[19] Rogel-Salazar, J. (2019a, Apr). *Star Wars* Network. https://doi.org/10.6084/ m9.figshare.7993292.v1

The network contains information for Episodes I through to VII and it is an undirected graph. The edges in the network are weighted by the amount of dialogue between the characters. As you may imagine, there are some assumptions that Gabasova has made to keep the network manageable. For example, separate nodes are kept for Anakin Skywalker and Darth Vader. But those for the Emperor and Senator Palpatine, or Queen Amidala and Padmé have been merged. Similarly, nonspeaking characters such as R2-D2 and Chewbacca were added via mentions in the screenplay. For further information on these aspects, please refer to the excellent post from Evelina Gabasova.

aka Darth Sidious too!

As usual, let us load some useful libraries, including
NetworkX, matplotlib, Pandas and numpy:

```
import networkx as nx

import numpy as np

import matplotlib.pyplot as plt
```

These libraries will be with you.
Always...

The network can be loaded as follows:

```
fname = 'starwars_network.gml'


S = nx.read_gml(fname)
```

As we did for the karate network, let us print some
information about the *Star Wars* network:

```
> print(nx.info(S))


Type: Graph

Number of nodes: 112

Number of edges: 450

Average degree:   8.0357
```

Our dataset contains 112
characters with 450 edges and the
average degree for this Universe is
8.0357.

We have 112 characters with 450 edges and the average
degree for this Universe is 8.0357, a bit higher than the
six-degrees of separation! Let us take a look at the network.

Before we do that, given the number of characters, it would
be good to pick out some of the nodes that we may be
interested in tracking. We will define a list of main
characters as follows:

```
main_characters = ['Darth Vader',
   'Emperor (Palpatine)', 'Luke', 'Leia',
   'Yoda', 'Anakin', 'R2-D2', 'Han',
   'Chewbacca', 'Padme (Queen Amidala)',
   'Poe', 'BB-8', 'Jabba', 'Count Dooku',
   'Jar Jar', 'Rey', 'Darth Maul',
   'Admiral Ackbar', 'Snoke', 'Qui-Gon',
   'Kylo Ren', 'Obi-Wan', 'C-3PO',
   'Darth Maul', 'Niv Lek', 'Boba Fett']
```

Oh, my dear friends. How I've missed you!

We will use this list to create a dictionary so that we can label these characters in the plots we will create as we go along this analysis:

```
labels = {}
for character in main_characters:
   labels[character] = character
```

Plotting labels in our network is managed with a dictionary.

In the original network, each node is assigned a value that represents the number of scenes where the character speaks, similarly a colour is also assigned. Although the plots in this book are in black and white, you can see the results in full colour in your machine. Let us extract these attributes from the network so that we can use them in our plots:

```
node_sizes = [3 * float(v) for v in
   nx.get_node_attributes(S, 'value').values()]

colors = [c for c in
   nx.get_node_attributes(S, 'colour').values()]
```

We extract node attributes such as size and colour from the network to create our plot.

We mentioned above that the edges are weighted and we can use the values to represent the thickness of the connections in the network:

```
edges = S.edges()
edge_width = [S[u][v]['value'] for u, v in edges]
```

We read the value for each existing connection in the network.

We know that both Jedis and Siths are able to use the Force and very appropriately we can use a force-directed layout to plot our network.

```
pos_force=nx.spring_layout(S)
```

May the (spring) Force be with you!

But our training is not yet complete!

We are now ready to use the Force too:

```
nx.draw_networkx_nodes(
   S, node_color=colors,
   with_labels=False, node_size=node_sizes,
   alpha=0.9, pos=pos_force)


nx.draw_networkx_edges(S, alpha=0.15,
   color='gray', width=edge_width, pos=pos_force)


nx.draw_networkx_labels(S, labels=labels,
   font_size=10, font_color='#000099',
   font_weight='bold', pos=pos_force)
```

We are plotting the nodes, edges and labels separately, but in the same figure and the same layout.

I could not help myself playing with the network and decided to show an initial rendering inspired by the famous Death Star space station. We can see the network in Figure 3.21.

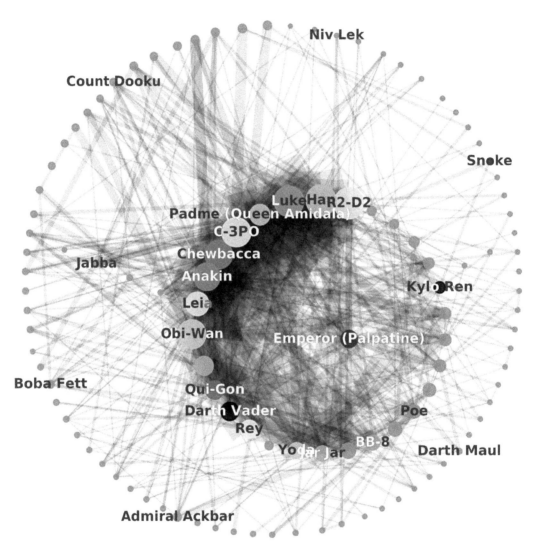

Figure 3.21: *Star Wars* network covering Episodes I-VII. Layout inspired by the famous Death Star.

Degree centrality is the first measure we will look at when analysing our network.

```
degree_centrality = nx.degree_centrality(S)
nx.set_node_attributes(S, degree_centrality, 'dc')
```

Remember that the degree centrality tells us how well connected a node is to the rest of the network.

The distribution of the degree centrality is shown in Figure 3.22 where we can see only a handful of characters with degree centralities higher than 0.20 and a large number of nodes with very small scores in this centrality measure.

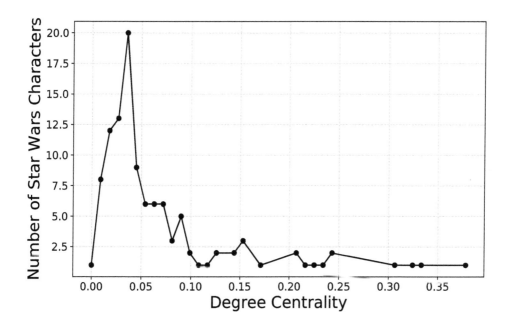

Figure 3.22: Distribution of the degree centrality for the *Star Wars* network.

Before we continue, in order to make our life a bit easier, let us define a function to plot networks in a more straightforward fashion. We will pass a network object, an attribute that will be encoded as the node sizes, a threshold to filter the network, a factor to modify the size of the nodes, the position where the nodes will be plotted and the width of the edges in the network. We will also accept a named parameter to show the labels of the chosen nodes. The function is as follows:

```
def plot_graph(G, att, att_threshold, size_factor,
    position, edge_width, **kwargs):

    labels = kwargs.get('labels', None)


    nodes = [x for x, y in G.nodes(data=True)
        if y[att] >= att_threshold]
    sg = G.subgraph(nodes)


    gcolors = [c for c in
        nx.get_node_attributes(sg,'colour').values()]


    nx.draw_networkx_nodes(sg, node_color=gcolors,
        node_size=[size_factor * v for v in
            nx.get_node_attributes(sg, att).values()],
        pos=position, alpha=0.5)


    nx.draw_networkx_edges(sg, alpha=0.2,
        color='gray', pos=position,
        width=edge_width)


    nx.draw_networkx_labels(sg, labels=labels,
        pos=position)
```

First we check if a set of labels is provided.

We then select the nodes that meet the threshold provided and obtain a subgraph.

We use the colour attribute to render our nodes.

We then draw the nodes with the appropriate size.

Then the edges.

And finally, the labels.

Using the same function that we defined in the previous section to obtain the top nodes for a centrality measure, we can see the top 5 characters by degree.

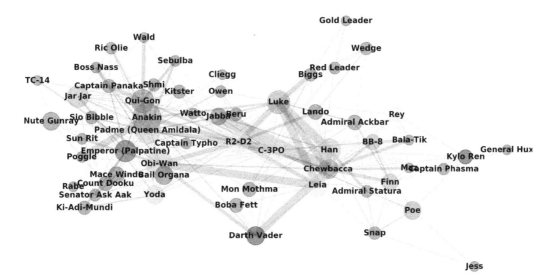

Figure 3.23: Degree measure of the *Star Wars* network. The size of the nodes denotes the degree centrality of the node.

```
> get_top_nodes(degree_centrality)


{'Anakin': 0.3783783783783784,

 'Obi-Wan': 0.3333333333333333,

 'C-3PO': 0.32432432432432434,

 'Padme (Queen Amidala)': 0.3063063063063063,

 'Qui-Gon': 0.24324324324324323}
```

Anakin and Obi-Wan are the characters with the highest number of connections.

It i s not surprising to see there Anakin and Obi-Wan, but Qui-Gon?? We can see the filtered network for degree centrality in Figure 3.23 and the code is as follows:

```
plot_graph(S, 'dc', 0.04, 5000, pos_force,
   edge_width)
```

You see, it only took a line with our new function!

The bridges in the network can be obtained with the help of the closeness centrality, let us take a look:

```
closeness_centrality = nx.closeness_centrality(S)
nx.set_node_attributes(S, closeness_centrality,
   'cc')
nodes_cc = get_top_nodes(closeness_centrality)
```

Closeness centrality shows us the bridge nodes in the network.

The bridge characters are:

```
> print(nodes_cc)

{'C-3PO': 0.5619021082938609,
   'Obi-Wan': 0.559020559020559,
   'Anakin': 0.5505505505505506,
   'Luke': 0.526613570091831,
   'R2-D2': 0.5166303744502797}
```

In this case, we have C-3PO and Obi-Wan as those bridges.

It is great to see both C-3PO and R2-D2 appear in the top 5 characters by closeness, together with Luke and Obi-Wan. Let us see the eigenvector centrality:

These were indeed the droids we were looking for!

```
eigenvector_centrality=nx.eigenvector_centrality(S)
nx.set_node_attributes(S, eigenvector_centrality,
   'ec')
nodes_ec = get_top_nodes(eigenvector_centrality)
```

The top 5 characters by eigenvector centrality are:

```
> print(nodes_ec)

{'Anakin': 0.29656614921513724,
  'Obi-Wan': 0.2810463592564618,
  'C-3PO': 0.2753430975993982,
  'Padme (Queen Amidala)': 0.2580025161393472,
  'Qui-Gon': 0.22896839403488994}
```

We have Anakin, Obi-Wan and C-3PO in the first three places.

Let us turn out attention to the PageRank for our network:

```
pagerank_centrality = nx.pagerank(S, alpha=0.9)
nx.set_node_attributes(S, pagerank_centrality,'pr')
nodes_pr = get_top_nodes(pagerank_centrality)
```

If we look at the top 5 characters by PageRange we have roughly the same order, but instead of having Qui-Gon in 5th place, we have Luke:

```
> print(nodes_pr)

{'Anakin': 0.042419290139533466,
  'Obi-Wan': 0.03851822264942938,
  'C-3PO': 0.035812500857126256,
  'Padme (Queen Amidala)': 0.03369795977341906,
  'Luke': 0.029121630268795225}
```

The order for PageRank is similar, but we finally get to see Luke!

The network resulting from encoding the eigenvector centrality in the size of the nodes and filtering for nodes with values higher than 0.06 can be seen in Figure 3.24.

```
plot_graph(S, 'ec', 0.06, 5000,

    pos_force, edge_width)
```

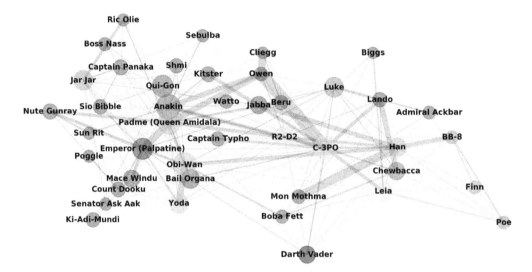

Figure 3.24: Eigenvector centrality for the *Star Wars* network. The size of the nodes denotes the eigenvector centrality of the node.

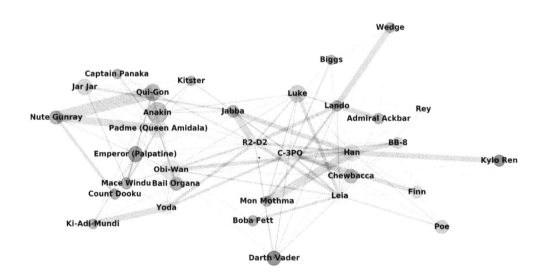

Figure 3.25: PageRange for the nodes in the *Star Wars* network. The size of the nodes denotes the PageRank score for the node.

The network encoding the PageRank scores for nodes with values higher than 0.006 is show in Figure 3.25.

```
plot_graph(S, 'pr', 0.006, 25000,
    pos_force, edge_width)
```

It is an inescapable fact of the *Star Wars* story that Anakin Skywalker gets seduced by the Dark Side of the Force and we can think of the two characters as being one and the same person. Let us consider the network where the nodes for these two central characters gets merged. The merging can be done with NetworkX with the `contracted_nodes` function:

Remember, fear is the path to the Dark Side.

```
V = nx.contracted_nodes(S, 'Darth Vader', 'Anakin')
```

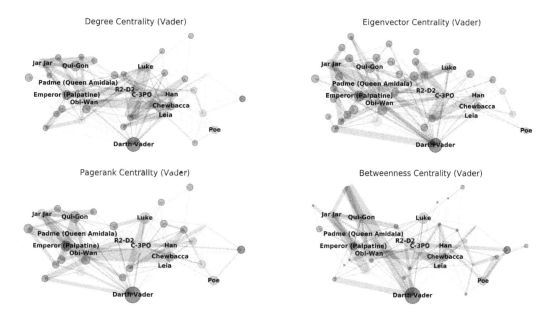

Figure 3.26: Vader networks for the following centrality measures: Degree centrality, eigenvector centrality, PageRank and betweenness.

Similar calculations to the ones carried out above can be done on this new network. The results for degree centrality, eigenvector centrality, PageRank and betweenness can be seen in Table 3.1. As we can see the rankings are very stable, keeping the first three places for Darth Vader, Obi-Wan and C-3PO, we then have Padmé, Luke, Qui-Gon and Han, followed by Leia, Chewbacca, the Emperor, R2-D2, Poe, and even Jar Jar.... Plots of the resulting (filtered) networks can be seen in Figure 3.26.

C-3PO!! Not R2!! Really??

Jar Jar... Oh well!!!

Ranking	Degree Centrality	Eigenvector Centrality	PageRank	Betweenness
1	Vader (0.4909)	Vader (0.3559)	Vader (0.0561)	Vader (0.2843)
2	Obi-Wan (0.3273)	Obi-Wan (0.2689)	Obi-Wan (0.0381)	Obi-Wan (0.1627)
3	C-3PO (0.3182)	C-3PO (0.2637)	C-3PO (0.0352)	C-3PO (0.1391)
4	Padmé (0.3091)	Padmé (0.2529)	Padmé (0.0344)	Luke (0.1309)
5	Qui-Gon (0.2455)	Qui-Gon (0.2243)	Luke (0.0284)	Han (0.104)
6	Luke (0.2364)	R2-D2 (0.2166)	Qui-Gon (0.0273)	Poe (0.073)
7	Han (0.2364)	Emperor (0.1966)	Han (0.0268)	Chewbacca (0.0681)
8	Leia (0.2273)	Jar Jar (0.183)	Leia (0.026)	Emperor (0.0641)
9	Jar Jar (0.2182)	Luke (0.1809)	Jar Jar (0.0251)	Padmé (0.0621)
10	R2-D2 (0.2)	Han (0.1765)	Emperor (0.0226)	Leia (0.0586)

Table 3.1: Character rankings for the most central characters in the *Star Wars* saga given by various centrality measures.

We can definitely see who the central characters in this galaxy are and how they interact. The story of the Light versus the Dark Side of the Force is right there with Darth Vader and Obi-Wan in the first places. The presence of the droids in the first 10 places plays homage to the influence that the feudal peasants from Kurosawa's film *The Hidden Fortress*.

This is definitely not a trap!

The data we have used contains information from Episodes I through VII, and having characters from the prequel (I-III) in the form of Qui-Gon, Padmé and even Jar Jar tells us that part of the story. It is interesting to see Poe as the only character from Episode VII that made the cut in the first 10 places and only for the betweenness centrality. This tells us about his importance in bringing together other characters in the story. This makes sense as he meets Finn first while escaping from the First Order, even giving him a name (FN-2187 is not deemed good enough) and introduces him to the rest of the resistance. Interesting to see that although the Emperor is an important character in the story, his presence is not outwardly revealed. This makes sense when we consider the plottings and cover-ups he had to concoct to get his plans to fruition.

Rey is not in the first 10 places. But then again, we only have data up to episode VI.

We finish this section by looking at the communities that arise from the connections in the network. Will we be able to distinguish the Dark Side from the Light one? Can we tell which are the shady characters? Let us take a look. We start by reducing the number of nodes in the network by concentrating on those that have degree centralities higher than 0.05:

Light versus Dark Side? Not quite, as we shall see.

```
nodes = [x for x, y in V.nodes(data=True)
   if y['dc'] >= 0.05]
VDC = V.subgraph(nodes)
```

We filter the graph for nodes with degree centrality higher than 0.05.

We can apply the Girvan-Newman algorithm as follows:

```
gn_side = community.girvan_newman(VDC)
sw_sides = tuple(sorted(c) for c
   in next(gn_side))
```

In this case, we have found two communities. We will now add this metadata to the network itself:

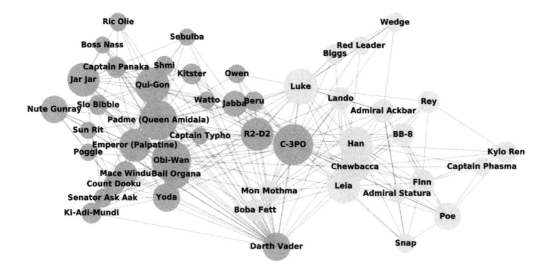

Figure 3.27: *Star Wars* sides (communities) obtained with the application of the Girvan-Newman algorithms.

```
comm = {}
for i, side in enumerate(sw_sides):
   for character in side:
     comm[str(character)] = 'side {0}'.format(i)
nx.set_node_attributes(VDC, comm, 'side')
```

If we colour the nodes in the network by the side that was found by the algorithm, we end up with the network shown in Figure 3.27. As we can see, it is perhaps telling us more about the episodes in the story, with the characters from Episodes I-III on one side, and the ones from IV-VI and VII on the other one. This makes sense when we consider the meaning of the edges in the network: They are dialogue interactions among characters; we know that Rey interacts with Han and Luke, but Poe never talked to Yoda or Padmé.

The communities tell us about the different chapters in the story, not about the two sides of the Force.

3.5 Summary

IN THIS CHAPTER WE HAVE covered many of the fundamental concepts used in the analysis of networks, whether social or otherwise. We have seen the wide variety of applications that networks have and the discussion was framed in terms of social network analysis, although I trust you can see the relevance in other areas of interest.

The work of the brilliant Leonhard Euler opened up a new way of understanding relationships between actors in a network. These actors are referred to as nodes or vertices, and the ties are known as edges. We understand the difference between directed and undirected graphs as well as some of the characteristics that make these networks interesting. Graph theory provides the basis to understand the relationships encoded in networks of interest.

We discussed the ideas behind a small-world network, leading to the popular idea of the six degrees of separation proposed by Milgram in the 1960s. Similarly, we talked about related measures such as the Bacon and Erdös numbers as ways to gauge the distance between actors, literally in the case of the Bacon number, in a network.

Encoding the information of a network in the form of a graph enables us to represent it using matrices and we described how an adjacency matrix can be used for this purpose. We covered other formats to encode this information in terms of edge and adjacency lists. In this way we introduced concepts around graphs such as trails, paths, cycles and semi-walks. We also described the use of NetworkX as a tool to analyse graph/network data with Python.

Furthermore, we described different measures that provide information about the importance of agents in the network. Measures such as degree centrality, closeness, betweenness, eigenvector centrality and PageRank let us describe the relationships in the graph and establish patterns that otherwise would not be easy to spot. We talked about cliques and clustering coefficients leading to the discussion of community detection with Girvan-Newman's and Louvain algorithms.

We finished the chapter with the application of these ideas to a couple of networks. The first one is the data provided by Wayne W. Zachary about a karate club with an infighting issue leading to the split of the club. The second one covers the interactions of the characters in the *Star Wars* films. So, do as Yoda says and pass on what you have learnt.

4

Thinking Deeply: Neural Networks and Deep Learning

AN ARTIFICIAL NEURAL NETWORK (ANN) is effectively a computing system that takes into account inputs that are combined, typically in a nonlinear manner, to calculate outputs that can be compared to expected outcomes. The motivation behind ANNs is loosely inspired by the biological neural networks that constitute animal brains.

For simplicity, we will also refer to them as neural nets.

The fact that expected outcomes are available to us should immediately make our Jackalope data scientist brains consider using neural nets for supervised learning. In that sense, neural nets are said to be able to *learn* how to carry out tasks based on the label data provided (data samples), without the need of being specifically programmed with rules.

Learning without having to be programmed!

Before we get into the deep end, understanding how neural networks work, we will first cover some historical aspects of their development. Then we will explain the general architecture of a neural network in terms of layers and nodes, cover forward and backward propagation and finish the chapter with a discussion on convolutional and recurrent neural networks.

4.1   A Trip Down Memory Lane

GIVEN ALL THE REPORTED ACHIEVEMENTS accomplished with the use of neural networks, we may think that the field is quite new. However, a lot of the ideas behind modern neural network implementations can be traced back to the 1940s. A good starting point is the work of McCulloch and Pitts[1] taking an electrical engineering approach to describing the use of *logical units* to model an artificial neuron. This can be seen as the basis of what we now call artificial neural networks. The inspiration was indeed the mimicking of the functions of a brain through electrical circuits, culminating with the coinage of the term *artificial intelligence* by John McCarthy.

Some ideas may be even older, but we need to draw the line somewhere.

[1] McCulloch, W. S. and Pitts, W. (1943). A logical calculus of the ideas immanent in nervous activity. *Bull. of Math. Biophysics* 5(4), 115–133

The neuron doctrine as proposed around 1888 by Spanish Nobel Prize winner Santiago Ramón y Cajal is the basis of modern neuroscience. It states that neurons are individual separate cells and they behave as biochemically distinct cells rather than a single entity in an interlinked network. A crude approximation to model some of the functions of the human brain is the electrical connectivity that takes place between the 10 billion plus neurons that compose it. The neuronal cell body, or soma, receives electrochemical signals

The inspiration is indeed the electrochemical activity of biological neurons.

(input) via the neuron's dendrites. If the combined signal received meets a given threshold, the neuron transmits a new signal (output) along its axon to other neurons' dendrites. This is the process the artificial neurons from McCulloch and Pitts emulated.

Continuing with the inspiration of a brain as a model, Frank Rosenblatt developed the concept of the *perceptron*[2] in which a neuron receives information from other neurons in the form of electrical impulses of varied strengths (positive or negative). The receiving neuron combines these impulses and if the result is larger than a certain given threshold the neuron "fires", transmitting the resulting impulse to other neurons. As we shall see in the rest of this chapter, today we refer to this as a one-layer neural network. Interestingly, the perceptron was conceived to be a custom-made machine, rather than an algorithm. If you find yourself in Washington D.C., you can pay a visit to the Mark I Perceptron in the Smithsonian Institution.

[2] Rosenblatt, F. (1962). *Principles of neurodynamics: perceptrons and the theory of brain mechanisms*. Report (Cornell Aeronautical Laboratory). Spartan Books

You can visit a perceptron in Washington D.C.

The perceptron combines the receiving inputs as a weighted sum and the firing happens if the sum exceeds the threshold C. With inputs x_1 and x_2 and weights w_1 and w_2 the output of the perceptron can be written as follows:

$$P_{output} = \begin{cases} 1, \text{ if } w_1 x_1 + w_2 x_2 > C, \\ 0, \text{ if } w_1 x_1 + w_2 x_2 \leq C. \end{cases} \qquad (4.1)$$

The perceptron is able to separate regions linearly.

We are effectively separating two regions in a plane with a line and thus the perceptron is able to separate regions linearly.

During the 1960s other advances helped bring these early neurons to be applied in the real world. For example, Bernard Widrow and Marcian Hoff devised the first learning rules for feedforward networks with multiple adaptive elements, naming their models "ADALINE" and "MADALINE". The rules relied on the examination of the values prior to adjusting the weights. The weight adjustment is proportional to the previous value times the error divided by the number of inputs. The idea is that even if one perceptron has a large error, it is possible to adjust the weights so as to distribute the error to adjacent perceptrons.

We will expand on feedforward nets in Section 4.2.3.

ADAptive LINear Elements and Multiple ADAptive LINear Elements, respectively.

With a perceptron, we can implement circuits that recreate operators such as AND and OR. However, it is not possible to implement a nonlinearly separable operation like XOR. Marvin Minsky and Seymour Papert showed[3] that not only it was not possible to compute an XOR operation with a single perceptron, but also provided arguments about it being achievable with multiple layers of perceptrons. The idea is to combine multiple neurons to perform more complicated tasks, if only we can add another and another layer of neurons to our model. As it turns out, the learning algorithm proposed by Rosenblatt did not work for multilayer neural nets.

[3] Minsky, M., S. Papert, and L. Bottou (2017). *Perceptrons: An Introduction to Computational Geometry*. The MIT Press. MIT Press

The supervised nature of the task means that the correct output expected is only specified for the final layer. We can use this information to adjust the weights for the layer in question, but... how do we get to the hidden layers sandwiched between the output and input ones? The answer, i.e., backpropagation, will have to wait for the lift of

We will cover backpropagation in Section 4.3.3.

the first AI winter to be widely spread. Nonetheless, the ideas behind it were floating around much before then.

In the early 1970s the work of Paul Werbos to extend beyond MADALINE enabled the development of a backpropagation algorithm[4]. This was largely unknown until 1986 when Rumelhart, Hinton, and Williams rediscovered it[5] and formalised it. They were able to set a clear framework for the technique, finally making it the well-known methodology we have today. Later in Section 4.3.3 we will address in more detail the workings of backpropagation. In the meantime, it suffices to say that the key aspect in its development is the realisation that if the neurons are not perceptrons per se, but instead they are able to compute their output with a nonlinear, differentiable function, then it is possible to use the derivative to minimise the errors incurred during training. In this way, with the aid of the well-known chain rule we can calculate the derivative for all the neurons in the prior layers.

[4] Werbos, P. (1994). *The Roots of Backpropagation: From Ordered Derivatives to Neural Networks and Political Forecasting.* Adaptive and Cognitive Dynamic Systems: Signal Processing, Learning, Communications and Control. Wiley

[5] Rumelhart, D. E., G. E. Hinton, and R. J. Williams (1986). Learning representations by back-propagating errors. *Nature 323*(6088), 533–536

With the advent of the backpropagation algorithm it was possible to train mutilayer architectures, opening the door to the development of convolutional neural networks (CNNs), first used by Yann LeCun et al.[6] to recognise hand-written digits with application in optical character recognition. By the end of the 1980s the interest in neural networks slowed down again as the approach to-date was not able to scale. Instead, algorithms such as the support vector machine gained prominence and it was not for another decade or so that neural nets regained interest.

[6] LeCun, Y., Boser, B., Denker, J. S., et al. (1989). Backpropagation applied to handwritten zip code recognition. *Neural Computation 1*(4), 541–551

We discussed SVMs on Chapter 9 of *Data Science and Analytics with Python.*

In 1997 a recurrent neural network (RNN) framework known as long short-term memory (LSTM) was proposed by Hochreiter and Schimdhuber[7], improving the efficiency and practical use of RNNs as we shall discuss in Section 4.4.3. By the mid-2000s, the term *deep learning* became ever more popular thanks to the use of the word "deep" by Geoffrey Hinton[8,9] and others to describe their approach to the development of large-scale neural networks. There are many more advances that merit more in-depth analysis than we can do justice here, and largely speaking, areas of research in Transfer Learning, Generative Adversarial Networks (GANs), Reinforcement Learning, hardware and software developments will give us more food for thought in the years to come.

[7] Hochreiter, S. and Schmidhuber, J. (1997). Long short-term memory. *Neural. Comput.* 9(8), 1735–1780

[8] Hinton, G. E., Osindero, S., and Teh, Y.-W. (2006). A Fast Learning Algorithm for Deep Belief Nets. *Neural Computation 18*, 1527–1554
[9] Hinton, G. E. and R. Salakhutdinov (2006). Reducing the dimensionality of data with neural networks. *Science 313 5786*, 504–7

All in all, for the different types of neural network architectures we have mentioned above, the analogy of neurons connecting with each other via their axons and dendrites is a first image that comes to mind. We can therefore start our journey by describing a general neural network architecture as a collection of nodes connected with each other so as to enable the transfer and manipulation of information. The nodes are aggregated into layers and thus the information flows from one layer to the next in a directed manner. A typical neural network architecture can be seen in Figure 4.1 where the nodes are represented by open circles, and the connections between them are shown as directed edges.

A neural network is a collection of nodes arranged in layers, enabling information to flow from one layer to the next.

As we can imagine, the graphical representation we have is similar to the graphs we discussed in Chapter 3. In this case

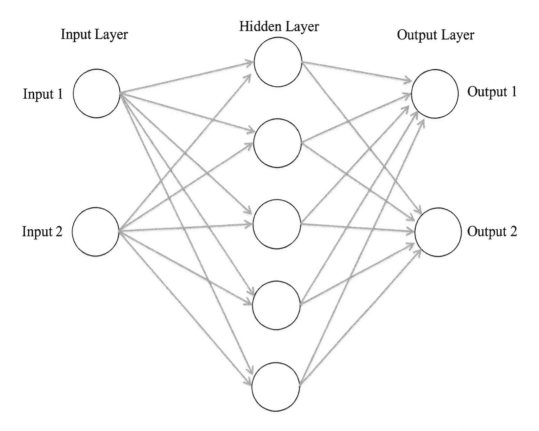

Figure 4.1: Neural network architecture with a single hidden layer.

we have a directed graph where the nodes belong to tiered layers and the information in the network flows in a single direction from one layer to the next.

Each of the edges in the network carries a weight and each node is able to take the inputs provided and combine them before passing them to the next tier of nodes. The learning process enables us to adjust or "learn" the optimal weights for the edges as the training proceeds, so that we make predictions with the network. Let us now go deeper inside this architecture.

Each edge in the graph has its own weight, and adjusting those weights is the learning process for a neural net.

4.2   No-Brainer: What Are Neural Networks?

AS WE HAVE SEEN IN the previous section, artificial neural networks can be understood in terms of their diagrammatic representations as graphs. Let us start delving into the workings of these graphs and see how they are able to *learn* patterns, *see* images, *recognise* speech and capture our collective imagination.

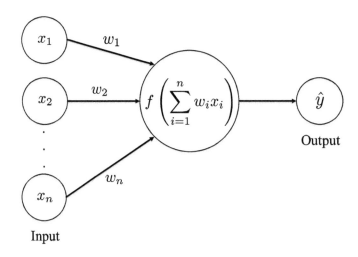

Input

Figure 4.2: An artificial neural network takes up an input and combines the contributions of the nodes to calculate an output $\hat{y}$ with the aid of a nonlinear function with the sum of its inputs.

The first thing to point out is that, unlike the graphs that we analysed in Chapter 3, the information present in the graph is not embedded in the architecture of the network. Instead an external input is required. This information is then used to compute an output with a function of the sum of its inputs. We can represent this as shown in Figure 4.2 where we can see n nodes providing a contribution to the calculation of the output $\hat{y}$ via a function $f(\cdot)$. Notice that each edge i has its own weight w_i.

Typically a nonlinear function.

The network architecture that we have in place is a weighted directed graph and our aim is to adjust the edge weights w_i as the learning takes place. We can think of this process as having a set of dials to adjust the strength of a signal at a given connection in the network. As it is the case in its biological counterpart, the synapses between neurons may actually fire, or be activated, if the aggregate signal is above a certain threshold.

To continue using the brain analogy, this would be the strength of the synapses between neurons.

4.2.1   Neural Network Architecture: Layers and Nodes

AN IMPORTANT FEATURE OF THE architecture of our neural networks is the fact that the nodes are arranged in layers. In other words, the information in the network flows from one layer to the next in the direction prescribed by the directed edges. We count the number of layers starting effectively from zero. That first layer is usually called the input layer and it is made out of passive nodes that take the input. The last layer is usually called the output layer and is made of active nodes. That is to say that they take the outcomes of the previous layer and modify the signals received. In between the input and output layers, we can have any number of so-called hidden layers. These hidden layers are also made out of active nodes. In Figure 4.1 we showed a typical example of a single layer neural network.

How Pythonic... but actually just a happy coincidence!

Each of the layers in the neural network architecture can have any number of nodes and as such, both the number of hidden layers as well as the number of nodes in each layer are a couple of the parameters you need to decide upon first.

We shall talk about the number of nodes later in this section.

As the number of hidden layers in our architecture increases, the deeper and deeper the input information needs to flow. I do use the word "deeper" with a bit of intent as this is what gives rise to the term *deep learning* to describe the work done with large artificial neural networks. Today, deep learning architectures have a wide range of applications including speech recognition, computer vision, automatic machine translation, text generation, image captioning, etc. We will talk more about deep learning in Section 4.4.

> Deep learning refers to the use of neural networks with a large number of hidden layers.

Different layers in the architecture will perform different kinds of manipulations and transformations on their respective inputs. The nodes in the input layer perform no computation; they simply, but importantly, pass on the information to the nodes in the first hidden layer. The hidden nodes carry out computation on the inputs received and transfer the result to the next layers, all the way through to the output layer. This process is usually known as *feedforward* where the information moves in one direction only; there are no cycles or loops.

> In other words, the nodes in a hidden layer.

> Not yet!

The single layer perceptron that we mentioned in the previous section is the simplest feedforward neural network: It does not have hidden layers and it is only capable of learning linear separable patterns. As the number of hidden layers grows, we are able to accomplish more complex tasks as shown in Table 4.1. The more layers we add, the more effectively we can perform automatic feature engineering.

> The more layers we add, the more effectively we can perform automatic feature engineering.

We mentioned above that each layer can contain, in principle, any number of nodes. Deciding how many nodes we put in each layer is as important as making up our

Number of Hidden Layers	Capability
0	Capable of representing only linear separable patterns.
1	Able to approximate any function with a continuous mapping from one finite space to another.
2	Able to represent any arbitrary decision boundary to arbitrary accuracy; can approximate any smooth mapping to any accuracy.
3 or more	Complex representations can be learnt by performing automatic feature engineering of sorts.

Table 4.1: Capabilities of neural networks with a different number of hidden layers.

minds about the number of layers. Although the hidden layers do not directly interact with the outside world, they do have a profound impact on the final output returned by the neural network. On the one hand, having too few nodes in the hidden layers gives rise to underfitting, as there are not enough nodes to detect the potential complex patterns in our data. On the other hand, the presence of too many nodes can also result in other issues. Overfitting is one of them, as the extra capacity in the network enables the system to memorise the attributes in the data, particularly when the set is not large enough. Even in cases where there is enough data, we need to take into consideration that the more nodes we have in the hidden layers results in longer

Deciding on the number of layers and the number of nodes in each is an important step.

training times. Some rule-of-thumb recommendations include having hidden layers with a number of nodes bounded by the size of the input and output layers. A good start is having around $60 - 70\%$ of the number of nodes in the input layer plus the number of nodes in the output layer. Finally, do not include more than twice the size of the input layer and remember that the ultimate architecture setup is a matter of striking a balance, as it is the case in many other areas of machine learning.

Choosing the size of the hidden layers is more data art than data science.

4.2.2   Firing Away: Neurons, Activate!

NOW THAT WE HAVE A better understanding of the architecture of our neural networks, we can delve deeper into their inner workings. Let us consider a one-hidden layer neural network as shown in Figure 4.3. Not only is this architecture able to represent linear functions, but also nonlinear ones. The input layer has three nodes, one of which we have marked as bias with a value of 1, the other two nodes take the values x_1 and x_2. These inputs are passed to the next layer along with their associated weights. Let us take a node in the (first) hidden layer of this neural network (highlighted in gray). Actually, we can zoom in to see what is happening there: See Figure 4.4. This hidden node receives the inputs $(1, x_1, x_2)$ along with the associated weights $(w_0, w_1 w_2)$ and uses the values to compute the function $f(\cdot)$ whose argument is a sum of the inputs as $\sum w_i x_i$. This function is referred to as the *activation function* and we shall talk more about it in the next pages.

Pun definitely intended!

We can extend this analysis to a larger number of nodes.

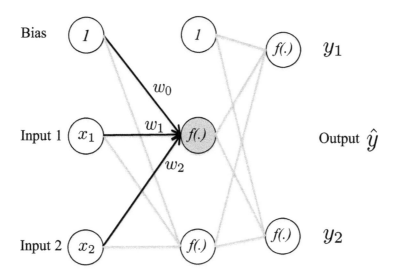

The process described above is carried out for each of the nodes in the first layer and the resulting value from the activation function is used as the input for the next layer, and so on. In the architecture shown in Figure 4.3, we have two output nodes. After executing the same process with the activation function $f(\cdot)$ their results (y_1, y_2) are the output of the neural network.

Figure 4.3: Neural network architecture with a single hidden layer, including bias. The inputs to a node (marked in gray) are used in conjunction with the weights w_i to calculate the output with the help of the activation function $f(\cdot)$.

The activation function is a nonlinear function. This is because we are interested in representing complex, real-world data with our neural networks. The activation function therefore introduces a nonlinearity to the outputs of the node, enabling the architecture to learn these complex representations.

The activation function is a nonlinear function.

We have been talking about the activation function as an important part of our neural network, but so far we have not said much about its structure. This is because there may

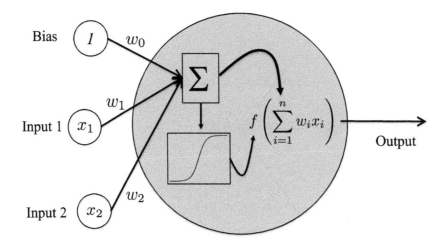

Figure 4.4: Zooming into one of the hidden nodes in our neural network architecture.

be many options available to us. Each of these options offers different ways in which the inputs are combined, and the most common activation functions include the following:

- **Sigmoid**: This function takes a real-valued input and maps it to a range of values between 0 and 1. The sigmoid function is given by the expression below and we can see a plot in the top panel of Figure 4.5

We have encountered this function in the context of logistic regression!

$$S(x) = \frac{\exp(x)}{1 + \exp(x)} \qquad (4.2)$$

- **Hyperbolic tangent**: This function also takes real-valued inputs and maps them to a range of values in the interval $[-1, 1]$. It is effectively a rescaling of the sigmoid function:

This is a rescaled sigmoid function.

$$\tanh(x) = 2S(2x) - 1 = \frac{\exp(2x) - 1}{\exp(2x) + 1}. \qquad (4.3)$$

We can see the shape of the tanh function in the middle panel of Figure 4.5.

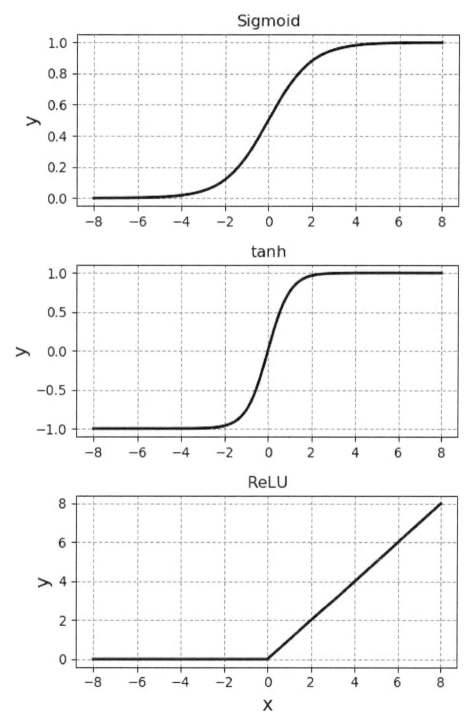

Figure 4.5: Some common activation functions, including sigmoid, tanh and ReLU.

- **Rectified Linear Unit** (ReLU): This function places a minimal threshold of zero to negative inputs, and maps positive values to themselves:

$$f(x) = \max(0, x).\qquad(4.4)$$

The bottom panel of Figure 4.5 depicts this function

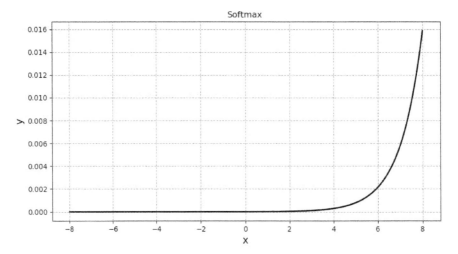

Figure 4.6: A plot of the softmax function.

It may be the case that in our application we are interested in generating probabilities as the outcomes of the activation layer. In this case, we can make use of the **softmax** activation function. This function is effectively a generalisation of the sigmoid function. It takes real values as input and maps them to a probability distribution where entry is in the range $(0, 1]$. Furthermore, all the entries add up to 1. The softmax activation function is given by Equation C.1 and a plot can be seen in Figure 4.6.

As the entries of a softmax function add up to 1, it can be used to draw probabilities.

$$\text{softmax}(x_i) = \sigma(z_i) = \frac{\exp(x_i)}{\sum_{j=1}^{N} \exp(x_j)}, \text{ for } i = 1, \ldots, k. \quad (4.5)$$

Once we have applied the activation function to the inputs of the node in question, we are ready to pass the outcome to the next layer in our neural network. We do this until we reach the last layer, where the outputs are actually the predictions made by the entire neural network architecture. Et voilà!

4.2.3   Going Forwards and Backwards

THE OUTPUT OF THE NEURAL networks we have discussed so far has been obtained by taking forward the inputs from one layer to the next. This kind of neural network is called a feedforward network and the flow of information goes in one single direction, not allowing for loops or cycles. Feedback is therefore not possible. What happens if the response we obtain from training our neural network is not satisfactory? Well, in the case of a feedforward network, as described above, there is not much we can do.

So far, we have only fed the information forward from the input to the output layers.

Nonetheless, it is possible to consider the following scenario: Once we have obtained the final output of our neural network, we can compare it to the labelled data used for training. If the error is negligible we are done; however, if the error is not acceptable we would like to provide this as feedback to the neural network. In other words, we would like the neural network to "learn from its mistakes".

We would like to be able to learn from our mistakes.

The process to enable this form of *learning* in a neural network is known as backward propagation of errors, or **backpropagation** for short. Following up the analogy about learning from our mistakes we are, in a sense, asking the

Or actually the neural network's mistakes!

machine to guess the value of the labelled data. The error in
the guess is calculated and backpropagated so that a better
estimate can be made.

OK! estimate...

In this way, we are going forwards and backwards, and
forwards again until the error is within an accepted level
of tolerance. The way in which backpropagation estimates
the error is by minimising a cost function, and therefore we
need to make use of calculus. A well-known optimisation
method used in this kind of tasks is **gradient descent**.
In the following sections we will cover in more detail the
implementation of backpropagation, but for the time being
let us spend some more time getting familiar with what is
happening at a high level. Let us start with our forward
propagation network as depicted in Figure 4.7, in panel a)
we have the situation described in the previous section. For
our purposes, we have a neural network with one hidden
layer and three nodes in the input layer.

Or until we give up...

We start we the forward
propagation step. Nothing
unusual here.

We need to bring the inputs (and bias) together with the
initial weights w_0, w_1 and w_2 and make the appropriate
calculations with them. In order to track what is happening
to the weights, we are adding the superscript $[0]$ to denote
the initial forward pass. In this way, the weights $w_i^{[0]}$ and
the inputs are combined in the hidden nodes by a given
activation function. The results are then passed forward to
the output layer, where we get a target prediction, in this
case the output is either a 1 or a 0. Please note that in Figure
4.7 we are only labelling the weights that go from the input
to the first hidden layer. The other edgs in the architecture
carry their own weights too.

We are not explicitly showing the
weights used from the hidden
layer to the output later, but the
same process applies.

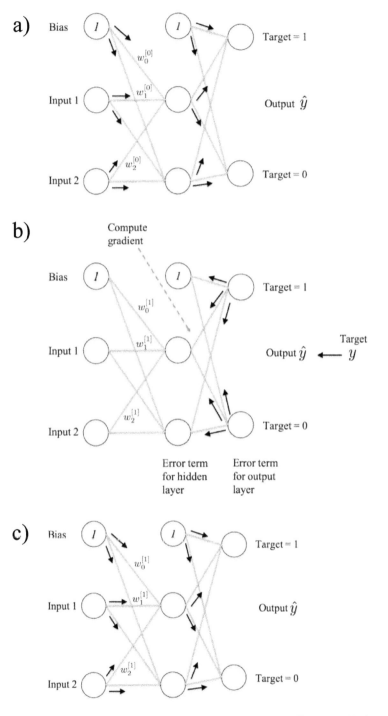

Figure 4.7: Backward propagation of errors, or backpropagation, enables the neural network to learn from its mistakes.

We are now interested in checking if the prediction labels obtained from the 0th forward pass are any good. We can denote the output result as $\hat{y}$ and compare it to the actual target y. The result of the comparison between y and $\hat{y}$ contains useful information for the neural network as it enables it to learn from its mistakes. In order to do this, we make use of a loss (or cost) function, which enables us to evaluate how well our chosen algorithm models the training data provided. If our predictions are off the mark, the loss function will return a higher value. However, if they are good, the result of the loss function will be a smaller number.

The comparison between actual and predicted values enables the network to learn from its mistakes.

It is possible to propagate this information from the output layer back to the hidden nodes, until it reaches the edges of the input layer. In this way it is possible to enable the neural network to identify the weights that need to be adjusted to improve the predictions made. On the one hand, in the cases where the prediction is different from the target label, the neural network can adjust the weight that made this prediction and improve the result. On the other hand, for labels that have been correctly predicted, no adjustment is needed. In order to propagate back the information, we are in effect solving an optimisation problem for the loss function chosen.

Please note that since the weights are combined by the activation, changes in one may require further changes in others.

As mentioned above, a well-known algorithm such as *gradient descent* can be used for the optimisation step, and it requires us to be able to compute gradients. We will provide further details about it in the next section. The backpropagation step is depicted in Figure 4.7, panel b).

We are now in the situation shown in panel c) of Figure 4.7 where we reach the start of our learning loop. Now that we have passed information back about the weights, the neural network can make adjustments and the new weights let us start a new forward pass. This step starts and follows exactly the same logic as before, except that this time we have new values $w_0^{[1]}$, $w_1^{[1]}$ and $w_2^{[1]}$. Notice that we are using the superscript 1 to denote the fact that we have a new iteration.

We start a new forward pass with the new adjusted weights.

From here on, the process continues as before: We use the weights and inputs to make calculations using the activation function, and pass the results to the next layer. When we reach the output layer, the new prediction results are compared with the targets. The fact that we are using a minimisation process indicates that we are expecting lower and lower values from our loss function. We continue iterating over our neural network sending information back and forth until we reach a chosen tolerance on the values of our loss function. At that point, we can stop the iterations and we have a neural network that has learnt from its mistakes in making predictions when comparing to the target labels provided. We are ready to unleash the model to the world and confront real data. Let us now take a look at implementing this workflow in more detail.

We iteratively adjust the weights until we reach an optimal solution, sending information forth and back through the layers of the network.. You are right, the phrase goes "back and forth" but that seems wrong for an ANN!

4.3   Neural Networks: From the Ground up

WE HAVE COVERED QUITE A few of the concepts behind a neural network architecture and understand the main ideas behind their "learning". In this section we are going to implement an artificial neural network with three layers: The input and output layers and one hidden layer.

The goal is to see how the concepts described above translate into code with Python. The code is not meant to be the most efficient implementation ever and there may be other ways to achieve the same results in a better way. Take this implementation for what it is, and we will cover other alternatives later on in this chapter.

Take this implementation with a "brain" of salt!

Let us imagine that we are interested in discriminating between two classes of animals, say cats and dogs. In Chapter 5 of *Data Science and Analytics with Python*[10], we encountered a friendly alien life-form that was tasked with clustering animals on Earth based on similarities and differences between them: Cats have pointy triangular ears, whereas rabbits have long oval ones; horses have manes and deer have antlers. This provided our alien friend with rules that can be used in classification based on the labels we have obtained for the animals shown to it. In this case we are assuming that the labels have already been identified and that we have a dataset containing animals with their corresponding label: Cat or dog. The next task for the alien is therefore to obtain a model that enables it to correctly predict whether she has a cat or a dog in front of him, given the different features provided to them.

[10] Rogel-Salazar, J. (2017). *Data Science and Analytics with Python*. Chapman & Hall/CRC Data Mining and Knowledge Discovery Series. CRC Press

It? him? her? them?

We should have asked for a name and preferred pronoun! Ma-Sha from Gazorpazorp? She may even have a Marc Jacobs top by now!

From our previous discussion, we know that training an artificial neural network involves choosing a number of nodes in our hidden layer(s). It stands to reason that the

more nodes we include, the more complex our neural
network becomes, and the hope is that we will be able to fit
more complex functions with it. However, we need to take
into account the balancing between high dimensionality and
hence complexity, versus the computational cost incurred.
We did mention in Section 4.2.1 that choosing the right
number of hidden nodes is more data art than data science.
For our current purposes we are going to consider playing
with the number of hidden nodes in the architecture and see
how this affects our output.

Higher complexity may mean higher computational cost.

4.3.1   Going Forwards

WE START BY MAKING OUR way forwards from the input
layer and into the depth of our neural network architecture.
In practice, the way to achieve this is via the application
of matrix multiplication, and of course of the activation
function chosen for the task. Let us consider our input to
be given by a 2-dimensional matrix X which will render
our prediction denoted by $\hat{y}$. We will denote the vector of
weights from the input layer to the first hidden layer as W_1
and thus we can calculate the combination of the inputs
with the weights as:

We will use matrices to represent our neural network model.

$$z_1 = XW_1 + b_1, \qquad (4.6)$$

This is the combined result of our inputs.

please note that both W_1 and b_1 are parameters of our
network that need to be learnt from training data.

We can pass the result z_1 to the activation function, and here
we will use the hyperbolic tangent for the hidden layer. This

means that the output will be given by:

$$a_1 = \tanh(z_1).\tag{4.7}$$

This is the output of the hidden layer.

We are now able to take the output a_1 of the hidden layer and pass it as the input to the next layer in our network. Remember that in this particular architecture this is actually the output layer. In this case we have that the combination of the input a_1 and the weight vector W_2 is given by:

$$z_2 = a_1 W_2 + b_2.\tag{4.8}$$

Once more, we calculate the combination of inputs.

For the activation function in the output layer, we will use the softmax function which will let us convert our scores to probabilities:

$$a_2 = \hat{y} = \sigma(z_2).\tag{4.9}$$

And this is the output of the entire network.

Although we have written the expressions above specifically for our three-layer neural network, it is easy to generalise the equations noting that z_i corresponds to the weighted sum of inputs of layer i and thus a_i is the output of the i-th layer after applying the activation function chosen for that layer. In effect we have a pipeline of matrices that transform our data from one layer to the next, enabling along the way some featuring engineering in an automatic way.

With one hidden layer.

Let us stop for a moment to consider the dimensionality of our matrices. For a 2-dimensional input X, with a single hidden layer comprising n hidden nodes we have that our parameters are $W_1 \in \mathbb{R}^{2 \times n}$, $b_1 \in \mathbb{R}^n$, $W_2 \in \mathbb{R}^{n \times 2}$, $b_2 \in \mathbb{R}^2$. We can see how the complexity becomes larger not only as we increase the number of nodes in the layer, but also as

Checking the dimensions of our matrices is a good practice.

we increase the number of layers, and indeed the number of nodes in them. Keeping track of all the transformations that larger, deeper neural networks perform could become a truly gargantuan task.

The calculations above can be generalised to a neural network with L layers. We denote the activation of the nodes in layer l as a column-vector $\mathbf{a}^l$, the edges from the nodes in layer $l-1$ to layer l are stored in the weight matrix $\mathbf{W}^l$ and the biases in the column vector $\mathbf{b}^l$. For the forward pass, given the activation function f_l, we have that:

Let us generalise the ideas above to L layers.

$$\mathbf{a}^l = f_l\left(\mathbf{W}^l \mathbf{a}^{l-1} + \mathbf{b}^l\right). \tag{4.10}$$

Note that we are taking into account the possibility that the activation function on each layer may be different, perhaps ReLU, softmax or even a hyperbolic tangent. The general architecture of the network can be seen in Figure 4.8.

The activation function can be different for each layer.

To calculate the input sums and move forward in the network, let us consider three adjacent layers in the architecture as shown in the middle part of Figure 4.8. Let us index the nodes in the layers $l-1$, l and $l+1$ as m, p and q, respectively. The input sum of a node p in layer l is:

$$z_p^l = \sum_m W_{mp}^l a_m^{l-1} + b_p^l, \tag{4.11}$$

This corresponds to the generalised combination of inputs.

where we are adding the contributions of all nodes m in layer $l-1$. We can calculate the activations in layer l as $a_p^l = f_l(z_p^l)$ and thus the input sum of a node q in layer $l+1$ is:

$$z_q^{l+1} = \sum_p W_{qp}^{l+1} a_p^l + b_q^{l+1}. \tag{4.12}$$

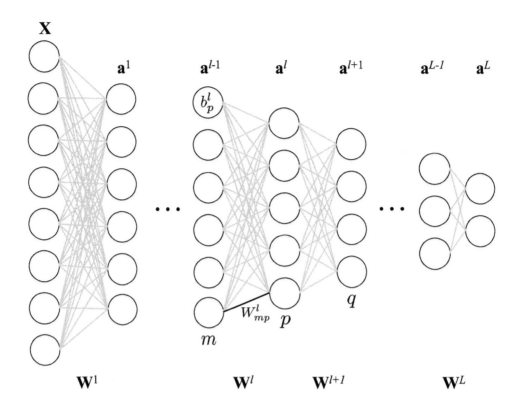

Figure 4.8: General architecture of a neural network; we are showing the labels of the different L layers in the network.

In this way we have moved forwards in the network from one layer to the next. We continue doing this until reaching the output layer. So far so good, and now how do we learn the parameters? Let us take a look.

4.3.2 Learning the Parameters

THE TASK DEFINED ABOVE REQUIRES us to determine the paramaters (W_1, b_1, W_2, b_2) such that we get a minimum error on our training data. The crucial part at this moment is defining that error in terms of a suitable loss function. In

We need to minimise a cost/loss function.

the high-level description in the Section 4.2.3 we mentioned that a comparison between our prediction $\hat{y}$ and the true class labels of y would be ideal.

A suitable choice, with the softmax activation function we have for our output layer, is the cross-entropy loss. Let us consider that given a model for which c classes are predicted, the hypothetical occurrence probabilities are $\hat{y}_1, \hat{y}_2, \ldots, \hat{y}_c$. If we observed k_1 instances for the first class, k_2 for the second, and so on we have that the likelihood is $P(data|model) = \Pi_c \hat{y}_c^{k_c}$. For $N = k_1 + k_2 + \cdots + k_c$ observations we can write the following expression:

The cross-entropy loss function is a suitable choice for many situations.

$$L(y, \hat{y}) = -\frac{1}{N} \log \Pi_c \hat{y}_c^{k_n}$$

$$= -\frac{1}{N} \sum_i k_i \log \hat{y}_i$$

$$= -\sum_i y_i \log \hat{y}_i \qquad (4.13)$$

where $y_i = k_i/N$ correspond to the empirical probabilities. For the case of two classes we have that the true observed probabilities are such that $y_2 = 1 - y_1 = 1 - y$, and the same applies to the predicted values. Therefore we can write Equation (4.13) as:

Binary classification is a good typical case.

$$L(y, \hat{y}) = -y \log \hat{y} - (1 - y) \log(1 - \hat{y}). \qquad (4.14)$$

In practice the loss function implemented in applications including logistic regression is an average of all cross-entropies. In the case where we have N data samples the loss function is calculated as:

$$L(y, \hat{y}) = -\frac{1}{N} \sum_{n=1}^{N} \sum_{i=1}^{C} y_i^{(n)} \log \hat{y}_i^{(n)}. \qquad (4.15)$$

Remember that it is possible to add a regularisation term to the loss function.

This expression lets us sum over each of our training data points and whenever we predict the incorrect class, we add to the loss. In other words, in cases where the two probability distributions y and $\hat{y}$ are far away, we have a greater loss. Our goal is to find parameters that minimise the loss, and thus maximise our predictions to match our training dataset. Let us see how the minimisation can be done.

4.3.3   Backpropagation and Gradient Descent

NOW THAT WE HAVE A loss function, we need to use an optimisation method to find its minimum. Gradient descent algorithms find the optimal for a loss or cost function by changing the parameters of a model such that the gradient of the errors points down to a minimum error value.

Gradient descent is a popular optimisation method.

We can make use of any optimisation technique we prefer and there are many out there from which to choose, ranging from brute force search all the way through to generic algorithms. The important thing is to be able to change the parameters of the neural network. However, as the complexity of our network increases we must take into account that the number of parameters to track becomes larger and larger and we would like it to be as computationally efficient as possible. Calculus is a good ally to every savvy Jackalope data scientist.

In principle, any good optimisation method can be applied.

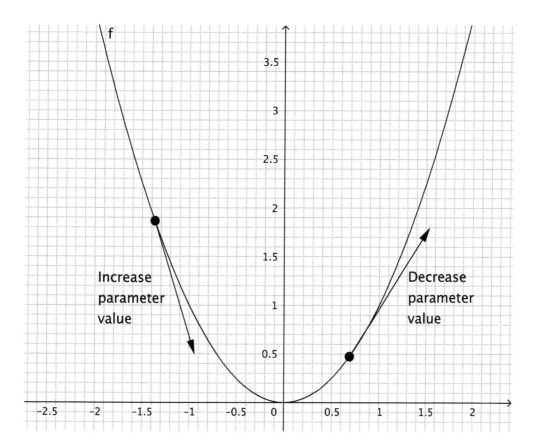

Figure 4.9: The derivative of a function f indicates the rate of change at a given point. This information lets us change our parameters accordingly.

A useful and fundamental concept from calculus is that of the derivative of a function. It basically provides a gauge to the rate of change the function experiences at a given point. In our case we can use this tool to check how much the error in our predictions changes when we change one of the parameters we would like to learn. Consider for instance the 2-dimensional function f depicted in Figure 4.9, where a clear minimum is shown.

If the function represents the cost, a positive value for its derivative indicates that the error increases if we increase the value of our parameter. If that is the case, we need to reduce it and hence we move towards the function's minimum. If, however, the derivative is negative, the error is decreasing, and therefore increasing the value of our parameter gets us closer to the minimum. If the derivative has a value of 0 we have reached a stable point, i.e., the minimum, and we are done.

Local minimum...

We can think of the description above as a skier who is trying to reach the valley and stop for a well-deserved refreshment. She would like to get to the lodge as swiftly as possible and that means finding the slope with steepest descent to reach her destination. If she chooses a path where the slope is increasing, she should change direction. That in a nutshell is what we are doing with the gradient descent algorithm. The case shown in Figure 4.9 can be described in terms of an ordinary derivative; however, when we have multiple parameters we will require the use of partial derivatives.

Think of the algorithm in terms of a skier that wants to reach the lodge as swiftly as possible.

Now, for the backpropagation of the errors in our neural network, we can apply the derivative trick and trace back our steps in the network architecture. Our starting point now is the output layer. We calculate the partial derivatives of the loss function with respect to our parameters and propagate the errors back to the input layer. The gradient descent algorithm requires as input the gradients of the loss function:

In other words, the vector of derivatives.

$$\frac{\partial L}{\partial W_1}, \frac{\partial L}{\partial b_1}, \frac{\partial L}{\partial W_2}, \frac{\partial L}{\partial b_2}.$$

Remember that our neural network carries out the following computations:

$$z_1 = XW_1 + b_1, \qquad (4.16)$$

$$a_1 = \tanh(z_1), \qquad (4.17)$$

We obtained these expressions in Section 4.3.1.

$$z_2 = a_1 W_2 + b_2, \qquad (4.18)$$

$$a_2 = \sigma(z_2) = \hat{y}. \qquad (4.19)$$

We use this information to update our parameters, and we do this with a particular **learning rate**, α, such that for a parameter W_i the update is given by:

$$W_i := W_i - \alpha \frac{\partial L}{\partial W_i}, \qquad (4.20)$$

and for b_i we have:

$$b_i := b_i - \alpha \frac{\partial L}{\partial b_i}. \qquad (4.21)$$

The learning rate, α, is a hyperparameter of our model.

We need to calculate each of the gradients and the application of the chain rule makes this task easier. Let us start with the derivative of the loss function with respect to the parameter b_2:

$$\frac{\partial L}{\partial b_2} = \frac{\partial L}{\partial z_2} \frac{\partial z_2}{\partial b_2}. \qquad (4.22)$$

We have that:

The chain rule to the rescue!

$$\frac{\partial z_2}{\partial b_2} = \frac{\partial(a_1 W_2 + b_2)}{\partial b_2} = 1. \qquad (4.23)$$

For the partial derivative of the loss function with respect to the variable z_2 we have that:

$$\frac{\partial L}{\partial z_2} = -y\frac{\partial \log \sigma(z_2)}{\partial z_2} - (1-y)\frac{\partial \log(1-\sigma(z_2)))}{\partial z_2},$$

$$= \frac{-y}{\sigma(z_2)}\frac{\partial \sigma(z_2)}{\partial z_2} - \frac{1-y}{1-\sigma(z_2)}\frac{\partial(1-\sigma(z_2))}{\partial z_2}, \quad (4.24)$$

We need to calculate the derivative of the softmax function.

$$= -y(1-\sigma(z_2)) + (1-y)\sigma(z_2),$$

$$= \sigma(z_2) - y = \hat{y} - y. \quad (4.25)$$

Expression (4.24) requires us to compute the derivative of the softmax function and more information can be found in Appendix C. Furthermore, a general derivative of the loss function with respect to parameter z_j can be found in Appendix D.

We have now all the information to calculate the derivative of the loss function with respect to the parameter b_2. Let us take a look:

$$\frac{\partial L}{\partial b_2} = \frac{\partial L}{\partial z_2}\frac{\partial z_2}{\partial b_2} = \hat{y} - y. \quad (4.26)$$

Once more we use the chain rule.

The derivative of the loss function with respect to the parameter W_2 is given by:

$$\frac{\partial L}{\partial W_2} = \frac{\partial L}{\partial z_2}\frac{\partial z_2}{\partial W_2} = a_1(\hat{y} - y). \quad (4.27)$$

And again...

In a similar way, we can make use of the chain rule to calculate the derivative of the loss function with respect to

b_1 as follows:

$$\frac{\partial L}{\partial b_1} = \frac{\partial L}{\partial z_2}\frac{\partial z_2}{\partial a_1}\frac{\partial a_1}{\partial z_1}\frac{\partial z_1}{\partial b_1},$$

We know the drill by now...

$$= (\hat{y} - y)W_2(1 - \tanh^2(z_1)). \qquad (4.28)$$

Following the same train of thought, finally the derivative of the loss function with respect to W_1 is:

$$\frac{\partial L}{\partial W_1} = \frac{\partial L}{\partial z_2}\frac{\partial z_2}{\partial a_1}\frac{\partial a_1}{\partial z_1}\frac{\partial z_1}{\partial W_1},$$

Don't we?

$$= (\hat{y} - y)W_2(1 - \tanh^2(z_1))X. \qquad (4.29)$$

Let us now go back to the generalisation introduced in Section 4.3.1 and use the indexing shown in Figure 4.8. Given a loss function L, we can calculate its derivative with respect to a single weight in layer l:

$$\frac{\partial L}{\partial W_{mp}^l} = \frac{\partial L}{\partial z_p^l}\frac{\partial z_p^l}{\partial W_{mp}^l},$$

We can now generalise our calculations.

$$= \frac{\partial L}{\partial a_p^l}\frac{\partial a_p^l}{\partial z_p^l}\frac{\partial z_p^l}{\partial W_{mp}^l},$$

$$= \left(\sum_q \frac{\partial L}{\partial z_q^{l+1}}\frac{\partial z_q^{l+1}}{\partial a_p^{l+1}}\right)\frac{\partial a_p^l}{\partial z_p^l}\frac{\partial z_p^l}{\partial W_{mp}^l},$$

$$= \left(\sum_q \frac{\partial L}{\partial z_q^{l+1}}W_{qp}^{l+1}\right)f_l'(z_p^l)a_m^{l-1}. \qquad (4.30)$$

We are including a sum to account for all the contributions from the nodes in layer $l + 1$. This is because their values have an effect on the overall error as they depend on the weights with respect to which we are taking the derivative.

Furthermore, in the expression above we are fixing p and m and as a result we can see what happens to the error when changing one single weight. We can also look at how the total error changes when the input sum to a node is modified:

$$\delta_p^l \equiv \frac{\partial L}{\partial z_p^l} = \left(\sum_q \frac{\partial L}{\partial z_q^{l+1}} W_{qp}^{l+1} \right) f_l'(z_p^l), \qquad (4.31)$$

Remember that we need to take into account the contributions from all input nodes.

This is the total error change given by the change in the input sum to a node.

where we have used the result in expression (4.30). This hints to a recursive formula such that:

$$\delta_p^l = \left(\sum_q \delta_q^{l+1} W_{qp}^{l+1} \right) f_l'(z_p^l) \qquad (4.32)$$

We have obtained a recursive function that can be applied to our model.

As for the derivatives of the loss function with respect to the biases we have:

$$\frac{\partial L}{\partial b_p^l} = \frac{\partial L}{\partial z_p^l} \frac{\partial z_p^l}{\partial b_p^l} = \frac{\partial L}{\partial z_p^l} (1) = \delta_p^l. \qquad (4.33)$$

Which turns out to be very handy!

We can now use our recursive formula to obtain the error of the nodes in the final layer L:

$$\delta_m^L = \frac{\partial L}{\partial z_m^L} = \frac{\partial L}{\partial a_m^L} \frac{\partial a_m^L}{\partial z_m^L} = \frac{\partial L}{\partial a_m^L} f_l'(z_m^L). \qquad (4.34)$$

Using these recursion formulas, we can verify the expressions we obtained before:

$$\delta^{(2)} = \frac{\partial L}{\partial b_2} = \frac{\partial L}{\partial a_2}\frac{\partial \sigma(z_2)}{\partial z_2} = \hat{y} - y \qquad (4.35)$$

$$\delta^{(1)} = \frac{\partial L}{\partial b_1} = \delta^{(2)}W_2\frac{\partial \tanh(z_1)}{\partial z_1}$$

$$= \delta^{(2)}W_2\left(1 - \tanh^2(z_1)\right) \qquad (4.36)$$

We obtained these expressions at the beginning of this section.

$$\frac{\partial L}{\partial W_2} = \delta^{(2)}\frac{\partial z_2}{\partial W_2} = \delta^{(2)}a_1 \qquad (4.37)$$

$$\frac{\partial L}{\partial W_1} = \delta^{(1)}\frac{\partial z_1}{\partial W_1} = \delta^{(1)}X \qquad (4.38)$$

Now that we have the equations that enable us to backpropagate errors, we can consider some aspects of the computational implementation of the optimisation algorithm. There are different variations and one of the most common is the so-called **stochastic gradient descent** where the model is changed for each training example in the dataset. In this case, the data effectively becomes available to the algorithm in sequential order. This kind of methodology is sometimes called *online machine learning*. Although we may get a more immediate view of the performance of the model, it is a computationally intensive affair as well as being prone to be affected by noise.

In stochastic gradient descent, we update the model for every training data sample.

A variation on this theme is the use of the so-called **batch gradient descent** where the changes in the model are calculated for each training sample, but crucially, the model

In batch gradient descent, the model is updated after all the training samples are considered.

is updated once all the training samples have been considered. A full loop through the complete training dataset is called an **epoch** and we update the model at the end of each epoch. The batch methodology makes our computation more efficient compared to the stochastic approach. It also provides us with a more stable error estimation. However, we need to be mindful of potential premature convergence given that stability. Similarly, large training datasets may give us very slow execution times.

An epoch is a full loop through the complete training dataset.

A variation on the batch methodology that splits the training dataset into small batches can be used too. This is called **mini-batch gradient descent** and serves as a balance between the stochastic and batch methodologies described above. Mini-batch lets us update the model with a higher frequency than batch while being more efficient than the stochastic approach. The batching of the training dataset also makes it more manageable for large sets. The batch size needs to be adjusted depending on our application.

In mini-batch gradient descent, we split the training set in smaller batches.

The batch size describes the size of the mini-batch!

Note that although our goal is to find the parameters of the model, we need to be aware of any hyperparameters for our model. In the case of mini-batch, not only do we need to find a suitable number of epochs but also the batch size. When the batch size is equal to the size of the training dataset we recover the batch methodology, whereas when the batch size is equal to a single data point we have the stochastic one. Masters and Luschi[11] advocate the use of small batch sizes, between 2 and 32 for example. Some popular batch sizes include values such as 32, 64 or 128.

[11] Masters, D. and C. Luschi (2018). Revisiting Small Batch Training for Deep Neural Networks. *Computing Research Repository* http://arxiv.org/abs/1804.07612

As for the epochs, let us recall that they refer to the number of iterations our algorithm runs through the entire training dataset. Each epoch has therefore one or more batches. When the number of batches per epoch is equal to 1, we have a batch gradient descent implementation! In cases where we have 2 or more batches per epoch we effectively have a couple of nested loops. One loop is over the number of epochs, where the entire training dataset is utilised; inside this loop we have another one that runs through the number of batches specified. In general the number of epochs can be typically on the order of hundreds so that the algorithm has enough time to learn the parameters that minimise the error.

Remember that an epoch has one or more batches.

Even thousands!

What does this all mean in more concrete terms? Let us assume that we have a dataset with 1000 data points and we have chosen a batch size of 32 with 2000 epochs. We are requiring our dataset to be divided into 31 batches of 32 samples and therefore we will update our model 31 times per epoch. With 2000 epochs we have 62,000 batches to go through while training our neural network.

Note that we are leaving 8 samples out... We can choose a better batch size to use all our data!

4.3.4 *Neural Network: A First Implementation*

WE HAVE BEEN THINKING ABOUT ANNs and the way they work, and you may be asking yourselves where the code is. Without further ado, let us provide a first implementation. Remember the caveat we clarified at the beginning of Section 4.3: This may not be the best implementation, and the aim is to demonstrate the concepts discussed above.

We did mention to take this implementation with a "brain" of salt!

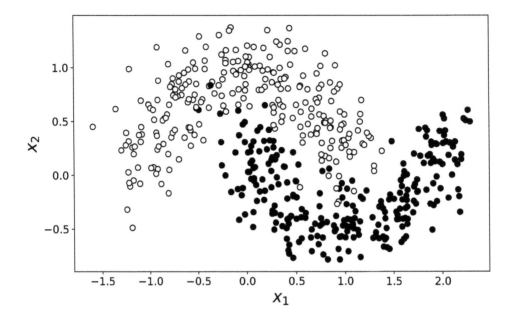

Figure 4.10: Observations corresponding to two classes, 0 and 1, described by features x_1 and x_2. We will use this data to train a neural network.

Let us consider the dataset shown in Figure 4.10. It contains observations corresponding to two classes labelled 0 and 1 described by two features x_1 and x_2. The dataset called `neuralnet_dataset.csv`[12] can be obtained at `https://doi.org/10.6084/m9.figshare.9249074.v1`. We can see that a linear classifier may be able to do an alright job in separating the two classes, but it would be a hard task to improve the discrimination given the semi-circular trends shown in the plot. Similar datasets can be generated with Scikit-learn with the help of the `make_moons` command. Let us start by reading the data:

[12] Rogel-Salazar, J. (2019b, Aug). Neural Network - Observation dataset. https://doi.org/10.6084/m9.figshare.9249074.v1

```
df = pd.read_csv('neuralnet_dataset.csv')
X = df[['x1', 'x2']].values
y = df['label'].values
```

We are reading our data into a Pandas dataframe.

Let us define a few parameters that will be used in determining the architecture of the neural network as described in the previous sections. We need to keep information about the number of samples in the training set as well as the number of nodes in the input and output layers. We are building a one-layer neural network, with its corresponding input and output layers. For the input layer we will have two nodes, one for each of the two features, x_1 and x_2 in our dataset. For the output layer we will also have two nodes, one for each class to be predicted. We can then see how this can be extended for multiclass problems. The architecture is the one shown in Figure 4.1.

We could actually use one node in the case of binary classification.

```
n_training = df.shape[0]
input_layer = 2
output_layer = 2
```

We have 2 nodes in the input and output layers.

We also provide a value for the learning rate α, and should we require a regularisation term in the cost function we also need the value for the hyperparameter λ:

```
alpha = 0.01
lambda_reg = 0.01
```

We define α and λ, our hyperparameters.

In order to keep track of the neural network parameters W_i and b_i, we will store and modify the values in a Python

dictionary. We will provide the number of nodes in each of
the layers to initialise the model. The number of nodes in
the hidden layer is one parameter we will need to decide
upon, and in this case we are going to show the effect of
the number of hidden nodes in the layer. Let us start with a
hidden layer comprising 3 nodes.

We also need to decide the
number of nodes in the hidden
layer.

```
def init_model(input_layer=2, output_layer=2,\
                hidden_layer=3):
    np.random.seed(42)
    W1 = np.random.randn(input_layer,\
      hidden_layer) / np.sqrt(input_layer)
    b1 = np.zeros((1, hidden_layer))
    W2 = np.random.randn(hidden_layer,\
      output_layer) / np.sqrt(hidden_layer)
    b2 = np.zeros((1, output_layer))

    nn_params = {}
    nn_params = {'W1': W1, 'b1': b1, 'W2': W2,\
      'b2': b2}
    return nn_params
```

This functions initialises our
model.

Our model can be initialised as follows:

```
nn_model = init_model(input_layer,\
    output_layer, 3)
```

In this case we have a model with
3 nodes in the hidden layer.

With the help of Equations (4.6)-(4.9), we can write a
function that implements the forward propagation step in
our neural network. For the hidden layer we are using a

hyperbolic tangent activation function. Since the output will be given in terms of probabilities for each of the two classes, we use the softmax activation function:

```python
def forwardprop(nn_model, X):
    W1, b1, W2, b2=nn_model['W1'], nn_model['b1'],\
        nn_model['W2'], nn_model['b2']
    z1 = X.dot(W1) + b1
    a1 = np.tanh(z1)
    z2 = a1.dot(W2) + b2
    e_scores = np.exp(z2)
    prob = e_scores / np.sum(e_scores, axis=1,\
        keepdims=True)
    return prob
```

This function implements the feedforward step in our neural network. We are using a hyperbolic tangent as the activation function.

Once we have the forward propagation step, we need to evaluate the loss incurred and therefore a function to this end is required. We will implement the cross-entropy loss function including a regularisation term as follows:

```python
def loss_eval(nn_model, X, y, lambda_reg):
    W1, b1, W2, b2=nn_model['W1'], nn_model['b1'],\
        nn_model['W2'], nn_model['b2']
    prob = forwardprop(nn_model, X)
    logprobs = -np.log(prob[range(n_training), y])
    data_loss = np.sum(logprobs)
    data_loss+=lambda_reg/2 *\
        (np.sum(np.square(W1))+\
        np.sum(np.square(W2)))
    return data_loss * (1./n_training)
```

We evaluate the cross-entropy loss function with this implementation.

Now that we have an evaluation of the loss, we can start the backpropagation step with learning rate α. In this case we are making use of our formulation from Equations (4.35)-(4.38).

And now the backpropagation step.

Remember that we are seeking to update the parameters of the model and thus we return a dictionary with the required information after the backpropagation step is completed. This in turn can be used as the input for the next forward propagation step:

```python
def backprop(nn_model, X, y, prob, alpha=0.01):
    W1, b1, W2, b2=nn_model['W1'], nn_model['b1'],\
        nn_model['W2'], nn_model['b2']
    z1 = X.dot(W1) + b1
    a1 = np.tanh(z1)
    delta2 = prob
    delta2[range(n_training), y] -= 1
    dW2 = (a1.T).dot(delta2)
    db2 = np.sum(delta2, axis=0, keepdims=True)
    delta1 = delta2.dot(W2.T)*(1-np.power(a1, 2))
    dW1 = np.dot(X.T, delta1)
    db1 = np.sum(delta1, axis=0)


    W1 += -alpha * dW1
    b1 += -alpha * db1
    W2 += -alpha * dW2
    b2 += -alpha * db2
    nn_model = {'W1': W1, 'b1': b1,\
        'W2': W2, 'b2': b2}
    return nn_model
```

Et voilà, the backpropagation implementation.

In order to get a final prediction from the model, we implement a function for this purpose:

```python
def predict(nn_model, x):
    prob = forwardprop(nn_model, x)


    return np.argmax(prob, axis=1)
```

We can obtain predictions with this piece of code.

Now that we have all the parts, we can build our neural network and implement a batch gradient descent for a chosen number of epochs:

```python
def neural_net(X, y, input_layer, output_layer,\
  hidden_layer, alpha=0.01, lambda_reg=0.01,
  epochs=30000, print_loss=False):
    nn_model = init_model(input_layer,\
        output_layer, hidden_layer)

    for i in range(0, epochs):
        prob = forwardprop(nn_model, X)
        nn_model=backprop(nn_model, X, y,\
            prob, alpha)

        if print_loss and i % 1000==0:
            print('Epoch {0} loss: {1:.{2}f}'.\
                format(i, loss_eval(nn_model,\
                X, y, lambda_reg), 4))

    return nn_model
```

We can now put it all together in a batch gradient descent implementation.

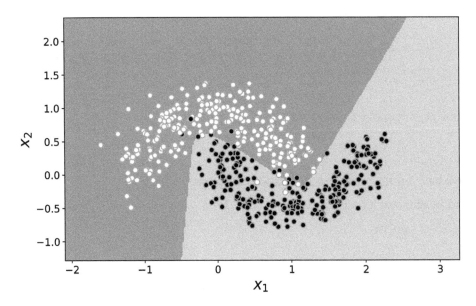

Figure 4.11: Classification boundary obtained with a 3-node hidden layer neural network. The discrimination is modelled well with a cubic-like function.

Let us train our neural network with a 3-node hidden layer:

```
nnet = neural_net(X, y, input_layer, output_layer,\
    3, alpha, lambda_reg, print_loss=True)


Epoch 0 loss: 0.4451

Epoch 1000 loss: 0.0942

...

Epoch 28000 loss: 0.0921

Epoch 29000 loss: 0.0922
```

A typical run of a neural net training provides information about the loss at the end of each epoch.

We can see the decision boundary obtained with this architecture in Figure 4.11 where we can see how the discrimination of the two classes is modelled with a cubic-like function.

It is now easy to implement a loop so that we investigate the effect that hidden layers of different sizes have in the predictions we make. Let us consider hidden layers with 1, 2, 3, 10, 30 and 50 nodes. We know that the larger the number of nodes in the hidden layer, the more complex the network, and hence the more complex the classification boundaries we can generate. This of course comes at the cost of potential overfitting.

Different hidden layer sizes provide different boundaries.

We will store the weights of each model in a dictionary called nn_models so that we can retrieve the chosen model with ease. Furthermore, we will make use of the time library to get a measure of the execution time for each of the architectures:

```python
hidden_layers = [1, 2, 3, 10, 30, 50]

import time
nn_models = {}

for hidden_node in hidden_layers:
  print('{0}-node hidden layer'.\
    format(hidden_node))
  start = time.time()
  nn_models[str(hidden_node)] = neural_net(X, y,\
    input_layer, output_layer, hidden_node,
    alpha, lambda_reg)
  stop = time.time()
  d = stop-start
  print('Execution time: {0:.{1}f} sec'.\
    format(d, 2))
```

We can see the effect of various layer sizes. In this case, a layer with 1, 2, 3, 10, 30 and 50 nodes.

A typical run of the loop defined above would look similar
to the following output:

```
1-node hidden layer
Execution time: 8.97 sec


2-node hidden layer
Execution time: 8.83 sec

...


50-node hidden layer
Execution time: 49.03 sec
```

Note that the times may vary
from run to run and computer to
computer.

In Figure 4.12 we can see some classification boundaries
resulting from the code above. Notice that the neural
network with 1 hidden node is effectively a linear classifier,
not dissimilar to an implementation of logistic regression for
example. The classification boundary is a straight line, and
empirically we can see a number of misclassified data
points.

A hidden layer with 1 node is as
good as a linear classifier.

As we move to 2 nodes we start seeing the non-linearity
in the boundary. We had already seen the 3-node case in
Figure 4.11 and it is great to see the result in context. By the
time we reach 10 nodes, the boundary starts becoming more
intricate. In the cases with 30 and 50 nodes the boundaries
are increasingly curvier, trying to separate the two classes
more and more. We can see the balancing act we need to
perform between getting a good enough prediction and
avoiding memorising our training dataset.

As we add more nodes, we get
more intricate boundaries and
separate our classes better. Beware
overfitting though!

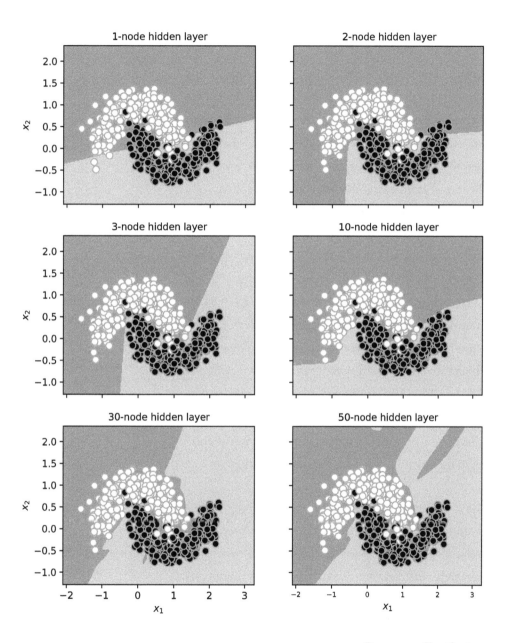

Figure 4.12: Classification
boundaries for a neural network
with one hidden layer comprising
1, 2, 3, 10, 30 and 50 hidden nodes.

4.4   Neural Networks and Deep Learning

WE HAVE SUCCESSFULLY BUILT OUR first neural network from scratch, deserving a celebration worth remembering. Not only have we covered a lot of the foundational concepts in neural networks, but also paved the road to addressing useful extensions to those ideas. A case in point is the recent explosion in the use of deep learning for a variety of applications, from automatic machine translation, to computer vision and even medical diagnosis.

Who's for fruit cake? Maybe two dozens fruit cakes, a dozen macaroons and some nice vanilla sponge would do for celebrations.

In Section 4.2.1 we first introduced the term *deep learning* in the context of explaining the layers and nodes inside a neural network. As we add more and more hidden layers to our network, with a larger and larger number of nodes we require for our inputs to flow deeper and deeper into the architecture we built. In that sense, we are moving from having 1, 2 or 3 hidden layers to having hundreds of them. A complex architecture like that is suitable to be used when having large sets of labelled data, with rich features and patterns to be learnt by the deep neural network.

Deep learning refers to the use or large multi-layer networks.

Given their usefulness, deep neural networks have gathered a lot of attention and constructing them in the way we did for our humble 1-layer network in the previous section is no longer feasible. Instead, there are a number of frameworks and libraries that make this task much easier and more understandable, as well as enabling us to make use of better implementations and the best in class in terms of hardware, such as graphics processing units (GPUs).

We need a better framework to build large networks.

Some of the most notable frameworks include Google's own TensorFlow[13] with low level implementations for deep learning and a low level API. Similarly, one can think of implementing things in Caffe[14] developed by the Berkley Vision and Learning Center with a focus on speed. Although neither TensorFlow nor Caffe is a Python library per se, they do offer bindings into Python making things more approachable for us. Other options include Theano[15] which can be compared to what scipy has done for scientific Python. We also have libraries such as Apache MXNet[16], Microsoft Cognitive Toolkit (CNTK)[17] and Facebook's PyTorch[18].

As you can see, the ecosystem is a vast one and there are many more tools out there than we could be able to cover in this book. All in all, we are interested in a framework that enables us to use some of the most up-to-date techniques in the deep learning arena, while keeping a high level language interface. This will enable Jackalope data scientists like us to abstract some of the low level implementations and use modular libraries to carry out deep learning tasks. For these reasons, we are going to cover the use or Keras in this book.

Keras[19] offers a high-level API written in Python supporting backends such as TensorFlow, CNTK and Theano. Keras enables experimentation and rapid prototyping, while keeping with the Pythonic philosophy of readability and user friendliness. It started life as part of the ONEIROS research effort. The name is the Greek word for "horn" ($\kappa\grave{\epsilon}\rho\alpha\varsigma$) in reference to the Hellenic literary image of the

[13] Abadi, M. et al. (2015). TensorFlow: Large-scale machine learning on heterogeneous systems. http://tensorflow.org/. Software available from tensorflow.org

[14] Jia, Y. et al. (2014). Caffe: Convolutional Architecture for Fast Feature Embedding. *arXiv preprint arXiv:1408.5093*

[15] Al-Rfou, R. et al. (2016, May). Theano: A Python framework for fast computation of mathematical expressions. *arXiv e-prints abs/1605.02688*

[16] Chen, T. et al. (2014). CMXNet: A Flexible and Efficient Machine Learning Library for Heterogeneous Distributed Systems. *arXiv preprint arXiv:1512.01274*

[17] Github (2018). CNTK: The microsoft cognitive tool. https://github.com/Microsoft/CNTK/. Accessed: 2018-08-13

[18] Paszke, A. et al. (2017). Automatic differentiation in PyTorch. In *NIPS Autodiff Workshop*

[19] Chollet, F. et al. (2015). Keras. https://github.com/fchollet/keras

ONEIROS stands for Open-ended Neuro-Electronic Intelligent Robot Operating System.

gates of horn and ivory that distinguish between true (horn) and false (ivory) visions or dreams. Homer makes reference to these gates in the Odyssey[20], when Penelope herself is trying to decide whether her dream about her husband's return to Ithaca is but a false vision.

In any event, Keras is a modular library that enables us to put together deep neural networks using a high-level syntax making it ideal for our purposes. In this particular case we are going to make reference to the TensorFlow backend, but other options are possible as we mentioned above. Keras lets the user build sequential networks, i.e., where the flow of information moves forward in a linear way as we have described in the previous sections. Similarly, it also lets us construct graph-based networks with the help of a functional API. With it we can let inputs "jump" to specific layers and obtain more complex network architectures as a result.

Here, we will use a TensorFlow backend.

For us to be able to use Keras with TensorFlow, we will need to make appropriate installations in our machines. We are assuming that we are working with Anaconda and creating a conda environment is probably the best option. You can try something like this:

Please make sure you check the documentation for your own system requirements.

```
> conda create -n tfenv pandas scikit-learn
    jupyter matplotlib
```

Remember to activate your environment (in this case called tfenv) every time you need to use Keras:

```
> conda activate tfenv

(tfenv)
> pip install tensorflow
> pip install keras
```

We are assuming the use of conda. Other virtual environments can also be used.

You can also consider installing other libraries to make your workflow better for you. Let us recreate with Keras the neural network architecture we built in Section 4.3.4. We will use the sequential API to create a layer-by-layer model and as usual we will import some useful libraries first:

```
import pandas as pd
import tensorflow as tf
import keras
from keras.utils import np_utils
from keras.model import Sequential
```

We will be using the sequential API.

We know why we require the first three import statements; as for the fourth one, we will use this to wrangle our data so that we can make appropriate type transformations to be used with Keras. The last import statement enables us to use the sequential API in Keras.

We instantiate a sequential model as follows:

```
model = keras.Sequential()
```

We need to instantiate our model.

Now that we have an instance of our model, we can proceed to the creation of each of the layers in our network. Keras offers different types of layers and one of the most common

is the dense layer. It is a layer where all the nodes have
edges to the previous layer. We need to provide the number
of units (i.e., nodes) that this layer must have. Since this is
our first hidden layer, we pass an argument to tell it how
many nodes are in the input layer. We can do this with a
shape tuple called input_shape, or for layers such as dense
ones we can use a parameter called input_dim. We also
need to specify the activation function that will be used at
this point of the neural network architecture. This is how we
do this:

A dense layer is a fully connected
layer.

```
hnodes = 3
hidden_layer = keras.layers.Dense(hnodes,
   input_dim=2, activation='tanh')
```

Our hidden layer.

In this case we are creating a hidden layer with 3 hidden
nodes, the input layer has 2 entries and the activation
function is the hyperbolic tangent. We can see how easy it
would be to change the number of hidden nodes in this case.
Notice that we did not have to declare explicitly the
existence of an input layer. We simply provide information
about its shape or dimensions.

This is only possible for Sequential
models.

The next layer in our architecture is the output layer, so let
us declare it in Keras:

```
output_layer = keras.layers.Dense(2,
   activation='softmax')
```

And our output layer.

In this case we have an output layer with two nodes and
the activation function applied is a softmax function. Notice
that we do not have to declare explicitly the shape of the

input received by this layer. It is implied by the sequencing of layers once we "stitch" them together. Let us do that:

```
model.add(hidden_layer)
model.add(output_layer)
```

Remember that the order in which you add the layers is important.

We simply use the add method of the sequential model to add the layers in the order they go in the architecture.

We need to decide on the optimisation algorithm that we are going to use in our neural network. Keras offers a variety of them including stochastic gradient descent (SGD), Adagrad, RMSprop or Adaptive Moment Estimation (Adam)[21] . In this case we will use SGD:

```
sgd = keras.optimizers.SGD(lr=0.01,
    decay=1e-6, momentum=0.9,
    nesterov=True)
```

[21] Kingma, D. P. and J. Ba (2014). Adam: A method for stochastic optimization. arxXiv:1412.6980. Comment: Published as a conference paper at the 3rd International Conference for Learning Representations, San Diego, 2015

where lr is the learning rate, decay applies a decay to the learning rate over each update:

$$\mathtt{lr} := \mathtt{lr} \left(\frac{1}{1 + \mathtt{decay} * \mathtt{iterations}} \right) ; \qquad (4.39)$$

The learning rate related to the decay and the number of iterations.

momentum is a parameter that encourages the algorithm to move in the direction of descent and is related to the velocity of descent:

$$\mathtt{v} := \mathtt{momentum} * \mathtt{m} - \mathtt{lr} * \mathtt{g}, \qquad (4.40)$$

The momentum is related to the velocity of descent.

where m is the previous weight update and g is the current gradient with respect to parameter p. We can use this velocity to calculate the new value of p:

$$p_{new} = \begin{cases} \texttt{p} + \texttt{v}, \text{ if } \texttt{nesterov} == \texttt{False}, \\ \texttt{p} + \texttt{momentum} * \texttt{v} - \texttt{lr} * \texttt{g otherwise}. \end{cases} \quad (4.41)$$

If you are interested in reading more about Nesterov momentum, take a look at the paper by Sutskever et al.[22] where a good description of initialisation and momentum is presented.

[22] Sutskever, I., J. Martens, G. Dahl, and G. Hinton (2013, 17–19 Jun). On the importance of initialization and momentum in deep learning. In S. Dasgupta and D. McAllester (Eds.), *Proceedings of the 30th International Conference on Machine Learning*, Volume 28 of *Proceedings of Machine Learning Research*, Atlanta, Georgia, USA, pp. 1139–1147. PMLR

We now need to compile our model, this step configures the learning process for our neural network architecture. We need to provide three arguments to the `compile` method: The optimisation algorithm to be used, the loss function to be optimised and a list of metrics:

```
model.compile(optimizer=sgd,
    loss='categorical_crossentropy',
    metrics=['accuracy'])
```

We compile our model to use stochastic gradient descent.

In this case we are using the stochastic gradient descent algorithm we instantiated above; the loss function is for categorical cross-entropy as we are trying to distinguish between two classes.

We are finally in a position to start the learning process with the aid of the `fit` method, but before we do that let us make a couple of manipulations to the input data. Remember that we read our data from a Pandas dataframe as follows:

```
df = pd.read_csv('neuralnet_dataset.csv')
X = df[['x1', 'x2']].values
y = df['label'].values
```

We use Pandas to read our data. Other methods can also be used.

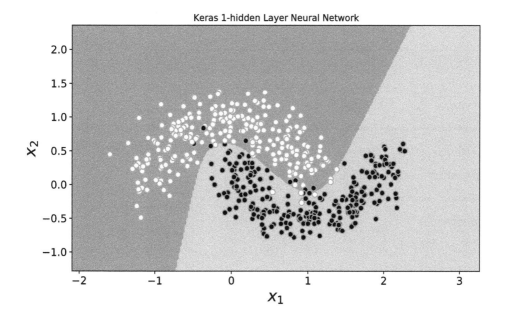

We will convert the labels in the y vector into a binary class matrix to be used with the categorical cross-entropy cost function:

```
y = np_utils.to_categorical(y)
```

and now we fit our model:

```
model.fit(X, y, batch_size=100, epochs=5000,
    verbose=0)
```

Notice that we can change the batch size and the number of epochs directly in the `fit` method. You can see how the learning progresses with `verbose=1`. The result of our learning process can be seen in Figure 4.13.

Figure 4.13: Classification boundary obtained with a sequential model for a neural network implemented in Keras.

We convert the target labels into categorical variables.

And finally, we train our model.

We can look at a summary of the architecture we just created as follows:

```
> model.summary()

Layer (type)            Output Shape          Param #
=====================================================
dense_1 (Dense)         (None, 3)               9

dense_2 (Dense)         (None, 2)               8

=====================================================
Total params: 17

Trainable params: 17

Non-trainable params: 0
```

We can see the layers created and the number of parameters to learn.

As we can see, there are 2 dense layers, one with 3 nodes and one with 2. There are thus 17 parameters that need to be fitted in this model and we can see the weights obtained with the get_weights method:

```
> model.get_weights()

[array([[ 2.1810133 , -2.1321995 , -2.4240587 ],
        [-0.41597274, -1.8568848 ,  1.0889707 ]],
        dtype=float32),
 array([1.0000919, 1.4230473, 3.3605928],
        dtype=float32),
 array([[-3.8464072,  3.5489938],
        [-3.4979208,  3.7599623],
        [ 4.5513706, -4.011438 ]], dtype=float32),
 array([-0.8270238 ,  0.82702374], dtype=float32)]
```

The weights are readily available to us. Beware their numbers for deep networks.

Please note that the weights you obtain in your machine may vary from the ones shown above, after all we are relying on different starting points. Finally, remember that you should apply best practices in your work by splitting your data into training and testing. You can also apply cross-validation while finding the best hyperparameters for your model.

Remember to apply best practices, and split your data into training and testing datasets.

We can see how the use of a high-level framework like Keras enables us to implement neural network architectures in an easy and friendly way. This opens up the opportunities to build more complex networks such as convolutional and recurrent neural networks. Let us take a look.

4.4.1   Convolutional Neural Networks

A CONVOLUTIONAL NEURAL NETWORK IS a type of artificial neutral network that relies on convolution to learn patterns in the training data provided. The architecture with input, hidden and output layers is the same as we have discussed above. The main difference is the fact that the hidden layers use more than a simple activation function; they also convolve their input with a filter or kernel. Convolutional neural networks (CNNs) have been gaining traction in applications such as image processing and computer vision for example.

CNN for short. Not to be confused with a certain news organisation!

Many image editing tools make use of convolution to apply different filters to a picture. Different kernels result in blurring, sharpening or detecting edges in the image. For example an identity kernel can help scale a picture down,

An identity kernel is given by
$$I = \begin{bmatrix} 0 & 0 & 0 \\ 0 & 1 & 0 \\ 0 & 0 & 0 \end{bmatrix}.$$

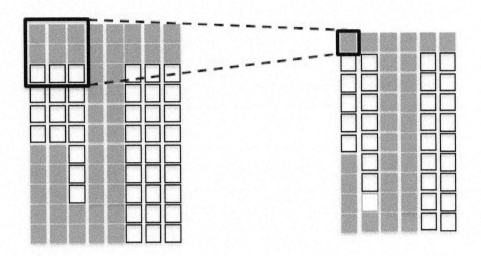

Figure 4.14: An image of a letter J (on the left). After applying an identity kernel the result is a scaled down version of the image (on the right).

while sharper images can result from the application of a sharpening kernel such as:

$$F_s = \begin{bmatrix} 0 & -1 & 0 \\ -1 & 5 & -1 \\ 0 & -1 & 0 \end{bmatrix}. \qquad (4.42)$$

Consider the image of a (pixelated) letter *J* as shown on the left-hand side of Figure 4.14. The application of an identity kernel to this image results in a smaller one. The convolution of the original picture with the kernel chosen requires the element-wise multiplication of a portion of the image of equal size as the kernel. We then add up all the product outputs as the result, which we show on the right-hand side of Figure 4.14.

Convolution requires element-wise multiplication of image portions of the same size as the kernel applied.

The application of the filter is done as if we were scanning the original image, moving the filter by a stride S. Think of the filter as a torch that is used to illuminate portions of the image as we move across it, letting us concentrate on the details highlighted by the torch's light. In our example above, for a stride $S = 1$ we have that we go from an image of 11×8 to a scaled image of 9×6. If you want to avoid the scaling down, you can apply **padding** to the image with zeros. You can determine the size of the final figure with the following formula:

Think of the convolution operation as a torch that scans the image to highlight details.

$$\text{output\_side} = 1 + \frac{1}{S}\left(\text{input\_side} + \text{kernel\_side} + 2(\text{padding})\right). \tag{4.43}$$

Figure 4.15: An image of a Jackalope icon (on the left). After applying a sharpening filter, we obtain the image on the right.

Let us take a look at a more realistic image manipulation. In Figure 4.15 we can see the result of applying the sharpening filter of Equation (4.42) to the image of a Jackalope icon.

Let us take a look at what is happening with a portion of the image. Here are is a 5×5 patch of the image:

$$P = \begin{bmatrix} 0 & 1 & 1 & 1 & 1 \\ 0 & 0 & 1 & 1 & 1 \\ 0 & 0 & 1 & 1 & 1 \\ 0 & 0 & 1 & 1 & 1 \\ 0 & 0 & 1 & 1 & 1 \end{bmatrix}. \tag{4.44}$$

We have chosen a portion containing an edge, 0 being blank and 1 black pixels.

The convolution of patch P with the filter F_s is given by:

$$P \circledast F_S = \begin{bmatrix} -2 & 2 & 1 \\ -1 & 2 & 1 \\ -1 & 2 & 1 \end{bmatrix}, \tag{4.45}$$

This is the result of convolving a 3×3 filter with a 5×5 image portion.

where $\circledast$ denotes the convolution operation, and the first element of the result is given by $(0)(0) + (1)(-1) + (1)(0) + (0)(-1) + (0)(5) + (1)(-1) + (0)(0) + (0)(-1) + (1)(0) = -2$.

The same sort of calculation is done for each of the entries in the given patch. For a color image, we have red, blue, green and transparency channels and the convolution has to be done for each layer. The output channel of the convolution is called a **feature map** and it encodes the degree of presence of the feature detected.

The same operation will have to be applied to each layer of the image.

Once the convolution is completed, it is possible to apply an operation to further reduce the size of the image and make the whole process more manageable. One such operation is

pooling: Given an $n \times n$ pooling window, we keep only the maximum value in the window. This is called *max-pooling*. Another option could be to obtain the average and this is called *average-pooling*. In the example above, max-pooling on a 2×2 window will result in:

Pooling is a down-sampling process that reduces the size of our matrices.

$$\text{max\_pooling}(P \circledast F_S) = \begin{bmatrix} 2 & 2 \\ 2 & 2 \end{bmatrix}. \qquad (4.46)$$

The operations outlined above will need us to sweep the entire image with our filter. The result is a filtered image with the resolution given by the formula shown in Equation (4.43).

Remember the analogy of using a torch.

So far so good, but... what is the relationship with neural networks. Well, if we use various filters that detect different features such as vertical and horizontal edges, curved features, etc. we can use the results to determine, for example, the presence of objects. In practice a CNN learns these feature maps as the training process is executed. A typical architecture for a CNN is shown in Figure 4.16.

This is useful in computer vision problems.

The setup involves the use of one or more convolutional layers with pooling and a ReLU activation, followed by a **flattening** layer. Flattening enables us to convert our 2D matrices into a column vector ready to be used in a dense layer. Sometimes it is useful to drop a random set of activations forcing the network to generalise better. These layers are referred to as **dropout** layers.

Or other activation functions.

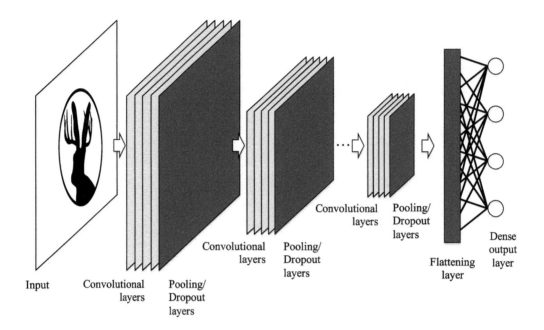

Figure 4.16: Architecture of a convolutional neural network.

4.4.2 *Convolutional Neural Networks in Action*

LET US CREATE A NEURAL network classifier for images based on the CIFAR-10 dataset[23]. The dataset contains 60,000 images with 32 × 32 resolution. They are divided into 10 balanced classes. The dataset is split into 50,000 training images and 10,000 testing ones. The ten classes in the dataset are: Airplane, automobile, bird, cat, deer, dog, frog, horse, ship and truck. An example for each of the classes is shown in Figure 4.17. Let us define a list with the classes:

[23] Krizhevsky, A. (2009). Learning multiple layers of features from tiny images. Technical report

```
class_names = ['airplane','automobile','bird',
   'cat','deer','dog', 'frog','horse','ship',
   'truck']
```

We will use this list to make human-readable predictions later on.

The dataset is included with Keras and can be imported as follows:

Figure 4.17: Example images for each of the ten classes in the CIFAR-10 dataset. The pixelation is the result of the images being 32×32.

```
from keras.datasets import cifar10
(X_tr, y_tr), (X_tst, y_tst) = cifar10.load_data()
```

The images are now given by integer numpy arrays. In order to ensure their correct manipulation, we will normalise our data. First we will cast the arrays as float.

Please note that the data will need to be downloaded the first time you use the dataset. This may take some time.

```
X_train = X_tr.astype('float32')
X_test = X_tst.astype('float32')
```

We will then calculate a mean and standard deviation and apply it to the data:

```
mean = np.mean(X_train,axis=(0,1,2,3))
std = np.std(X_train,axis=(0,1,2,3))
X_train = (X_train-mean)/(std+1e-7)
X_test = (X_test-mean)/(std+1e-7)
```

We obtain the mean and standard deviation to normalise our data.

In order to use categorical cross-entropy as our loss function, we will use one-hot encoding to get suitable classes for our task. We will have to specify the number of classes in our dataset so that we have the appropriate number of nodes in the output layer:

```
from keras.utils import np_utils
y_train = np_utils.to_categorical(y_tr)
y_test = np_utils.to_categorical(y_tst)
num_classes = y_train.shape[1]
```

In this way we ensure the labels are categorical variables.

We are going to build our convolutional neural network using the Keras functional API. Let us import some useful libraries first:

```
import numpy as np
import keras
from keras.models import Model
from keras.layers import Dense, Activation,\
    Flatten, Dropout, BatchNormalization, Input
from keras.layers import Conv2D, MaxPooling2D
from keras import regularizers
from keras.callbacks import LearningRateScheduler
from keras.preprocessing.image import\
    ImageDataGenerator
```

We import a number of useful libraries from Keras.

We can see some familiar words such as `Dense` and `Flatten`.
As for others, they tend to do what they describe:
Convolutional layers can be defined with `Conv2D` and
max-pooling can be achieved with `MaxPooling2D`. For others
we will provide explanations as we use them.

> `Conv2D` implements a convolutional layer.

When using the functional API, we must define an input
layer explicitly with a shape argument determining the
dimensionality of the training data. In this case we have
images of size $32 \times 32 \times 3$.

> Remember that we have 3 channels in the images.

```
model_input = Input(shape=(32, 32, 3))
```

The layers are connected pairwise and the connection
specifies the source of the input as given by the arrangement
in our architecture. We explicitly name the inputting layer in
parentheses after the desired connecting layer. It is easier
when we see it; let us create a first convolutional layer
taking input from `model_input` defined above:

> We explicitly name the inputting layer in parenthesis.

```
weight_decay=1e-4
conv1 = Conv2D(32, kernel_size=(3, 3),\
    activation='relu', padding='same',\
    kernel_regularizer=\
    regularizers.l2(weight_decay))(model_input)
```

Our convolutional layer takes first the number of filters
to be learnt. This represents the dimensionality of the
output space for the layer. In this case we request 32 filters.
`kernel_size` specifies the window size for the convolution.
The activation function applied to the layer is specified with
`activation` and in this case we are using a ReLU function.

> The `kernel_size` is a tuple defining height and width of the window.

It is possible to apply padding; here we request for the
output to be the same size as the input. We also apply a
penalty to the parameters of this layer, in this case an $L2$
penalty with a weight decay of 1×10^{-4}. Finally, we can
see that model_input is the input for this convolutional
layer. The next step in our architecture is the application
of a normalisation[24] transformation maintaining the mean
activation close to 0 and its standard deviation near 1.

Other padding options include
valid and casual.

```
batchn1 = BatchNormalization()(conv1)
```

[24] Ioffe, S. and C. Szegedy (2015).
Batch normalization: Accelerating
deep network training by
reducing internal covariate shift.
CoRR abs/1502.03167

We apply another combination of a convolution layer and
batch normalisation:

```
conv2 = Conv2D(32, (3, 3), activation='relu',\
    padding='same', kernel_regularizer\
    = regularizers.l2(weight_decay))(batchn1)
batchn2 = BatchNormalization()(conv2)
```

We can easily add more layers to
our architecture.

Our next layer is a pooling layer. MaxPooling2D takes an
argument defining the pooling window size:

```
pool1 = MaxPooling2D(pool_size=(2,2))(batchn2)
```

As we can see, the input for this layer is given by the
batchn2 layer. In order to help with generalisation, we will
now set a random fraction of the input units to 0:

In this case we drop out 20%.

```
drop1 = Dropout(0.2)(pool1)
```

We are getting the hang of this. We will add a few more
convolution layers together with batch normalisation,

pooling and dropout. Here, we will be requesting 64 filters in each of the next two convolution layers, followed by two more with 128 filters, with dropouts of 30% and 40%, respectively:

```
conv3 = Conv2D(64, (3, 3), activation='relu',\
    padding='same', kernel_regularizer\
    =regularizers.l2(weight_decay))(drop1)
batchn3 = BatchNormalization()(conv3)
conv4 = Conv2D(64, (3, 3), activation='relu',\
    padding='same', kernel_regularizer=\
    regularizers.l2(weight_decay))(batchn3)
batchn4 = BatchNormalization()(conv4)
pool2 = MaxPooling2D(pool_size=(2,2))(batchn4)
drop2 = Dropout(0.3)(pool2)
conv5 = Conv2D(128, (3, 3), activation='relu',\
    padding='same', kernel_regularizer=\
    regularizers.l2(weight_decay))(drop2)
batchn5 = BatchNormalization()(conv5)
conv6 = Conv2D(128, (3, 3), activation='relu',\
    padding='same', kernel_regularizer=\
    regularizers.l2(weight_decay))(batchn5)
batchn6 = BatchNormalization()(conv6)
pool3 = MaxPooling2D(pool_size=(2,2))(batchn6)
drop3 = Dropout(0.4)(pool3)
```

We are adding layer upon layer to our convolutional neural network: Convolutional, batch normalisation and pooling, one after the next.

We can add as many convolutional layers as we desire, and remember that as you add more, the number of parameters to be fitted grows too. Let us flatten the input up until now, and add a dense layer.

```
flat = Flatten()(drop3)
dense1 = Dense(num_classes,\
   activation='softmax')(flat)
```

Finally, we connect to a dense output layer.

Note that the output layer has `num_classes=10` nodes, one for each class in our training data and the activation function is a softmax function. We can see the final version of our architecture with the summary:

```
> model.summary()

---------------------------------------------------------

Layer (type)             Output Shape           Param #

=========================================================

input_1 (InputLayer)     (None, 32, 32, 3)      0

conv2d_1 (Conv2D)        (None, 32, 32, 32)     896

batch_normalization_1    (None, 32, 32, 32)     128

conv2d_2 (Conv2D)        (None, 32, 32, 32)     9248

batch_normalization_2    (None, 32, 32, 32)     128

max_pooling2d_1 (Max     (None, 16, 16, 32)     0

dropout_1 (Dropout)      (None, 16, 16, 32)     0

conv2d_3 (Conv2D)        (None, 16, 16, 64)     18496

batch_normalization_3    (None, 16, 16, 64)     256

conv2d_4 (Conv2D)        (None, 16, 16, 64)     36928

batch_normalization_4    (None, 16, 16, 64)     256

max_pooling2d_2 (MaxP    (None, 8, 8, 64)       0

dropout_2 (Dropout)      (None, 8, 8, 64)       0

conv2d_5 (Conv2D)        (None, 8, 8, 128)      73856

batch_normalization_5    (None, 8, 8, 128)      512

conv2d_6 (Conv2D)        (None, 8, 8, 128)      147584

batch_normalization_6    (None, 8, 8, 128)      512
```

We can see the different layers in our CNN, and the number of parameters to learn.

```
max_pooling2d_3 (MaxP   (None, 4, 4, 128)   0

dropout_3 (Dropout)     (None, 4, 4, 128)   0

flatten_1 (Flatten)     (None, 2048)        0

dense_1 (Dense)         (None, 10)          20490

=================================================

Total params: 309,290

Trainable params: 308,394

Non-trainable params: 896
```

In this case we have 308, 394 parameters to train.

This model has a total of 309, 290 parameters, of which we need to train 308, 394. Let us now compile our model. We define a batch size of 64 and use an RMS optimiser:

```
batch_size = 64
opt_rms = keras.optimizers.rmsprop(lr=0.001,\
    decay=1e-6)
model.compile(loss='categorical_crossentropy',\
    optimizer=opt_rms, metrics=['accuracy'])
```

Do not forget to compile the model before training.

We can define a schedule for the learning rate: As the number of epochs increases, our learning rate gets smaller.

```
def lr_shedule(epoch):
    if epoch>100:
        lrate = 0.0003
    elif 75 < epoch <= 100:
        lrate = 0.0005
    else:
        lrate = 0.001
    return lrate
```

As training goes on, we make our learning rate smaller.

We will also use Keras to augment our data by making transformations to the inputs, we will use the `ImageDataGenerator` function to create modifications enabling for rotation of the image, height and width shifts and even horizontal flips:

```
datagen = ImageDataGenerator(
    rotation_range=15, width_shift_range=0.1,
    height_shift_range=0.1, horizontal_flip=True)


datagen.fit(X_train)
```

With `ImageDataGenerator` we can augment our images by applying transformations.

We are ready to fit our model: Keras enables us to fit the model on batches with real-time data augmentation through the `fit_generator` method for the model, and the `flow` method for the data augmentation.

```
model.fit_generator(datagen.flow(X_train, y_train,
    batch_size=batch_size), steps_per_epoch=\
    X_train.shape[0]//batch_size, epochs=125,
    verbose=1, validation_data=(X_test, y_test),
    callbacks=[LearningRateScheduler(lr_schedule)])
```

Please note that this step may take several hours, depending on the computer architecture you use.

We can evaluate the model on the test data as follows:

```
> scores = model.evaluate(X_test, y_test,\
    batch_size=128, verbose=1)
> print('Evaluation result: {0:.2f}, Loss:\
    {1:.2f}'.format(scores[1]*100, scores[0]))


Evaluation result: 88.45, Loss: 0.47
```

Evaluating our model is very easy.

Let us pick 10 images at random to create predictions for them.

```
import random
ixs = []
for i in range(10):
  ix = random.randint(0, X_test.shape[0])
  ixs.append(ix)
  sub_X_test[i] = X_test[ix]
```

Using the good old random package.

First let us look at the indices of the pictures:

```
> print(ixs)

  [8804, 4028, 7066, 5241, 1648,
  8330, 1202, 2210, 2055, 2153]
```

In case you want to check the labels predicted...

For the pictures chosen randomly, the prediction can be calculated as:

```
> mypred = np.argmax(model.predict(sub_X_test), 1)
> print([class_names[x] for x in mypred])

['frog', 'airplane', 'frog', 'deer',
'ship', 'dog', 'bird', 'bird', 'dog', 'ship']
```

We are able to compare the labels predicted with the actual ones. You may want to use something like a confusion matrix instead.

The actual labels can be retrieved as follows:

```
> print([class_names[y_tst[i][0]] for i in ixs])

['frog', 'airplane', 'frog', 'deer',
'ship', 'dog', 'bird', 'bird', 'dog', 'ship']
```

Finally, let us make a prediction with a totally new image. Let us try the picture shown in Figure 4.18 saved into a file called `picbo001.jpg`. First we will need to read the image and ensure that it has the right dimensions:

You can also make predictions for images not in the dataset!

```
import matplotlib.image as mpimg
from skimage.transform import resize

img=mpimg.imread('picbo001.jpg')
img_resized = resize(img, (32, 32),\
    anti_aliasing=True)
```

Figure 4.18: A picture of a nice feline friend to test our convolutional neural network.

In this case, the resized image has values between 0 and 1. We will therefore multiply the image by 255 to apply the normalisation used for the training images:

```
img_resized = (img_resized*255-mean)/(std+1e-7)
proc_img = img_resized.reshape((1,) +\
  img_resized.shape)
```

The last step is needed so that the image has dimensions $(1, 32, 32, 3)$ as expected by the model. Finally we can make our prediction:

```
> pr = model.predict(proc_img)
> pr_label = np.argmax(pr, axis=1)[0]
> print('The image has a {0}'.format(\
  class_names[pr_label]))


The image has a cat
```

Indeed, the convolutional neural network can see our feline friend and tell us about it!

Et voilà, we have an image classifier from a convolutional neural network ready to be used.

4.4.3 Recurrent Neural Networks

MEMORY IS AN IMPORTANT FUNCTION that our brains enable us to perform. We are not pretending to explain here what memory is or is not, or even what it is for. I recommend reading A. Glenberg's paper on the subject instead[25]. If we think of memory as the function to encode, store and subsequently retrieve information, we would expect that, given the inspiration, an artificial neural network may be able to support a similar ability. So far, that has not been the case. The neural networks we have discussed pass information forwards and backwards but at

[25] Glenberg, A.M. (1997). What memory is for. *Behav. Brain Sci.* 20, 1–55

no point we have mentioned anything about retaining any memories. Carrying memories forwards is a helpful thing, as the Queen of Hearts[26] would remark , "It's a poor sort of memory that only works backward."

[26] Carroll, L. and J. Tenniel (1897). *Through the Looking Glass: And what Alice Found There.* Altemus' illustrated young people's library. Henry Altemus Company

The premise of a recurrent neural network architecture is such that we require it to remember previous inputs to be used in subsequent steps of the training. Up until now we have made the assumption that all inputs are independent of each other. However, there are certain tasks where this is not necessarily true. Think for example of applications where the past history is important in the prediction, such as in the time series we discussed in Chapter 1, or for example in speech recognition, language translation or image captioning. Remembering what the inputs that came before the current time provide important information to the network.

And outputs for that matter...

Performing the same task for every element of a sequence of inputs makes the task *recurrent* and hence the name of this type of neural networks. The output, as explained above, is dependent on the previous calculations carried out by the network and therefore having the equivalent of a *memory* function that captures that information is important. Consider a section A of a neural network that receives an input X_t. The output of this section is a value y_t as shown in Figure 4.19. In a recurrent neural network we enable a loop that lets us pass the information from one portion of the network to the next. We can think of this loop in an unfolded way as shown in the right-hand-side of Figure 4.19.

RNN for short.

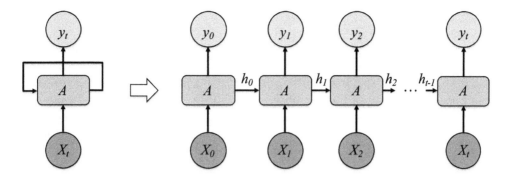

Figure 4.19: A diagrammatic representation of the architecture of a recurrent neural network.

The unfolded version of the recurrent neural network lets us clearly see the importance of the sequence of inputs and outputs during training. We have already mentioned some of the applications where RNNs have become the norm. A particular architecture that is widely used is the so-called *long short-term memory* or LSTM proposed in 1997 by Hochreiter and Schmidhuber[27], with several adjustments added in subsequent years. Before we get to see how LSTM works, let us highlight some of the differences between RNNs and the neural network architectures we have seen.

[27] Hochreiter, S. and Schmidhuber, J. (1997). Long short-term memory. *Neural. Comput.* 9(8), 1735–1780

Let us consider the task of predicting what the next word in a sentence is. We can choose a large corpus as our training data, think for example of a book such as *Erewhon, or Over the Range* [28] by Samuel Butler. First published in 1872, the book tells us about the adventures our narrator experiences in the eponymous country he discovers. Upon arrival on the land, the protagonist learns that, 500 years prior, Erewhonians were made aware of the danger of technological revolt, banning the use of anything but the most primitive machines. The decision is explained in a manifesto called *The Book of the Machines*. This is the literary

Indeed a sentence is a sequence of words.

[28] Butler, S. (2005). Erewhon; Or, Over the Range. Project Gutenberg https://www.gutenberg.org/ebooks/1906. Accessed: 2019-09-03

mechanism that Butler uses to raise the possibility of conscious machines by Darwinian selection.

But we digress... After training our neural network with the text from *Erewhon*, if we input the sequence:

> "There is no security"– to quote his own words– "against the ultimate development of mechanical ...

The title of the novel is the word "Nowhere" spelt backwards, with the letters "w" and "h" transposed.

we would expect a reasonable word to follow, based on the training text provided. During training, we will take each word at a time and produce a result as in the feedforward neural networks we know and love. However, in this case we also need to be aware of the previous inputs that have been provided before we look at the result. This is what we are doing in the unfolded version of the RNN shown in Figure 4.19 where each $X_0, X_1, X_2, \ldots, X_t$ corresponds to the input words from the corpus. In turn, we produce the predicted follow-up word $y_0, y_1, y_2, \ldots, y_t$, and we hold in memory the information $h_0, h_1, h_2, \ldots, h_{t-1}$ about the previous words.

Refer to the unfolded version of our RNN shown in Figure 4.19.

In order to make the most out of our recurrent neural network architecture, we will need to consider using something like word embeddings to help us map words to vectors, for instance with the help of Word2Vec[29]. In this case, to make the explanation simpler we consider a simplistic approach such as one-hot encoding to obtain vectors with dimension $(V, 1)$ where V is the number of words in the vocabulary. The values of the vectors are all zeros, except for a 1 at the position that corresponds to the entry in our dictionary of words. So if the vocabulary has

[29] Mikolov, T., I. Sutskever, et al. (2013). Distributed Representations of Words and Phrases and Their Compositionality. In *Proceedings of the 26th International Conference on Neural Information Processing Systems - Volume 2*, NIPS'13, USA, pp. 3111–3119. Curran Associates Inc

three words: [aardvark, iberian_lynx, zebra], the vector
for *iberian_lynx* will be $[0, 1, 0]$.

Back to *Erewhon*, let us imagine that we would like to use
the RNN in Figure 4.19 to predict the next word in the
proposed sequence. The network applies a recurrence
formula in A to the input vector as well as to its previous
state. For the first word (*There*) there is nothing before it, so
nothing to remember. When we move to the next word (*is*)
the network applies the recurrence formula to it and takes
the previous state into consideration, i.e., the word *There*.
The two words are used to calculate a new state, which will
be fed back to the network in the next time step. We say that
at time t the input is *is*, at time $t - 1$ the input was *There*. We
continue like this for the rest of the inputs, one at a time.

RNNs apply a recurrence formula to the input vector as well as to its previous state. This latter is the memory we want the network to retain.

We can think of the current state of the network to be given
by a combination (via an activation function) of the previous
state and the input vector as the current time step:

$$h_t \simeq f(h_{t-1}, X_t), \qquad (4.47)$$

where f is the activation function. From our discussions
about the training of feedforward neural nets, we have seen
that the weights associated with each of the nodes are the
parameters we need to fit. We therefore need to take them
into account here too. Let us denote the weight at the input
node as W_{xh}, and the weight at the current node as W_{hh}, the
state at time t will then be given by:

Not only the input and previous states, but we also need the weights.

$$h_t = \sigma(W_{hh}h_{t-1} + W_{xh}X_t). \qquad (4.48)$$

where we are applying a softmax activation function. In this case the memory of the network is only of the immediate previous step. We can say that it has a short memory. Remembering more steps will require appropriate storage.

Remembering more steps requires more storage.

With this state we can calculate the output at time t as $y_t = W_{hy}h_t$. At this point, if this is the final output of the network, we can use backpropagation to enable us to update the weights as we have done before. In the case of our sample sentence, after obtaining the optimal weights, we input each of the words in the sequence, the RNN will produce $(h_1, h_2, h_3, \ldots, h_{15})$ and we calculate y_{16} using h_{15} and X_{16} (the one-hot encoded vector of the word *mechanical*). A successful training will give us a vector y_{16} corresponding to the word *consciousness*, which would have been the correct prediction.

The application of backpropagation still stands for recurrent neural networks.

The main difference between RNNs and the other neural nets we have discussed is the application of the feedback loop connecting the present state to the past decisions made. This is what we refer to as **memory** in the context of neural networks and its main goal is to exploit the information contained in the sequence of inputs.

The feedback loop is the distinguishing feature of RNNs.

We mentioned above the application of backpropagation in a recurrent neural network. In this case we need to backpropagate through time (BPTT). We treat the full sequence (in this case the sentence) as a single training sample; the error is given by the sum of errors at each time step (each word). So for the total error E we have that:

In this case, backpropagation is actually backpropagation through time.

$$\frac{\partial E}{\partial \mathbf{W}} = \sum_t \frac{\partial E_t}{\partial \mathbf{W}}, \tag{4.49}$$

As before we can apply the chain rule and as we can see from the unrolled version of the RNN, the gradient needs to be calculated for each time step with respect to the weight parameter. For example for E_5 we have that:

$$\frac{\partial E_5}{\partial \mathbf{W}} = \frac{\partial E_5}{\partial \hat{y}_5} \frac{\partial \hat{y}_5}{\partial f_5} \frac{\partial f_5}{\partial \mathbf{W}}, \tag{4.50}$$

The chain rule still rules for BPTT.

where f_5 is the activation function at this time step. In turn, this activation function depends on $\mathbf{W}$ and f_4, which depends on f_3, and so on. With the weight being the same for all the time steps in one single pass, we can combine all the gradients so long as we express the calculations with a well-defined, ordered sequence of calculations. It is sometimes preferred to use a truncated BPTT approach as the cost and time of going back over many time steps can be quite high.

It is clear now that recurrent neural nets get their predictive power from the dependency on previous time steps. However, they may have some trouble remembering over long time dependencies. If the memory is only over one time step, a recurrent neural network may have trouble with a sentence such as:

Not dissimilar to a lot of us humans anyway!

The knight fleeing from the Jackalope is a coward,

This must be the Jackalope of Caerbannog of course!

where the description of being a coward is for the knight and not for the Jackalope. The issue is not just one of interval length. As we propagate forward in the network, if we were to encounter a gradient that is smaller than 1 and we multiply it by a suitably small learning rate, the values becomes ever smaller. We then use this information to propagate the errors back through time making the problem bigger. This leads to an issue with recurrent neural networks called the **vanishing gradient** problem where the network has problems remembering information from far away in the sequence, making predictions based only on the most recent time steps.

Vanishing gradients indicate issues with remembering long sequences.

Conversely, we can experience **exploding gradient** issues where the gradient values become increasingly large assigning undue importance to certain weights for no good reason. Exploding gradients can be successfully managed by imposing a threshold on the gradients for example. Another option is the truncated BPTT we mentioned above. In comparison, vanishing gradients are more concerning and they can be dealt with by using architectures such as LSTM.

Whereas exploding gradients assign undue importance to certain weights.

4.4.4   Long Short-Term Memory

A LONG SHORT-TERM MEMORY NEURAL net is a type of RNN able to remember over longer-term dependencies. The chain of repeating modules we have described above still holds true in an LSTM. However, the inner workings of the module A shown in Figure 4.19 is no longer the simple application of an activation function such as a ReLU or a hyperbolic tangent.

Long short-term memory, or LSTM for short.

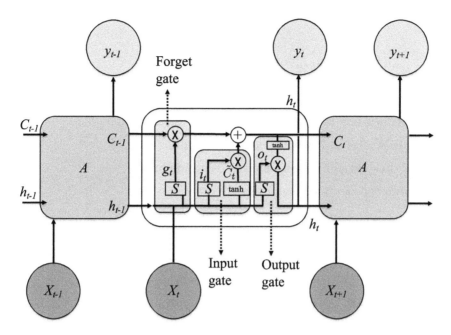

Figure 4.20: The inner workings of a long short-term memory neural network.

Instead, each module of the LSTM has 3 gates, namely the Forget Gate, the Input and the Output Gates. These are shown in Figure 4.20, and we will consider each of them in turn. The main cell state of the LSTM is the horizontal line that runs straight through the top of the diagram. The architecture of the network relies on the addition or removal of information to this cell state through the gates mentioned above.

For example, in the Forget Gate we have a sigmoid neural network layer (the box marked with S) followed by a pointwise multiplication operation (the circle marked with X). This lets us decide what information is allowed to pass to the cell state. It takes information form the previous state h_{t-1} and the input X_t generating a value between 0 and 1 for each cell state C_{t-1}. The output g_t of this gate can be

Refer to the Forget, Input and Output Gates in Figure 4.20.

expressed as:

$$g_t = S\left(W_g \cdot [h_{t-1}, X_t] + b_g\right). \qquad (4.51)$$

If the value generated is a 0, it indicates that the information will be forgotten, whereas a 1 will enable the information to be remembered. In short, the Forget Gate lets us decide how much past information we should remember

The next stage in the process is the Input Gate where we are able to decide the amount of information that this module will add to the current cell state. In other words, if the Forget Gate enables us to forget information of the past state, this gate lets us decide what to remember in this cell state. The Input Gate has two stages, first a sigmoid layer that picks what values will be updated:

Also called Update Gate as we shall see.

$$i_t = S\left(W_i \cdot [h_{t-1}, X_t] + b_i\right). \qquad (4.52)$$

Remember the 0s and 1s thrown by a sigmoid function.

Then we have a hyperbolic tangent layer that proposes new potential cell state values $\tilde{C}_t$:

$$\tilde{C}_t = \tanh\left(W_C \cdot [h_{t-1}, X_t] + b_C\right). \qquad (4.53)$$

The importance of values is modulated by the $[-1, 1]$ output of the hyperbolic tangent.

The outputs of the two layers are then combined (circle marked with X in Figure 4.20 inside the Input Gate boundary), which will be used to update the state given by the top horizontal line in our diagram.

We need to update the old cell state C_{t-1}. In reality all the decisions have already been made in the previous stages we just need to apply the calculations. First we multiply the output of the Forget Gate g_t with the previous state C_{t-1}, forgetting parts of the old state. We then add the result to the filtered candidate values $\tilde{C}_t$ from the Input Gate (in the top horizontal line in the diagram)

At the circle marked with + in Figure 4.20.

$$C_t = g_t C_{t-1} + i_t \tilde{C}_t. \tag{4.54}$$

That is why we also call it the Update Gate.

We are now at the Output Gate of our module, where we decide the portion of the current cell that will make it to the output. We apply a sigmoid layer for this purpose:

$$o_t = S\left(W_o \cdot [h_{t-1}, X_t] + b_o\right). \tag{4.55}$$

And finally, to the Output Gate.

At the same time we put the cell state obtained from the previous stages C_t through a hyperbolic tangent layer to map the values between -1 and 1 and combine the outputs filtering out the portions of the cell state we want to output, i.e., h_t:

$$h_t = o_t \tanh(C_t). \tag{4.56}$$

The description presented above covers the main components in an LSTM. There are other variations such as the Gated Recurrent Unit (GRU)[30] which combines the Forget and Input Gates into a single unit. It also merges the cell state and hidden state resulting in simpler inner architecture.

[30] Cho, K., B. van Merrienboer, et al. (2014). Learning phrase representations using RNN encoder-decoder for statistical machine translation. *CoRR abs/1406.1078*

If you are interested in a comparison of different LSTM architectures, take a look at "LSTM: A Search Space Odyssey"[31] were the authors present such comparison. They find that different LSTM architectures perform more or less the same as standard LSTM. They show that the Forget Gate and the output activation function are the most critical components.

[31] Greff, K., Srivastava, R. K., Koutník, J., et al. (2017). LSTM: A Search Space Odyssey. *IEEE Trans. Neural Netw. and Learning Sys. 28*(10), 2222–2232

4.4.5 *Long Short-Term Memory Networks in Action*

LET US CREATE A NEURAL network that is able to generate a plausible sequence given a set of training data. We will use a character-level language model. This means that we will give our LSTM recurrent neural network a number of character sequences and request for the probability distribution of the next character in the sequence. We can use the model to generate new sequences (hopefully coherent sentences) one character at a time. An interesting blog entry called *The Unreasonable Effectiveness of Recurrent Neural Networks*[32] covers this same challenge including different types of corpora.

This kind of models is called generative... for obvious reasons.

[32] Karpathy, A. (2015). The Unreasonable Effectiveness of Recurrent Neural Networks. https://karpathy.github.io/2015/05/21/rnn-effectiveness/. Accessed: 2019-09-09

Our starting point requires us to get hold of a large piece of text. We will use the text mentioned in Section 4.4.3, i.e., the 1872 fiction novel *Erewhon, or Over the Range*[33] by Samuel Butler. The text can be found in the Project Gutenberg site.

[33] Butler, S. (2005). Erewhon; Or, Over the Range. Project Gutenberg https://www.gutenberg.org/ebooks/1906. Accessed: 2019-09-03

After downloading the text in UTF-8 format and it is saved in a plain file called `erewhon.txt` we can start our journey over the range. As usual we start by loading some libraries:

```
import numpy as np

import random

from keras.models import Sequential

from keras.layers import Dense

from keras.layers import Dropout

from keras.utils import np_utils

from keras.layers import LSTM

from keras.callbacks import ModelCheckpoint
```

We already know how to do this with our eyes closed.

We are familiar with the calls made above, expect perhaps for the last two entries. LSTM, however, should be pretty straightforward after reading the preceding section. ModelChekpoint helps us request information from our architecture at desired points, e.g., at the end of every epoch. Let us load the text:

```
book = 'erewhon.txt'

with open(book, 'r') as file:

    text = file.read().lower()

n_text = len(text)
```

We open and read the file as usual.

We can see what the length of our corpus is:

```
> print('Book Text Length: {}'.format(n_text))


Book Text Length: 483134
```

The number of characters is the length of our text.

We have over 480k characters in the text. We will be generating text character-by-character and therefore we require a set of the characters used in the text. It is this set that becomes our "vocabulary" for this task.

```
chars = sorted(list(set(text)))

n_vocab = len(chars)
```

We calculate a set from the characters in the corpus.

We can now ask about the cardinality of the character set used in the corpus:

```
> print('Number of characters used: {} '.\
    format(n_vocab))


Number of characters used: 62
```

There are 62 entries in the set, more than the usual 26 letters in English.

There are 62 different characters used, more than the typical 26 characters in the English alphabet. This is because there are some symbols, punctuation and other characters too:

```
> print(chars[:5], chars[-5:])


['\n', ' ', '!', '"', '#']
['y', 'z', '{', '}', '\ufeff']
```

Perhaps an opportunity to pre-process our data.

We will need to keep track of the characters used, but not only that, we will need to pass a numerical representation to the neural network. To that end, we will create an index for the characters:

```
char_ixs = dict((c, i)
    for i, c in enumerate(chars))
```

We are using a dictionary to create our vocabulary index. Great!

It may be needed to reverse back the index, so that any prediction can be traced back to the character in question:

```
ixs_char = dict((i, c)
    for i, c in enumerate(chars))
```

We also need the reverse index.

Another important decision that needs to be made is the length of the training sequences we will feed into the LSTM. In this case we are going to use a fixed length of 40 characters. Other approaches may include partitioning the text into sentences and pad them to take into account long and short sentences.

You can try other length sequences.

In order to keep things in check, we will generate sequences jumping a few characters. We do this with a step of 3. Finally, the training sequences, along with the next character in the sequence, will be stored in lists:

```
seq_len = 40
step = 3
rawX = []
rawy = []
```

We store the training sequences in rawX and the next characters in rawy.

Let us generate the sequences, i.e., sentences, that will be fed to the neural network:

```
for i in range(0, len(text) - seq_len, step):
    rawX.append(text[i: i+seq_len])
    rawy.append(text[i+seq_len])

n_sentences = len(rawX)
```

We append the sequences to the lists above.

We can check how many sequences have been generated:

```
> print(n_sentences)


161032
```

This is the number of sequences that will be used to train our recurrent neural network.

We have over 160k sentences to train our network. Let us take a look at one of them:

```
> print(rawX[900])


machines as an attempt to reduce mr. dar
```

This is sequence 900 in our dataset.

and the next character in this sequence is:

```
>   print(rawy[900])


w
```

And this is the next character for sequence 900.

We can get a glimpse to the Darwinian references used by Butler in the description of the Erewhonian machines. We need to encode these sentences and next characters to be able to pass them to the neural network. We will create some Boolean arrays to hold the information. For the sequences we need an array to hold the number of sentences (161032) by the length of the sentence (40) by the number of characters in our vocabulary (62). For the next characters we only need the number of sentences by the number of characters:

I am no RNN, but surely that would be a reference to Darwin himself!

```
X = np.zeros((len(rawX), seq_len, len(chars)),
    dtype=np.bool)

y = np.zeros((len(rawy), len(chars)),
    dtype=np.bool)
```

Our sequences and next characters are now transformed into Boolean arrays.

Each character in each sentence can now be encoded with the help of the index we created earlier on:

```
for i, sentence in enumerate(rawX):
    for t, char in enumerate(sentence):
        X[i, t, char_ixs[char]] = 1
    y[i, char_ixs[rawy[i]]]=1
```

We use our dictionary to encode the characters.

We have completed our data processing and we are ready to define the architecture of our LSTM neural network. We will use the sequential API and try to keep the architecture simple at this stage:

```
model = Sequential()
model.add(LSTM(128, input_shape=(seq_len,
    len(chars))))
model.add(Dropout(0.2))
model.add(Dense(len(chars), activation='softmax'))
```

We use the sequential API in Keras for this implementation.

We start with a long short-term memory layer with 128 units expecting an input with dimensions of the length of the sequence by the number of characters. We then apply a dropout layer setting 20% of the inputs units to 0. Finally, we connect this to a dense output later with a softmax activation function. Let us look at a summary of the model:

```
> print(model_summary())


-----------------------------------------------------------

Layer (type)              Output Shape           Param #
===========================================================

lstm_1 (LSTM)             (None, 128)            97792

dropout_1 (Dropout)       (None, 128)            0

dense_1 (Dense)           (None, 62)             7998

===========================================================

Total params: 105,790

Trainable params: 105,790

Non-trainable params: 0
```

This model requires us to train $105,790$ parameters. For that purpose we need to compile our model while providing an optimiser and an appropriate loss function:

```
from keras.optimizers import RMSprop


opt = RMSprop(lr=0.01)

model.compile(loss='categorical_crossentropy',\
    optimizer=opt)
```

We need to train $105,790$ parameters in this model.

We may be interested in a very accurate model that predicts each character in the text perfectly. That may take a more intricate architecture and a longer training time. In this case, we will request the model to provide us with a view of the improvements achieved in the training by recording a model to a file whenever this happens at the end of an epoch. This is why we are interested in the ModelCheckpoint method introduced earlier on in this section.

This model may not be the most accurate, but then again it is a very simple one.

We start by defining a file name including information about the given epoch and loss, we will pass this information to the model checkpoint and provide this as a list of callbacks to the model:

```
fname= 'weights-improv-{epoch:02d}-{loss:.4f}.hdf5'
checkpoint = ModelCheckpoint(fname,\
    monitor='loss', verbose=1,\
    save_best_only=True, mode='min')
```

ModelCheckpoint lets us keep track of the improvements in the model during training.

We can now start training our model:

```
model.fit(X, y, epochs=60, batch_size=128,
    callbacks=[checkpoint])
```

We are training the model for 60 epochs with batches of 128 sequences. In the instance when this model was run, the model did not manage to get any further improvements in the optimisation of the loss function after the 59th epoch. The latest file produced by the check point was `weights-improv-59-1.3969.hdf5`.

The model obtained can be used to generate some text. But before we do that, let us make sure that we are able to obtain appropriate samples out of the probability array. We will use the fact that we are using a softmax function and apply a "temperature" to control the randomness of the predictions made. If the network produces class probabilities with logit vector $\mathbf{z} = (z_1, z_2, \ldots, z_n)$ by applying a softmax function, then we are able to calculate

We need to ensure that we can obtain appropriate samples out of a probability array.

the probability vector $\mathbf{q} = (q_1, q_2, \ldots, q_n)$ with q_i given by the following expression:

$$q_i = \frac{\exp(z_i/T)}{\sum_{j=1} \exp(z_j/T)},\tag{4.57}$$

where T being the temperature parameter. When $T = 1$, we are computing the softmax function directly on the logits without scaling. When $T = 0.5$ for instance, we are effectively doubling the logits and therefore we have larger values of the softmax function. This makes our predictions more confident but also more conservative. Let us create a function to calculate the sample:

```
def sample(p, temperature=1.0):
    p = np.asarray(p).astype('float64')
    p = p**(1/temperature)
    p_sum = p.sum()
    sample_temp = p/p_sum


    return np.argmax(np.random.multinomial(\
        1, sample_temp, 1))
```

This function lets us obtain those samples.

Let us pick a random number to get a sequence. We will generate characters one at a time and they will be added to the initial sentence:

```
start_ix=random.randint(0, len(text) - seq_len - 1)
generated= ''
sentence = text[start_ix: start_ix + seq_len]
generated += sentence
```

We pick a sequence at random.

An initial sentence will be given for example by:

```
> print(sentence)


ily believe to be faithful representatio
```

Your sentence will surely be different.

Let us generate 400 characters with the model. Remember that we will get predictions in terms of indices and they will need to be translated back into characters using the dictionaries we defined earlier on in this section:

```
for i in range(400):
    x_pred = np.zeros((1, seq_len, len(chars)))
    for t, char in enumerate(sentence):
        x_pred[0, t, char_ixs[char]] = 1.


    preds = model.predict(x_pred, verbose=0)[0]


    next_index = sample(preds, diversity)
    next_char = ixs_char[next_index]
    generated += next_char
    sentence = sentence[1:] + next_char
```

We generate 400 characters with our LSTM. Remember that we need to translate back using our reverse index.

The generated text for the sequence above would look similar to the following:

```
ily believe to be faithful representation with
their body had a secress of a strong to be one of
the first and single something that we really on
the ancery and reason in the country as a sense
of the mainty of me the work and well all the wood
```

Not bad, particularly when considering that this was generated character-by-character with a simple LSTM.

> in the most concesing the work down his attant on
> the world that the stubles, and seemed to a does
> we should be dead, and the england for my proports
> of for the statue to the parents for the mos

It may not seem like much, but bearing in mind that the text
was generated one character at a time and without prior
knowledge to the English language, the model was able to
generate word-like groups of characters most of which are
actual English words such as "reason", "work", "england",
"country or "dead". The results are by no means perfect, but
remember that the neural network architecture we build
only had a single LSTM layer.

4.5   Summary

IT HAS BEEN A LONG journey, and I hope you have enjoyed
the ride. In this chapter we have covered some of the most
important aspects behind the magic and "unreasonable
effectiveness" of neural networks. Given the influence
that neural networks and deep learning have and with the
number of use cases growing, this is truly an area in data
science that any Jackalope data scientist needs to cover.

We started our journey with a trip down memory lane,
where we looked at an abridged historical account of some
of the developments that have made neural networks shine.
We saw how some of the ideas behind modern architectures
started life much earlier than a lot of us imagine. Indeed

the inspiration provided by biological neurons is a useful analogy but realising the main differences is also important. The development of the perceptron is a clear step in the development of what we call deep learning and a good undestanding of its capabilities and limitations is a must.

Looking at the directed graphs used to represent neural nets, made out of nodes and layers, we get a clear picture of the flow of information, from layer to layer and node to node. We saw how the receiving nodes take both the input information and the weight of the connecting edges to compute a combined output. All this, with the aid of an activation function. In turn this output is sent to the next set of nodes in the following layer. Deciding on the number of layers and nodes is an important task and we saw how we can go from representing linear patterns through to more complex representations simply by changing the number of nodes in a hidden layer.

After getting a good understanding of the feedforward step in a neural network, we described the way the model can learn from its mistakes by looking at the errors incurred by the predictions after a single feedforward pass. The key to adjusting the weights in the network relies on the application of the chain rule to backpropagate the errors. Several round trips of feedforward and backpropagation enable the model to improve its predictions. With this information we were able to create our first neural network from scratch and looked at the effect that the number of nodes in a layer has in the overall classification boundaries generated by the model.

At this point we were able to take a look at expanding the number of layers, nodes and connections within a neural network and entered the world of deep learning. We used Keras to implement these architectures as it offers a friendly and powerful manner to build our networks. We recreated the network we built from scratch and discussed the implementation of two popular architectures, namely convolutional neural networks (CNNs) and recurrent neural networks (RNNs). We created an image classification network to exemplify the work of CNNs, and generated character-level language with the help of a long short-Term memory RNN.

No brainer!

5

Here Is One I Made Earlier: Machine Learning Deployment

WE HAVE COVERED A LOT of ground in this and its
companion book *Data Science and Analytics with Python*[1]. We
have discussed the trials and tribulations of Jackalope data
scientists, seen the differences between supervised and
unsupervised learning, and talked about models such as
regression, decision trees, time series, neural networks,
logistic regression and natural language processing
techniques among others. It is a large landscape and there
are many areas into which we could delve much deeper, or
indeed some others we have not even touched.

[1] Rogel-Salazar, J. (2017). *Data Science and Analytics with Python*. Chapman & Hall/CRC Data Mining and Knowledge Discovery Series. CRC Press

Of all those areas, in this chapter we will discuss some
aspects that we need to take into account in order to not
only build a powerful model, but also make it part of a data
product that can be used by its intended consumers. Not
only does this require the close collaboration of the
triumvirate formed by a Jackalope data scientist, project

We can build powerful models,
but who will use them?

manager and data architect, but also the support of a product owner and subject matter experts.

We will first talk about data products, the requirement to build pipelines and processes and the need for creating machine learning models able to perform scoring on device. We will then provide an example for deploying a simple machine learning model in a mobile device such as an Apple iPhone. To that end we will use some of the capabilities that the ecosystem for these devices offers, including the use of XCode and the Swift programming language.

We will build an iOS app!

5.1   The Devil in the Detail: Data Products

NOTHING AS PERVASIVE AS A product. We all recognise them, buy them, sell them and/or use them. A product is a good idea, method, information, object or service that has been created as a result of a process in order to satisfy a need or want. Typically we think of products as tangible objects. With that being the case, it could be surprising to us when we first hear about a data product. We can think of a data product as any other product, but one whose existence meets the need or want we mentioned above through the employment of data.

Products are not exclusively tangible objects!

That definition is still quite broad and wide-encompassing; after all, a number of digital products out there use data. Things such as websites or portals for example. In our case we would like to concentrate on those data products whose main *raison d'être* is centred around data. You may think that we are splitting hairs here, but hear me out. A data product is still a product, and thus the standard considerations of developing a product do apply: Meet a customer need, improvement through feedback, competition, prioritisation, etc. You name it. That is true even for those super expensive products in fictional planet *Algon*, the fifth world in the system of Aldebaran, the Red Giant in the constellation of Sagittarius.

Ok, read me out... This is not a podcast after all!

No bananas on Algon though!

Nonetheless, a data product distinguishes itself for the development considerations we need to make around the availability, processing and meaning of data. No wonder that the powers of a Jackalope data scientist are in high demand around the creation of data products. The main consideration is therefore the incorporation of data, and data science techniques while going beyond data analysis, to the provision of value for the customer. It is the idea of putting data understanding into production.

Or indeed of a rangale of Jackalope data scientists.

We can think of different categories of data products including:

- Raw data - Making data available though appropriate pipelines.

- Derived data - Processing and calculating fields that can be used later in the funnel.

- Algorithms - This has been the main topic of our discussions. We pass some (raw/derived) data through an algorithm to obtain understanding useful to the users.

A categorisation of data products in increasing order of complexity.

- Decision support - Enabling the user to make a decision based on better information. The aim is to provide the information in an easy way to be consumed. These are the products we will talk about in this chapter.

- Automated decision-making - This is closer to the overall goal of artificial intelligence where the process of making a decision is delegated to the machine without user intervention.

As we move from raw data into automated decisions, not only do we move in an increasing scale of complexity, requiring different skills in the development of the product, but also the products have different intended audiences. For raw and derived data products, as well as algorithms, the audience tends to be technical. However, for the decision support and automated decision-making, the end users will tend to be more specialised and perhaps not even technical at all.

The different data product categories above have very different intended audiences.

We have been considering the usage of algorithms as data products to be consumed by us (Jackalope data scientists) to understand the patterns available in our data. In this chapter we are concerned with the next level in the scale above, where the available data is provided to a suitable algorithm to extract an insight and we are then interested in providing this power to our users or customers, particularly non-technical ones.

I know, I know... actionable insights...

As it is the case with many other products, they do not simply arise fully formed, like Venus from the sea-foam. Instead, we need to apply investigation, feedback and expertise to hone in on the problem we are trying to solve. A methodology that comes to mind in these situations is Agile[2], which gives us the opportunity of exploring and understanding our problem, while being flexible providing us with an opportunity to learn, evolve, pivot and create better products. The idea of a unicorn data scientist is not the ideal in an agile development cycle, instead a team of shrewd Jackalope data scientists will enable the wider team to be nimble and multi-functional.

The multi-functional team we refer to is not just made out of data scientists. In general we require data architects, engineers, product managers and subject matter experts in order to create a successful data product. Data scientists need to liaise with engineers to obtain a reliable dataset; subject matter experts need to provide their know-how at crucial development stages and verify how useful results may be, while informing product managers about the direction of travel for the product. Communication among all these agents is therefore paramount and Agile may be able to facilitate this as part of the ceremonies that form part of a good implementation of the methodology.

There is no magic number for the amount and number of data sources required by a data product. Data science is a hungry, even greedy, affair: The more data available, the better. In that sense, the assessment that the team will need to make is not only about the data quantity and quality, but also about the timeliness of data availability, as well as the data combinations that can be pursued in order to create models that benefit/improve the product. Furthermore,

[2] Stellman, A. and J. Greene (2014). *Learning Agile: Understanding Scrum, XP, Lean, and Kanban.* O'Reilly Media

Working in a multi-functional team under a methodology such as Agile enables the successful creation of good products.

The fact, you have standups in the morning, does not mean you are applying Agile.

Data science is a greedy discipline, the more data the better!

depending on the type of algorithms employed in the data product, it may be possible to make indirect observations of signals in the data to predict useful information.

All in all, as any data product is still a product it will need to meet the needs or solve the problems that real users/customers/people have. The important thing therefore is to start with the problem statement and iterate it. There is no doubt that technology is an important factor in the successful development of a data product, but it is not a panacea. Starting up with the technology and finding a problem to solve is the equivalent of using a hammer to tighten a screw. In some cases it may work, but it would be better to find technology that helps solve the problem at hand.

Starting with the problem statement is paramount.

Or any product actually!

The success of a good data product relies on the collaboration and effort of the team behind it and, to a larger extent, on the users whose pain points the product helps mitigate. As such, our task as Jackalope data scientists is to use the most appropriate data to employ in our development, make use of suitable algorithms and collaborate with data engineers, architects, product and project managers, and yes, even users. We can then let our tools, languages and platforms deliver a solution to the problem statement.

After all, if the users do not see the value in the product, they will not use it.

This may take many forms and one way to tackle this challenge is through the creation of user-friendly interfaces. These applications let users consume the results of the data product. For instance, consider a product that applies a

The creation of a user-friendly interface may help in serving the need of our customers better than handing them a Python script.

multivariate regression algorithm to predict house prices. It supports users that are interested in climbing the property ladder and they can be better served with the help of a purpose-built application that makes the prediction easier to compute. Compare this to handing them a programming script or a table with numbers.

We will build a similar solution later on; stay tuned!

The deployment of machine learning algorithms as part of a data product can be achieved in various ways. Depending on the ultimate goal of the product and its intended audience this may range from programmatic authoring, scheduling and monitoring of data pipelines with tools such as Apache Airflow[3] or Luigi[4]; within platforms such as Dataiku, IBM Data Science Experience and Azure; or in device, where processing happens directly in a smart phone for example. The extension to this is the concept of machine learning at the edge, where computing power is distributed across a network of devices, making use of the Internet of Things, instead of a centralised system in the cloud. We may not cover here computing at the edge, but let us take a look at deployment on a single device.

[3] Apache Airflow (2014). Apache Airflow Documentation. https://airflow.apache.org. Accessed: 2019-09-30
[4] Spotify (2014). Luigi. https://github.com/spotify/luigi. Accessed: 2019-09-30

IoT for short.

5.2 Apples and Snakes: Core ML + Python

WITH THE HIGH AVAILABILITY OF a large number of connected devices, the computing power that can be harnessed for the application of machine learning is huge. A lot of these devices are small enough to be carried around with us and are part of our daily lives. Furthermore, they come with a variety of sensors and monitors that can gather

Here, we are interested in harnessing the power of mobile devices.

data, which in turn can be used by the data products we build for the benefit of our users.

It is possible to implement our data products to be deployed in a mobile device, enabling the machine learning algorithms to process and execute directly there, without the need of sending data or information to a server and coming back to the user. This has advantages for data privacy as the information never leaves the user's device and reduces friction in terms of latency for the user, for example. As you can see, this offers a number of advantages, as the machine learning models we develop are delivered into the hands of your users, quite literally.

The processing happens directly in the device!

We want to deliver our models into the hands of our users.

There are some tools that enable the deployment of machine learning models into a device, taking a trained model and encapsulating it in a format that is compatible with the ecosystem of the device in question. In this case we are going to concentrate on some of the tools that Apple has made available to developers in order to integrate machine learning workflows into applications, aka apps. One such tool is Core ML which is a computer framework, in other words a software abstraction that enables generic functionality to be modified as required by the developer to transform it into software for specific purposes. This enables us to develop complex projects or simple apps.

Although we are concentrating our discussion in the Apple ecosystem, there are other solutions out there!

Our aim is to deploy a machine learning model into an app.

Core ML is a framework created and provided by Apple to speed up the development of apps that use *trained* machine learning models. Notice that word we wrote in italics in the description of the framework: trained. This means that the model has to be developed externally with appropriate training data for the specific project in mind. For instance if you are interested in building a classifier that distinguishes Jackalopes from hares, and horses from unicorns, then you need to train the model with lots of images of Jackalopes and hares, horses and unicorns first. Then you can apply the Core ML framework to integrate the model within an app.

Core ML supports a variety of machine learning models, from generalised linear models (GLMs for short) to neural networks. A summary of the models that can be used with Core ML is shown in Table 5.1. It is possible for you to develop your own custom conversion tool in case your model is currently not supported. Core ML also helps with the task of adding the trained machine learning model to your application by automatically creating a custom programmatic interface that supplies an API to your model. All this is within the comfort of Apple's own IDE: Xcode.

There is an important point to remember. The model has to be developed externally from Core ML, in other words you may want to use your favourite machine learning framework, computer language and environment to cover the different aspects of the data science workflow. You can read more about this in Chapter 3 of *Data Science and Analytics with Python* book[5]. In any case, whether you use Scikit-learn, Keras or another supported framework, the model you develop has to be trained (tested and evaluated) beforehand. Once you are ready, Core ML will support you in bringing it to the masses via your app.

Core ML takes pre-trained machine learning models and makes them available with in an app.

Check the Apple Developer documentation for further model supported in the future.

API stands for Application Programming Interface

That word again; in this case think Python libraries such as Scikit-learn for instance.

[5] Rogel-Salazar, J. (2017). *Data Science and Analytics with Python*. Chapman & Hall/CRC Data Mining and Knowledge Discovery Series. CRC Press

Model Type	Supported Models	Supported Frameworks
Neural networks	Feedforward, convolutional, recurrent	Caffe v1, Keras 1.2.2+
Tree ensembles	Random forests, boosted trees, decision trees	Scikit-learn 0.18 KGBoost 0.6
Support vector machines	Scalar regression, multi-class classification	Scikit-learn 0.18, LIBSVM 3.22
Generalised linear models	Linear regression, logistic regression	Scikit-learn 0.18
Feature engineering	Sparse vectorisation, dense vectorisation, categorical processing	Scikit-learn 0.18
Pipeline models	Sequentially chained models	Scikit-learn 0.18

Table 5.1: Models and frameworks supported by Core ML.

In 2019 Apple announced the release of an application called Create ML[6] bundled within the set of tools they make available to the developer. It lets us create and deploy a machine learning model and the aim of the tool is to democratise training of models as the output from Create ML is already in the Core ML format. This means that the step of converting your model is not required. Create ML supports workflows for computer vision, natural language processing, sound classification, activity classification (using

[6] Apple Inc. (2019b). Core ML. https://developer.apple.com/ documentation/createml. Accessed: 2019-10-01

motion sensor data) and tabular data. We will not cover
the use of Create ML here, as it is outside the remit of this
book. However, the interested reader can refer to the Apple
Developers' site for more information.

As for the advantages of Core ML, Apple mentions[7] that
it is optimised for on-device performance. This minimises
the memory footprint and power consumption of the app.
Also, the fact that the model runs strictly on the device
ensures the privacy of user data and guarantees that the
app remains functional and responsive when a network
connection is unavailable. In order to use our model within
our app, we need to translate our implementation into a
`.mlmodel` format. Let us find out more about how we can do
that by building our own app.

[7] Apple Inc. (2017a). Core ML. https://developer.apple.com/documentation/coreml. Accessed: 2019-10-01

5.3   Machine Learning at the Core: Apps and ML

IN THIS SECTION WE WILL cover the end-to-end creation
of a simple app with machine learning at its core. Starting
with the creation of a suitable Python environment for the
creation of the model and its translation to Core ML format,
all the way to running it in your iPhone. We are largely
following the workflow depicted schematically in Figure
5.1, starting with the development in Python using libraries
such as Scikit-learn and Keras. We then will convert our
Python model into Core ML using Core ML Tools. We then
integrate the translated model into our app development
and finally deploy the app to our users.

Yes, at its (Apple) Core (ML)!

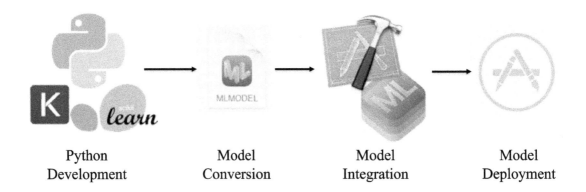

| Python
Development | Model
Conversion | Model
Integration | Model
Deployment |

Figure 5.1: We follow this workflow to deploy our machine learning models to our app.

5.3.1   Environment Creation

IN PREPARATION TO TRAINING A model which will be converted into Core ML so as to be integrated within our application, it is best practice to make sure we have a suitable environment to work on. When Core ML first came to light, the Core ML module only supported Python 2! Fortunately, things have moved on since then and now Python 3.x is also supported.

Creating an environment for Core ML is best practice.

In order to ensure reproducibility of the stack, we will create an environment with the appropriate modules. In this case we are using Anaconda and will create a conda environment called coreml with Python 3.7; it will include some of the libraries we may be using such as Scikit-learn, Pandas, matplotlib, etc.

You may use your favourite Python distribution.

```
> conda create --name coreml python=3 ipython
  jupyter scikit-learn pandas matplotlib
```

We need to install the Core ML Tools module[8] and the easiest way to do this is to use `pip install`

[8] Apple Inc. (2017b). Core ML tools. https://github.com/apple/coremltools. Accessed: 2019-10-01

```
> conda activate coreml

(coreml)
> pip install coremltools
```

5.3.2 Eeny, Meeny, Miny, Moe: Model Selection

NOW THAT WE HAVE A suitable environment to carry out our development, we need to get to the ever so difficult task of choosing a model. This is not as simple as picking up one of the many algorithms available to us, and the decision depends to a large extent on the use case at hand. The main recommendation is therefore to consider the problem statement that we are trying to address, obtain the appropriate data to help with answering the problem and brainstorm with the rest of the team to assess best actions.

Remember to use the data science workflow. Start with the problem statement and use appropriate data.

Model selection will also be dictated by the metrics of your algorithm and indeed the application of best practices in terms of data splitting, feature engineering, cross-validation, etc. We will not cover these steps here, as they have been addressed in Chapters 1 and 3 of *Data Science and Analytics with Python*[9]. Instead, we are interested in the steps that follow the successful selection of the model. Let us consider for the sake of argument and without loss of generality that we are relying on our good old friend, the dependable linear regression model.

[9] Rogel-Salazar, J. (2017). *Data Science and Analytics with Python*. Chapman & Hall/CRC Data Mining and Knowledge Discovery Series. CRC Press

We are indeed all familiar with a line of best fit, and surely many of us remember doing some of it by hand! Also, who has not played with Excel's capabilities to perform a linear regression? Let us remind ourselves of some of the basics: A linear regression is a model that relates a variable y to one or more explanatory (or independent) variables x_i.

The parameters that define the model are estimated from the available data relevant to the problem. Remember that there are a number of assumptions about the explanatory variables. You can find more information in Chapter 4 of the companion book mentioned above. We can think of the goal of a linear regression model to draw a line through the data as exemplified in Figure 5.2. In such a case, data for the independent variable x_1 is used to determine the value of y.

We can think of the goal of linear regression as finding a line of best fit.

Let us take the case of 2 independent variables x_1 and x_2. The linear regression model to predict our target variable y is given by:

$$y = \alpha + \beta_1 x_1 + \beta_2 x_2 + \epsilon, \qquad (5.1)$$

where α and β_i are the parameters to be estimated. Once the estimation is obtained, we use these parameters to generate predictions. With the aid of techniques such as least squares, it is possible to estimate the parameters α, β_1 and β_2 by minimising the sum of the squares of the residuals, i.e., the difference between an observed value, and the fitted value provided by a model. Once we have determined the parameters, we are able to score new (unseen) data for x_1 and x_2 to predict the value of y.

Once we have estimations for α, β_1 and β_2 we can use the model to score new, unseen data points.

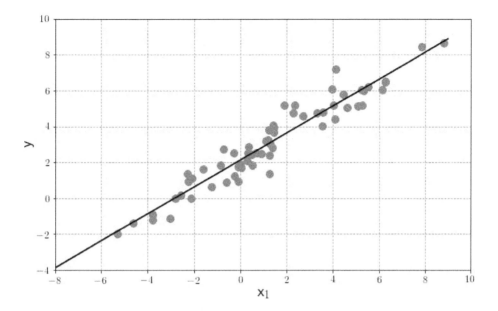

Figure 5.2: A line of best bit for the observations y dependent of features x_1.

In this case, we will show how we can do this for a famous dataset called "Boston House Prices" where our aim is to predict the price of a house in Boston given a number of features or attributes of the property. We will use a couple of variables such as the number of bedrooms in the house and a crime index for the area. Remember that the aim will be to show how to build the model to be used with Core ML and not build a perfect model for the prediction.

We will use the "Boston House Prices" dataset in the rest of this chapter.

5.3.3   Location, Location, Location: Exploring the Data

WE CONSIDER THAT OUR PROBLEM statement is the challenge of predicting the price of properties in a city.

What about concentrating in Boston? It seems like a great location to explore. There is a bit of a caveat in this case; we will transport ourselves with our TARDIS to the 1970s as the dataset we will use comes from that time.

Other time travelling methods may be available... at some time or other...

The dataset in question has information collected by the U.S. Census Service concerning housing in the area of Boston, Massachusets and originally published by Harrison and Rubinfeld[10]. The original aim for this dataset was to assess the willingness that market participants would have to pay for clean air. That is the reason the dataset includes date on the concentration levels of nitric oxides.

[10] Harrison, D. and D. Rubinfeld (1978). Hedonic prices and the demand for clean air. *J. Environ. Economics and Management 5*, 81–102

To make our discussion more manageable, we will use our knowledge of one of the most well-known models in statistics and yes, machine learning: Linear regression. We know that we can relate the values of input parameters x_i to the target variable y to be predicted. Let us however do some basic exploration of our dataset.

The dataset contains 506 data points with 13 features:

- CRIM - per capita crime rate by town

- ZN - proportion of residential land zoned for lots over $25,000$ sq.ft.

These are the features or attributes that are included in the "Boston House Prices" dataset.

- INDUS - proportion of non-retail business acres per town

- CHAS - Charles River dummy variable (1 if tract bounds river; 0 otherwise)

- NOX - nitric oxides concentration (parts per 10 million)

- RM - average number of rooms per dwelling

- AGE - proportion of owner-occupied units built prior to 1940

- DIS - weighted distances to five Boston employment centres

- RAD - index of accessibility to radial highways

- TAX - full-value property-tax rate per $10,000$

- PTRATIO - pupil-teacher ratio by town

- B - $1000(Bk - 0.63)^2$ where Bk is the proportion of black population by town

- LSTAT - percentage of lower status of the population

The target is called MEDV and it represents the median value of owner-occupied homes in the $1,000$s.

We are going to use Scikit-learn and fortunately the dataset comes with the module. The input variables are included in the data method and the price is given by the target. We are going to load the input variables in the dataframe boston_df and the prices in the array y:

That is awesome, right?

```
from sklearn import datasets
import pandas as pd


boston = datasets.load_boston()
boston_df = pd.DataFrame(boston.data)
boston_df.columns = boston.feature_names


y = boston.target
```

We retrieve the dataset directly from Scikit-learn!

We are going to build our model using only a limited number of inputs. The reason for this decision is two-fold: We are simplifying the workflow to fit our discussion, but more importantly when we put the data product in the hands of our users, we would like them to use a friendly version of the prediction where they are able to modify a few features, rather than a bloated application no one would like to use. In a more realistic situation, these are decisions that would need to be carefully considered as part of the product development and testing sprints.

For ease of discussion, we will only use two variables in our model: Crime rate and number of rooms.

In any event, here we will pay attention to the average number of rooms and the crime rate:

```
X = boston_df[['CRIM', 'RM']]
X.columns = ['Crime', 'Rooms']
```

We select the variables of interest.

The description of these two attributes is as follows:

```
> X.describe()

              Crime        Rooms
count   506.000000   506.000000
mean      3.613524     6.284634
std       8.601545     0.702617
min       0.006320     3.561000
25%       0.082045     5.885500
50%       0.256510     6.208500
75%       3.677083     6.623500
max      88.976200     8.780000
```

We can see the descriptive statistics for our variables of interest.

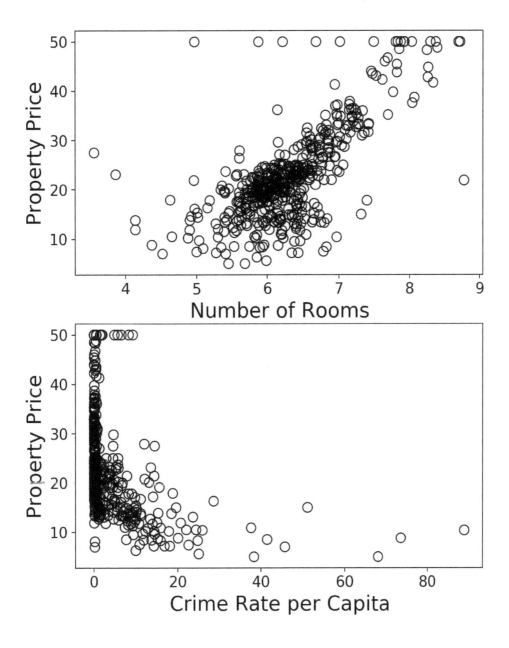

Figure 5.3: Boston house prices versus average number of rooms (top) and per capita crime rate (bottom).

As we can see the minimum average number of rooms is 3.56 and the maximum is 8.78. The median is 6.20. In the case of the per capita crime rate by town, the minimum value is 0.006 and the maximum is 88.97, nonetheless the median is 0.25. We will use some of these values later to define the ranges that will be provided to our users to find price predictions. We can see the relationships of these two features versus the house price values in Figure 5.3.

These figures will inform the parameters that we will make available to our users through the app.

5.3.4   Modelling and Core ML: A Crucial Step

IN THE LAST SECTION WE have taken a look at the Boston House Prices dataset, loaded it directly from Scikit-learn and looked at some of the features of interest for our predictive model. It is now time to build the linear regression model we talked about earlier on. Then we will convert it into a .mlmodel to be used in an iOS app. As usual, we are going to need some modules:

We will build a linear regression model for this dataset.

```
import pandas as pd
from sklearn import linear_model
from sklearn.model_selection\
    import train_test_split
from sklearn import metrics
import numpy as np
import coremltools
```

Importing modules is second nature to us!

We are familiar with the modules and methods mentioned above. The newcomer in this case is coremltools which will enable the conversion of our model to be used in iOS.

We have already loaded our data in the previous section and created a subset of features including the crime rate score and the number of rooms in the property. We also need to have our target variable, i.e., the price of the property:

```
y = boston.target
```

We need to define our target variable.

We know we need to separate the target variable from the predictor variables so that the model can be built. Although this dataset is not too big, we are going to follow best practices and split the data into training and testing sets:

```
X_train, X_test, y_train, y_test=train_test_split(
    X, y, test_size=0.2, random_state=7)
```

We split our data into training and testing.

In this case we are reserving 20% of the dataset for testing and the split is initialised with a random seed equal to 7. Remember that the idea is to use the training set only in the creation of the model. We then test with the remaining data points.

Let us now create a self-contained function to build a generalised linear model:

```
def glm_boston(X, y):
    print('Implementing a linear regression')
    lm = linear_model.LinearRegression()
    gml = lm.fit(X, y)
    return gml
```

This function implements and fits a linear regression model from Scikit-learn.

This creates an instance of the LinearRegression algorithm in Scikit-learn and fits it with the data in X to predict the target y. Let us use this function with our training data:

```
my_model = glm_boston(X_train, y_train)
```

The linear regression model we are implementing is of the form:

$$y = \alpha + \beta_1 x_1 + \beta_2 x_2 + \epsilon, \qquad (5.2)$$

Here, we refer to α as the intercept and β_i as the coefficients.

and the fitting of the model we just performed will let us extract the fitted parameters α and β_i that will enable us to make predictions. Let us see our coefficients:

```
coefs = [my_model.intercept_, my_model.coef_]
```

We can check what the values are:

We can see the estimated value of our coefficients with the aid of the properties .intercept and .coeff_ of our model.

```
> print('The intercept is {0}'.format(coefs[0]))


The intercept is -33.5555348465913.


> print('The coefficients are {0}'.\
    format(coefs[1]))


The coefficients are [-0.28631372  9.0980796 ].
```

The model is ready to be tested against the test data:

```
y_pred = my_model.predict(X_test)
```

The .predict method of the model lets us score unseen data and make predictions.

We can take a look at some metrics that let us evaluate our model against the test data:

```
> print('The mean absolute error is {0}'.format(\
     metrics.mean_absolute_error(y_test, y_pred)))


The mean absolute error is 4.868982830602648.


> print('The mean squared error is {0}'.format(\
     metrics.mean_squared_error(y_test, y_pred)))


The mean squared error is 65.8994897857804.
```

It is important to look at evaluation metrics for our model.

Another important metric we would like to take a look at is the R-squared:

```
> print('The r-squared is {0}'.format(\
     metrics.r2_score(y_test, y_pred)))


The r-squared is 0.18447543902501917.
```

R-squared is a typical metric used in linear regression.

We know that a value of 1 means that we have a perfect prediction. In other words, the variance of the data will be explained fully by the model. In this case we have less than 20% of the variance explained... Not great, but not terribly bad. Let us continue with this model. Remember that our aim here is to look at the deployment of the model rather than the accuracy we achieve with it.

Remember that our aim here is to look at the deployment of a model. You can spend more time finding a better model than this good enough one (for our purposes!)

Let us take a look at one of the test samples and its prediction. We will set up a dictionary for the input features, and see the prediction that the model has made for these values:

A dictionary will be used in passing values to the Core ML model!

```
sample = { 'crime': X_test.iloc[0]['CRIM'],
    'rooms': X_test.iloc[0]['RM'] }
ypred_sample = y_pred[0]
```

Making a prediction with a pair of values for our chosen attributes.

In this case we are extracting the first set of values in the testing dataset. The prediction for this set of values is stored in the first element of the array y_pred we calculated before:

```
> print('A property with {0} is valued\
    {1} thousand dollars'.format(\
    sample, ypred_sample))


A property with {'crime': 3.8497, 'rooms': 6.395}
is valued 23.524462257014 thousand dollars
```

We can easily check the predicted value for the chosen parameters.

A property with an average number of rooms equal to 6.39 in a location with a crime rate score of 3.84 is predicted to be valued as 23.52 thousand dollars.

If we imagine that this is the model that we are interested in deploying to our users, then we are ready for the big moment: Converting our model to an .mlmodel object!! Ready?

In reality, you will probably have to spend more time pondering this.

```
coreml_model = coremltools.converters.\
    sklearn.convert(my_model,\
    input_features=['crime', 'rooms'],
    output_feature_names='price')
```

The named parameters in the translation will be used in the app implementation later on.

Since we are using Scikit-learn to develop our model, we need to employ the `sklearn.convert` method of `coremltools.converters` to convert the model into Core ML format. Remember that currently you can also convert models developed with Caffe, Keras, LIBSVM and XGBoost. In the code above we are passing the name of our model from Scikit-learn, together with the names we would like to use for our input features, i.e., `crime` and `rooms`; we also provide a name for the output, in this case `price`.

We are using `sklearn.convert` as our model is originally developed with Scikit-learn. Core ML supports other frameworks too.

Now that we have a Core ML objects, we can edit some of the metadata attached to it. This will make it easier to be integrated to the rest of the deployment stack via XCode. For instance, information about the author, licensing and others can be consumed by XCode UI. Also the input and output descriptions can be used as comments in the code generated by Xcode for the model consumer. Finally, we can save the model. We will import the saved model in our app later on, but for now we store it in a file with the name `PriceBoston.mlmodel`.

Adding metadata to our Core ML model is easy.

```
coreml_model.author = 'JRogel
coreml_model.license = 'BSD'
coreml_model.short_description = 'Predicts the
    price of a house in the Boston area (1970s).'
coreml_model.save('PriceBoston.mlmodel')
```

In this case we are adding metadata about the author, the license and a description.

We can use the support that Core ML provides for visualising converted models, letting us see the building blocks of the model itself. We can do this with the help of

We can even visualise the model.

the `.visualize_spec` method, and an example of the result
can be seen in Figure 5.4.

```
coreml_model.visualize_spec()
```

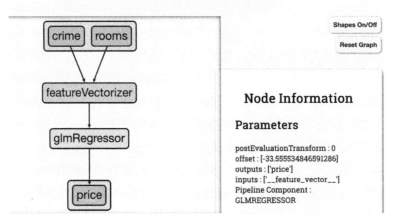

Figure 5.4: Visualisation of
the Boston house price model
converted into Core ML format.

Let us check that the converted model returns the same
predictions as the Scikit-learn model. All we need to do is
pass to the Core ML model a dictionary with the features
defined in the conversion, in this case `crime` and `rooms`. This
can be for instance the dictionary called `sample` we defined
above:

```
cml_pred = coreml_model.predict(sample)
```

Let us print the result:

```
> print(cml_pred)

{'price': 23.524462257014}
```

We can check that the prediction
of the Core ML model matches
that of the original Scikit-learn
one.

and as we can see the result is a dictionary with `price` as a key and its value matches the prediction obtained with our linear model defined in Scikit-learn. We are ready for the next step and that is to deploy our model in an app. We will be using Xcode for that purpose.

5.3.5   Model Properties in Core ML

WE HAVE CREATED OUR CORE ML model out of a linear regression algorithm developed with Scikit-learn. The model predicts prices for properties in the Boston area based on two predictors, namely crime rate and average number of rooms. It is by no means the best model out there and our aim is to explore the creation of a model (in this case with Python) and convert it to a Core ML model that can be deployed in an iOS app.

Before we move on to the development of the app, it would be good to take a look at the properties of the converted model. If we open the `PriceBoston.mlmodel` we saved in the previous section, we will see the information shown in Figure 5.5.

Opening it in Xcode of course!

We can see the name of the model (`PriceBoston`) and the fact that it is a "Pipeline Regressor". We saw that the model can be given various metadata attributes such as Author, Description, License, etc. We can also see the listing of the Model Evaluation Parameters:

We can see the metadata we added to the model.

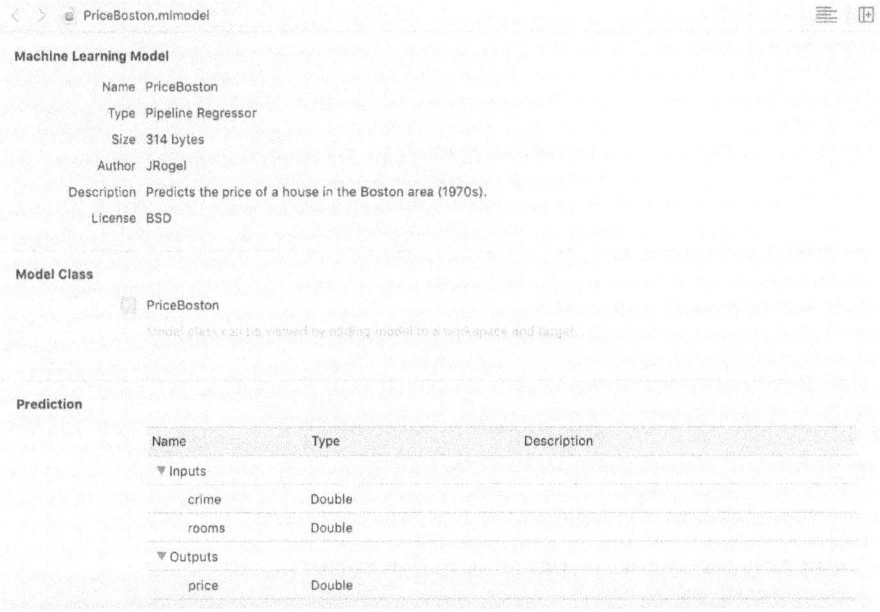

Figure 5.5: Properties of the Boston Pricer Core ML model created from Scikit-learn.

```
Inputs

===============================================

    crime           Double''

    rooms           Double


Outputs

===============================================

    price           Double
```

Note that the inputs and outputs are expected to be doubles.

They take the form of Inputs (crime rate and number of rooms) and Outputs (price). There is also an entry to describe the Model Class (PriceBoston) and you can see that since the model is not part of a target, the target class is not present. Once we integrate this model to an app, Xcode will generate the appropriate code automatically.

Although there is a Model Class, the target class is not present.

The autogenerated Swift code will define the input variables and feature names as well as a way to extract values out of the input strings. It will set up the model output and other components such as defining the class for model loading and prediction. All this is taken care of by Xcode in one go, making it very easy for us to use the model in our app. We will start building that app in the next section.

Once we add our model to a project, Xcode will autogenerate the target class for us.

5.4   *Surprise and Delight: Build an iOS App*

WE HAVE COME A LONG way and we are now ready to unleash our Boston pricer algorithm to the World! An implementation in Scikit-learn will be useful for a number of cases. In many others, we need to take into account the shocking fact that not everyone is interested in openning a Jupyter Notebook to run a prediction. Instead, if we are interested in deploying our algorithm to, say, non-technical users, we will have to surprise and delight them with a well-built app.

If only everyone could use Jupyter notebooks, or, even better, Python scripts in the terminal... not!

In this section we will cover the overall steps that will get our algorithm encapsulated into a very simple iOS app. The intention is to provide a flavour of the steps that need to be covered, and I would encourage you to spend more time thinking about the functionality of the app, the interactions that your users will need to go through, the flow of the application, the look and feel, the design, logos and images. And perhaps more importantly user testing and acceptance. With that warning, let us get started.

The app will be very simple, and I hope you take some time to improve it!

5.4.1   New Project: Xcode

LET US START BUILDING AN iOS app that will use the
model we created above, and enable our users to generate a
prediction for the price of a property based on input values   An estimate? A valuation?
for the parameters used in the model, namely average
number of rooms and crime rate score. Our aim is to build
a simple interface where the user enters the values of the
chosen features and the predicted price is shown in the
device. Make sure you have access to Xcode and the Core
ML model we created earlier on. Ready?

Figure 5.6: Creating a new XCode
project for a Single View App.

Open up Xcode and select "Create a new Xcode project".
That will open up a new dialogue box; from the menu at
the top make sure you select "iOS" and from the options
shown, please select the "Single View App" option and then   We are building a "Single View
click the "Next" button. See Figure 5.6 where the options   App".
mentioned above are highlighted with a black square.

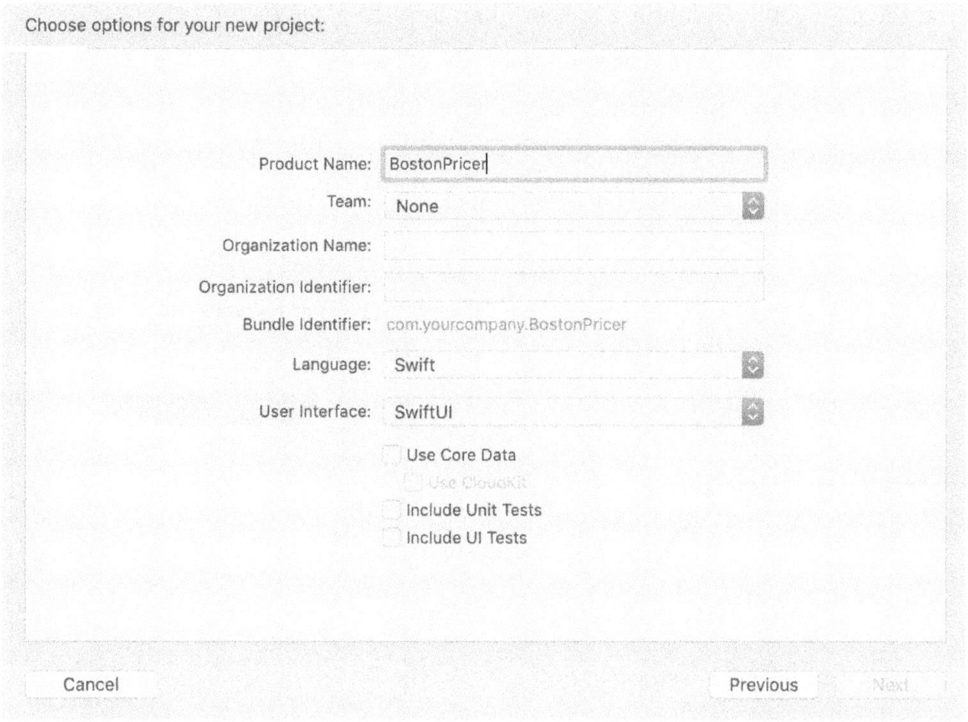

Choose options for your new project:

Product Name:	BostonPricer
Team:	None
Organization Name:	
Organization Identifier:	
Bundle Identifier:	com.yourcompany.BostonPricer
Language:	Swift
User Interface:	SwiftUI

Use Core Data

Use CloudKit

Include Unit Tests

Include UI Tests

Cancel   Previous   Next

Figure 5.7: We need to provide some metadata for the project we are creating.

The steps above will let us create an iOS app with a single page. If you need more pages or views, this is still a good place to start, as you can add further "View Controllers" and/or "Content Views" while you develop the app. In the next dialogue box, shown in Figure 5.7, Xcode will be asking for options to create the new project. Give your project a name, something that makes it easier to elucidate what your project is about. In this case, let us call the project "BostonPricer". You can also provide the name of a team (team of developers contributing to your app for instance) as well as an organisation name and identifier. In our case, these are not that important and you can enter any suitable values you desire. Please note that this becomes more

You can add more views to your project, if needed.

We are using SwiftUI to build our user interface.

important in case you are planning to send your app for approval to Apple. Make sure that you select "Swift" as the programming language and "SwiftUI" as the User Interface. We are leaving the option boxes for "Use Core Data", "Include Unit Tests" and "Include UI Tests" unticked.

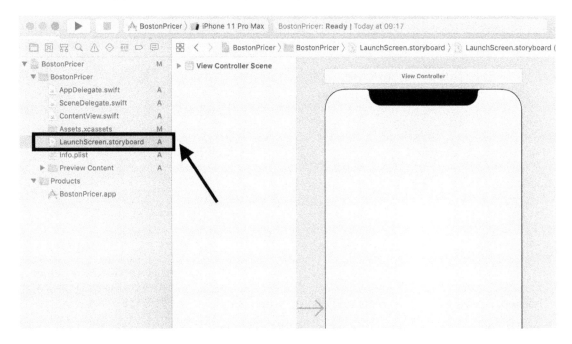

After clicking "Next", Xcode will automatically open a new editor and you will see some autogenerated code. Now, on the left-hand side you will see the Project Navigator, look for and click on the "LaunchScreen.storyboard" element as shown in Figure 5.8. This is the main view that our users will see when the application is launched. You can see on the right-hand side the shape of our target device, in this case an iPhone 11 Pro Max, and you can change that to fit your needs and those of your users.

Figure 5.8: The LaunchScreen.storyboard element is the main interface presented to our users.
How cool is that!

The Launch Screen is effectively a splash screen that will be shown when the app is started.

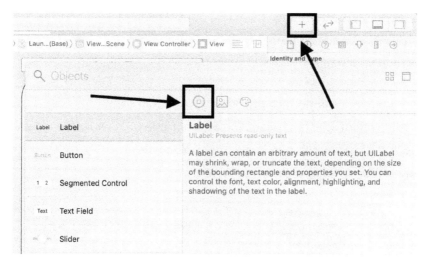

Figure 5.9: Open the Library with the plus icon, and the Object Library with the icon that looks like a square inside a circle.

Let us add a title and a couple of labels to our splash screen. We will need three labels and an image view. To do that, we will use the "Object Library". In the current window of Xcode, on the top-right corner you will see an icon with a plus sign (Figure 5.9); this opens up the Library which will be shown in a separate window. Look for an icon that looks like a little square inside a circle (Figure 5.9); this is the "Object Library" icon. Select it and, at the bottom of the area, you will see a search bar. There you will search for the following objects:

The Object Library lets us add different objects to our screen to build our app.

- Label

- Image View

In this case we are building a very simple splash page and all we will need is three labels and one image. You can drag each of the elements from the Object Library into the story board. You can edit the text for the labels and the button

Add three Labels and an Image View to the device screen.

by double clicking on them. Change the name of the labels to "Boston Pricer", "Advanced Data Science and Analytics with Python" and your name.

For the Image View, we will need to provide a picture. On the left-hand side menu select the `Assets.xcassets` folder. You can drag and drop your chosen image there. You will see something similar to what is shown in Figure 5.10.

Make sure you add a picture to your project.

Figure 5.10: Drag and drop your image into the `Assets.xcassets` folder.

Go back to the Launch Screen storyboard and select the Image View. From the menu on the top right-hand side select the Attribute Inspector. Here you can use the Image drop-down menu to select the picture you just added to your project (see Figure 5.11).

This is the icon that looks like a bookmark or an unfilled arrow pointing down.

Figure 5.11: Select your image in the Attribute Inspector.

You will notice that Xcode is giving some warnings about the "Auto Layout" of the application—See Figure 5.12. This is because we have not provided any constraints to the objects in the screen. If you were to change the target device (for example from the iPhone 11 Pro Max to an iPad Pro) you will see that the location of the objects changes. Let us first add some constraints to our image.

Figure 5.12: Auto layout errors.

Figure 5.13: Let us centre the image vertically and horizontally.

Select the Image Viewer and open the Align menu in the bottom right-hand side of the canvas (see Figure 5.13). Align the image vertically and horizontally in the container by ticking the appropriate boxes and click the button to add the two constraints.

Align the picture horizontally and vertically.

We now need to ensure the picture maintains a reasonable size and keeps its aspect ratio. Control-click and drag at the same time inside the image. You will see a blue arrow appearing as shown in the left-hand side of Figure 5.14. When you let go, a pop-up dialogue box will show (as in the right-hand side of Figure 5.14). Select "Width" in the pop-up dialogue box.

We need to Control-click and drag at the same time!

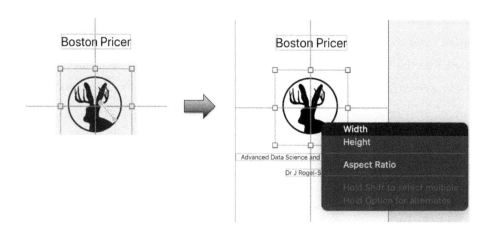

Figure 5.14: We can put constraints on the height, width and aspect ratio of our image.

A new constraint will appear in the menu on the right-hand side of Xcode. There you can edit the constraint. In this case we would like the image to be less or equal to 200 pixels, as shown on the left-hand side of Figure 5.15. Control-click and drag inside the image again. This time select "Aspect

You can manage the constraints on the boxes that appear in the right-hand side menu of the Xcode window.

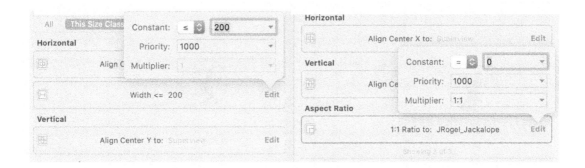

Figure 5.15: We can edit the added contraints for width and aspect ratio.

Ratio" and edit the constraint for the ratio to be 1:1, as shown in the right-hand side of Figure 5.15.

Select the "Boston Pricer" label and click on the "Add New Constraints" tool at the bottom of the canvas. In the dialogue box click on the bottom bar to make the space to the nearest neighbour to be 50 pixels—See the left-hand side of Figure 5.16. Select now the "Boston Pricer" and the Image and click on the Align tool bar. Align the two objects horizontally by ticking in the box as shown on the right-hand side of Figure 5.16.

The one that looks like a square between two vertical bars.

We will do a similar thing to our other two labels. For the "Advanced Data Science and Analytics with Python" label, add new constraints to neighbours at the top, right and left to be 20 pixels. Make sure that you have the "Constraints to margins" option ticked. For the label with your name, add a new constraint to have 20 pixels to the top nearest neighbour. Then align the centres of this label with the centre of the image. These steps would have made the warnings disappear.

Adding constraints could be a time-consuming task. All this can be more easily managed with SwiftUI as we shall see.

Figure 5.16: We are now adding constraints to one of the labels.

You can now marvel yourself and run your first iOS app. All you need to do is click on the play button on the top left-hand side of the Xcode window. This will launch an iPhone simulator. First you will see the splash screen we just created, and then, once the app starts you will see the message "Hello World" in the best style of first programmes in any programming language. The screens will look similar to those in Figure 5.17.

Clicking on the play button in Xcode will launch an iPhone simulator where our app will run!

As you can see, it is possible to create the look-and-feel of the application using the so-called *Interface Builder*, where we can drag and drop windows, buttons, labels, and more. The caveat is that the functionality for each of these objects needs to be developed independently using the Model-View-Controller pattern.

Covering the Model-View-Controller pattern is out of the scope of this book. However, we are going to use the

Figure 5.17: Running our app up until this point will show the splash page created, followed by the "Hello Word" message shown in all its glory.

SwiftUI which is a toolkit that enables us to build our apps in a declarative manner. We can also drag-and-drop components and the framework supports previews of our design without having to launch the simulator. Furthermore, the declarative nature of the framework means that we do let the operating system take care of the state of the objects and even their location in the canvas.

SwiftUI will actually make a lot of us Pythonistas feel more at home.

We mentioned at the beginning of this section that some autogenerated code is shown when creating our project. It is this code the one that is responsible for displaying the "Hello World" message as seen on the right-hand side of Figure 5.17. We can see this code by clicking on the `ContentView.Swift` file on the Project Navigator on left-

The autogenerated code we mentioned before is responsible for the "Hello World" message.

hand side of our screen. You will see an editor similar to
the one shown in Figure 5.18. If you cannot see a preview of
the app, make sure you click on the Resume button on the
canvas view.

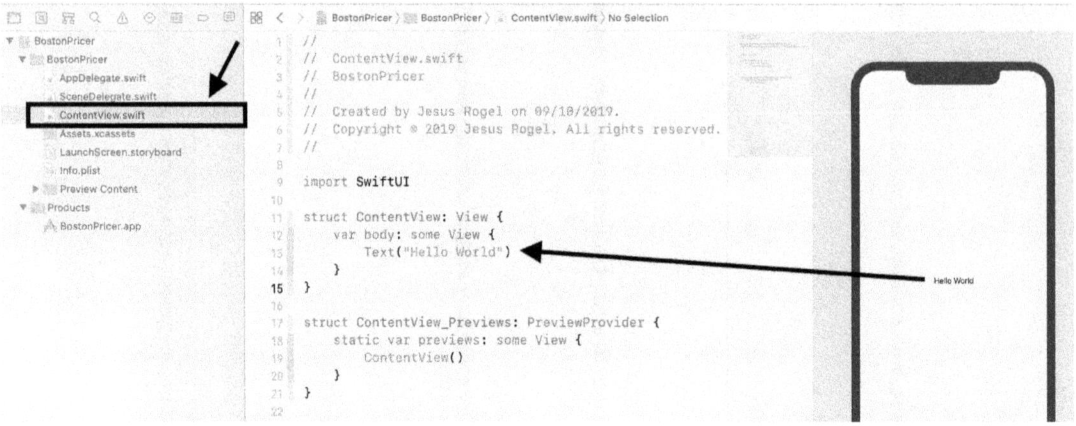

Figure 5.18: The autogenerated
code that prints "Hello World" to
the screen can be found in the
ContentView.Swift file.

Let us change the text of the autogenerated code from
"Hello World" to "Boston Pricer". We can also add some
formatting to the label by making the font title size and
centring the text:

Swift

```
struct ContentView: View {
    var body: some View {
        Text(''Boston Pricer'').font(.largeTitle)
            .multilineTextAlignment(.center) }
}
```

You can actually make the attribute modifications in the
preview. Command-click on the label and select "Show
SwiftUI Inspector". There you can select the font and

alignment; the code in the editor will change automatically (see Figure 5.19).

We need to ensure that the different objects we add to our interface are part of a navigation view. Also, since we are letting the operating system organise these objects, we need to ensure they are contained in either horizontal or vertical stacks. For that, Swift lets us create VStack and HStack objects, respectively. We can create a NavigationView with a vertical stack, or VStack, containing our text label:

Figure 5.19: The attributes can be changed in the preview.

```swift
struct ContentView: View {
    var body: some View {
        NavigationView {
          VStack {
            Text(''Boston Pricer'')
                .font(.largeTitle)
                .multilineTextAlignment(.center) }
        }
    }
}
```

Swift

We will start placing a few other objects in our app. Some of these objects will be used simply to display text (labels and information), whereas others will be used to create interactions. In particular, we are interested in letting our users select input values and generate a prediction. In this case we will start by adding a couple of labels in a horizontal stack (HStack) and a button. After the line of code starting with .multilineTextAlignment, type the following code:

We are adding objects in a horizontal stack, or HStack.

```
HStack {

    Text(''Crime Rate'').padding(.trailing, 40)

    Text(''No. Rooms'').padding(.leading, 40)

 }


Spacer()


Button(action: {}) {

    Text(''Get Prediction'')

}


Spacer()
```

Swift

Figure 5.20: The app layout is automatically handled with SwiftUI.

The horizontal stack creates two labels side-by-side, one with the text "Crime Rate" and the other one with "No. Rooms". The button has the label "Get Prediction" and thanks to the use of Spacer() the layout of the app is handled with ease by the operating system and in any screen size required. See Figure 5.20.

5.4.2   Push My Buttons: Adding Functionality

WE NOW HAVE A NICE looking app. If we were to run the simulator with the code we have, things will work. However, nothing will happen. We need to add functionality to our objects. In this case we only expect the user to tap on the button to trigger an action. This eventually will show the prediction for the property price with the attributes selected. First, let us make sure that we can add an action to the button such that when it is tapped it displays a message.

We need to add functionality to our app.

Before we delve into the code, let us talk about states. Consider a real object such as a lightswitch that is used to turn the lights on and off in a room. The switch may have an indicator for on and off. The *state* of the room is such that it is illuminated when the switch is in the on position, and it is plunged into darkness when the switch is in the off position. The actions of the person in the room can change the state of the room by changing the position of the switch. Furthermore, the state of the room can also be changed by other circumstances such as the time of day, the number of people in the room, the temperature of the room, etc. We refer to these variables as *state variables* and all possible combinations of every possible value for the state variables is referred to as the *state space*.

Bear with me... we will get there.

The state of illumination in a room is controlled by a variable state that takes the values *on* or *off*.

The state space of our current app is the equivalent of the on and off switch. There are two states:

Our app also has two states: before and after pressing the button.

1. The screen shown before the user presses the button. This is shown in Figure 5.20.

2. A pop-up message after the user hits the button. When the user dismisses the message, we revert back to state 1.

We need a state variable to keep track of the two states mentioned above. In this case a Boolean will suffice. We declare a state variable in SwiftUI with @State. At the top of the code in the content view, make the following modifications:

A state variable is declared with @State in Swift.

```
struct ContentView: View {

    @State var popUpVisible: Bool = false

    var body: some View {

        ...
```
Swift

We are declaring a Boolean state variable called popUpVisible and assign it the value of false. We can now tell our app to change its state when the user presses the button. To that end, let us make the following changes to the button we implemented before:

```
Button(action: {
    self.popUpVisible = true
}) {
    Text(''Get Prediction'')
}
.alert(isPresented: self.$popUpVisible) {
    Alert(title: Text(''Prediction''),
        message: Text(''Prediction will be
            shown here.''),
      dismissButton: .default(Text(''Cool!'')))
}
```
Swift

An alert takes a title, a message and an action for when the alert is dismissed.

The first thing to note is the addition of a line in the action for the button. In this case we assign the value of true when the user presses the button. After the label of the button, we are also adding a few lines of code. The alert() method of the button will present a popup alert to the user. The title is the bold title of the window; the message displayed is handled by message and importantly the dismissButton is a button that dismisses the window when the user is done. The result of pressing the button can be seen in Figure 5.21.

5.4.3   Being Picky: The Picker View

WE NEED TO PROVIDE OUR users with an easy way to pick the attributes of the property they need to value. Currently our app contains three labels and one button. We need to add a couple of pickers, one for the crime rate score and another one for the number of rooms.

Let us start creating constants to hold the potential values for the input variables. At the top of the ContentView struct make the following changes:

Figure 5.21: The app state after pressing the button.

```
struct ContentView: View {
  let crimeData = Array(stride(from: 0.05,
    through: 3.7, by: 0.1))
  let roomData = Array(4...9)
  @State var popUpVisible: Bool = false
  ...
```

Swift

The modifier let declares constants in Swift.

These values are informed by the data exploration we carried out in Section 5.3.3 earlier on. We are going to use the arrays defined above to populate the values that will be shown in our pickers. For this we need to define a data source for each picker as well as a state variable. Right below the definition of the constants crimeData and roomData, let us add the following state variables:

Crime from 0.05 to 3.65 in steps of 0.1, and Rooms from 4 to 9.

```
@State var pickerCrime = 0

@State var pickerRoom = 0
```

Swift

Let us now add a couple of pickers. In the `NavigationView`, between the "Boston Pricer" title and the button, remove the `HStack` with the two labels and replace it with the following `VStack`. The result will be similar to the one in Figure 5.22.

Swift

```
VStack {
  Picker(selection: .constant(1),
    label: Text(''Crime'')) {
    Text(''1'').tag(1)
    Text(''2'').tag(2)
  }
    .padding(.leading, 10)
  Picker(selection: .constant(1),
      label: Text(''No. Rooms'')) {
    Text(''1'').tag(1)
    Text(''2'').tag(2)
  }
    .padding(.leading, 10)
}
```

Figure 5.22: Adding a couple of pickers to our app.

Currently the pickers have the values 1 and 2 but what we really want is to show the values from the constants we defined above. Let us look at the Crime Rate picker first:

```
Picker(selection: $pickerCrime,
  label: Text(''Crime'')) {
  ForEach(0..<crimeData.count) { ix in
    Text(''\(self.crimeData[ix],
      specifier: ''%.2f'')'').tag(ix)
  }
}
```

Swift

We are first specifying that the variable state `pickerCrime` is used in this picker's selection. The content of the picker is then given by each of the indexed entries in the `crimeData` array. We need to convert the doubles into text. We do this by string interpolation by enclosing the name of the variable between "`\( ...)`". Think of this operation as a substitution of the variable value. Finally, we specify that we only require two decimal points with the formatter "`%.2f`".

Figure 5.23: The pickers are now showing the correct values we specified.

Let us now change the second picker to show valid values for the number of rooms:

```
Picker(selection: $pickerRoom,
  label: Text(''No. Rooms'')) {
  ForEach(0..<roomData.count) { ix in
    Text(''\(self.roomData[ix]'').tag(ix)
  }
}
```

Swift

In this case we simply convert the integers into text, as there is no need to specify a format for these strings. The result of the code above can be seen in Figure 5.23.

We can check that the state variables are indeed capturing the state of the app. Let us change the alert shown by the button so that it shows the values picked by the user. At this stage, we are not going to worry about formatting the value of our double array `crimeData`. Modify the button implementation as follows:

Let us check that we can capture the current state of the app.

Swift

```
Button(action: {
  self.popUpVisible = true
}) {
  Text("Get Prediction")
}
.alert(isPresented: self.$popUpVisible) {
  Alert(title: Text(''Prediction''),
    message: Text(''The values picked are\n
      Crime Rate: \(crimeData[pickerCrime])\n
      Rooms: \(roomData[pickerRoom])''),
    dismissButton: .default(Text(''Cool!'')))
}.padding()
```

The result can be seen in Figure 5.24. It is now time to bring the model into our app. Ready?

5.4.4 Model Behaviour: Core ML + SwiftUI

LOOK HOW FAR WE HAVE come... We started this chapter looking at what Core ML does and how we can use the tools provided by Apple to translate our Python models. In this case we decided to use linear regression as our model, and chose to use the Boston Price dataset in our exploration for this implementation. We built our model using Python

Figure 5.24: We can see that the app is capturing the correct state for the pickers.

and created our `.mlmodel` object. We have put together
an app that can be run in an iPhone and we are ready to
include our Core ML model in our Xcode project. The aim is
to use the inputs selected from our pickers and calculate a
prediction based on our model and display the result to our
users.

Perhaps we may want to refer to
our prediction as a valuation?

Let us start by adding the `.mlmodel` we created earlier on so
that it is an available resource in our project. In the Xcode
project navigator, select the "BostonPricer" folder. At the
bottom of the window you will see a plus (+) sign, click on
it and select "New Group" (see Figure 5.25). This will create
a sub-folder within "BostonPricer". Select the new folder
and hit the return key, this will let you rename the folder to
something more useful. In this case we are going to call this
folder "Resources".

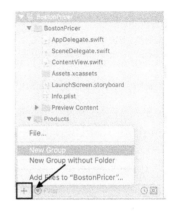

Figure 5.25: Adding a New Group
to our project.

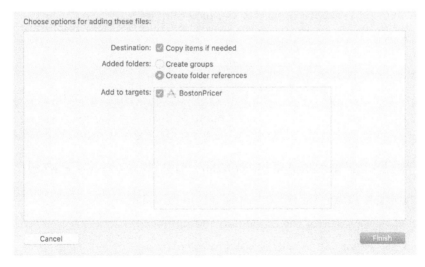

Figure 5.26: Adding resources to
our Xcode project.

In your Mac, open Finder, and navigate to the location of
the `PriceBoston.mlmodel` we created earlier on. Drag the

file inside the "Resources" folder. This will open a dialogue box asking for some options for adding this file to our project (see Figure 5.26). Leave selected the "Create Folder References"; make sure that you copy the items as needed. Click on the "Finish" button and you will see the model now being part of the project.

It is a good idea to keep our Xcode project tidy with the help of groups.

Go to the code in the Content View where we are going to make a few changes. The first change is to tell our project that we are going to need the powers of the Core ML framework. At the top of the file, locate a line of code that imports SwiftUI, right below it type the following:

```swift
import CoreML
```

Swift

Inside the definition of the ContentView struct, let us define a constant to reference the model. Look for the declarations of the crimeData and roomData constants and next to them type the following:

We need to instantiate a our model, just like we have done in Python.

```swift
let model = PriceBoston()
```

Swift

You will see that when you start typing the name of the model, Xcode will suggest the right name as it knows about the existence of the model as part of its resources, neat!

As Xcode now knows about our model, autocomplete is available for it.

We are now going to create a method that is able to read the values selected by the user for the crime rate and number of rooms pickers. These values will be used to calculate a valuation. Our method will return a string containing the predicted price. After the NavigationView code enter the following:

```
var body: some View {

  NavigationView{...}

}


func predictionMsg() -> String {

  let crime = crimeData[pickerCrime]

  let rooms = Double(roomData[pickerRoom])


  guard let PriceBoston = try? model.prediction(

    crime: crime, rooms: rooms) else {

      fatalError(''Unexpected runtime error.'')

  }


  let price = String(format: ''%.2f'',

    PriceBoston.price*1000)

  let Msg = ''Your property value is\n $\(price)''


  return Msg

}
```

Swift

We are collapsing the NavigationView view code to be clear about where the changes need to be placed.

The model has a .prediction method to calculate our prediction.

Finally, we format our result to be ready for display.

Note that in the code above we have collapsed the NavigationView for ease of clarity. Our method is called predictionMsg and it returns a string. First it reads the values of the pickers and assigns them to two constants crime and rooms. These are the input names expected by our model, remember?

Notice that we have cast the rooms constant as a double.

In Section 5.3.5 we saw that our PriceBoston class has a prediction(crime:rooms:) method used to predict the median value of a property from the model's input values.

The result of this method is assigned in the code above to a `PriceBoston` output instance. The `price` property of this instance is used to get the prediction. We know that the values are in thousands of dollars and that is why we are multiplying the predicted value by 1000 before using it in a string to be returned by the function.

That is the line starting with `guard`.

Figure 5.27: The final app producing predictions for our users out of a linear regression model first developed with Python.

We can now run our app with the simulator and the result will be a fully functional model, first developed in Python, producing predictions in the hands of our users through an iOS app. See Figure 5.27 to get an idea of what to expect, and the final version of the app is available in GitHub[11]. There are many more things that we can do to improve the app. For instance, we can test that the layout works for

[11] Rogel-Salazar, J (2017). Boston Pricer. https://github.com/rogelj/coreml_boston. Accessed: 2019-10-23

a variety of screen sizes. Also, having a picker may be a
bit cumbersome for some of the inputs, perhaps a stepper
would be more appropriate. Another important aspect
in the experience that we want to give to our users is the
overall look-and-feel and usability for the app. This includes
the design of appropriate icons in various sizes. You can
now enroll a test device to run your application and use
the app as intended, in a mobile device. You can find more
information about that in the Apple Developers site[12].

[12] Apple Inc. (2019a).
Apple Developer.
https://developer.apple.com.
Accessed: 2019-10-23

5.5   Summary

AS WE SAID AT THE beginning of this chapter, we have
indeed covered a lot of ground. And yet, there are still quite
a few areas that we can explore in a deeper way. There are
also many more subjects we have not touched on at all. In
this last chapter we have looked into the perennial issue
of bringing our models, predictions and solutions to our
customers, users and stakeholders.

We provided a working definition for a data product as
one that meets the needs, wants and/or requirements of
our users through the use of data. We saw that it is of
particular importance to take into account any development
considerations around data. This may include things such
as its availability, processing, meaning and understanding,
to name a few. We also need to include in our development
cycles the usage of data science techniques, going beyond
data analysis.

We have also explored the complexity of data products: Ranging from raw data and algorithms through to automated decision making. The vast majority of our discussions before this chapter have been centred around the usage of data, and data science techniques, by Jackalope data scientists. In this chapter we were actually interested in bringing the fruit of our efforts to a non-technical audience too. To that end we explored the requirements of a multi-functional team including the need, not just for data scientists, but also data architects, engineers, product managers and subject matter experts.

As a way to bring our trained models to our potential users, in this chapter we looked at building an application that can be deployed in a mobile device. In this case we have chosen to explore the Apple ecosystem including Xcode, Swift and Core ML. We saw how Core ML offers us Pythonistas a way to convert our trained models into a format that can be integrated within an app, and be brought to the hands of our users. Core ML tools enable us to translate a Scikit-learn model into the `.mlmodel` format used by the iOS and MacOS applications we intend to develop.

In this case we used a well-known dataset to make predictions of the mean value of a property in the Boston area (in the 1970s). In order to keep our discussion manageable for the scope of the chapter, we used a linear regression model, covering the different stages of the data science workflow: From data understanding to exploration, model training and testing and finally deployment.

Although the book has been primarily dedicated to the use of Python in the practice of data science, in this chapter we made reference to Swift. The intention was not to do a comprehensive coverage of this programming language. The hope, however, was that the snippets of code used are easy enough to understand the gist of the language. We covered the usage of the SwiftU framework, which gives us the opportunity to add programmatically new elements to our application, while letting the operating system handle not only the location of the elements, but also track the state space of the application.

We finished this chapter by incorporating our Core ML model into the app, letting the user provide input values for the features used in the model to make a prediction. As we noted in the previous volume of this book, *there is no such a thing as a perfect model, only good enough ones*, and thus the model we present to our users may not be the one and only model we develop, tweak, improve and supersede. We can continue using anthropomorphic language to refer to models that *learn, see, understand* and *recognise*, but we will not be able to disguise the fact that mathematics, statistics and software development sit at the heart of our efforts. Enabling those efforts has been the intention of this, and its companion, book.

Enjoy!

A

Information Criteria

IN OUR TIME SERIES DISCUSSION in Chapter 1 we mentioned our interest in determining the current value of a series based on the past observations. We saw a few models that can be used, and in many cases it involves how many lag terms we need to include. The coefficients of these terms provide us with information about the effects of the past in predicting future values.

When adding more terms we are effectively gaining information, but inevitably at the same time we make our model more complex. In order to balance this dichotomy, in many other cases we use regularisation. Various information criteria help us with this regularisation task by balancing the information gained by including additional lag terms versus increasing the complexity of our model.

Some of the most frequently used information criteria include the Akaike information criterion or AIC[1], the Bayesian—sometimes referred to as Schwarz—information

[1] Akaike, H. (1969). Fitting autoregressive models for prediction. *Annals of the Institute of Statistical Mathematics* 2(1), 243–247

criterion (BIC)[2], or the Hannan and Quinn information criterion (HQIC)[3].

[2] Schwarz, G. (1978). Estimating the dimension of a model. *The Annals of Statistics* 6(2), 461–464
[3] Hannan, E.J. and Quinn, B. G. (1979). The determination of the order of an autoregression. *Journal of the Royal Statistical Society, Series B* 41, 190–195

In general, the information criteria mentioned above have the form:

$$IC_k = \log \hat{\sigma}_k^2 + \frac{kp_n}{n}, \tag{A.1}$$

where $\hat{\sigma}_k$ is the standard deviation to be estimated when k parameters are to be determined, and n is the number of observations. The first term in the expression above is the goodness-of-fit, which is to be balanced with the second term which effectively measures the complexity of the model. For each of the information criteria, the coefficient in this penalty term takes the form:

$$p_n = \begin{cases} 2, & \text{for AIC.} \\ \log n, & \text{for BIC.} \\ 2\log\log n, & \text{for HQIC.} \end{cases} \tag{A.2}$$

In each case, the aim is to find the model with the lowest value of the selected information criterion.

B

Power Iteration

Let A be an $n \times n$ matrix. We start with an arbitrary initial vector $\mathbf{x}^{(0)}$ and we form the the the vector sequence $\left\{ \mathbf{x}^{(k)} \right\}_{k=0}^{\infty}$ by defining:

$$\mathbf{x}^{(k)} = A\mathbf{x}^{(k-1)}, \quad k = 1, 2, \dots \tag{B.1}$$

It is clear from the expression above that:

$$\mathbf{x}^{(k)} = A^k \mathbf{x}^{(0)}. \tag{B.2}$$

The main idea behind power iteration is that $\mathbf{x}^{(k)}$ will converge to an eigenvector associated with the eigenvalue of the largest magnitude.

In general, we are interested only in the direction, not necessarily in the length, of the eigenvector. In practical terms, it is best practice to include a normalisation step to Equation (B.1). This leads us to the power iteration algorithm as follows:

1. Start with a vector $\mathbf{x}^{(0)}$ with $\|\mathbf{x}^{(0)}\| = 1$

2. $k = 0$

3. repeat

4. $k = k + 1$

5. $\mathbf{y}^{(k)} = A\mathbf{x}^{(k-1)}$

6. $\mu_k = \|\mathbf{y}^{(k)}\|$

7. $\mathbf{x}^{(k)} = \mathbf{y}^{(k)}/\mu_k$

8. until a convergence criterion is satisfied.

All the vectors $\mathbf{x}^{(k)}$ generated by the algorithm have a norm equal to one. In other words, $\left\{\mathbf{x}^{(k)}\right\}_{k=0}^{\infty}$ is a sequence on the unit sphere in n dimensions.

C

The Softmax Function and Its Derivative

WE HAVE ENCOUNTERED THE SOFTMAX function in Chapter 4 and given its importance in the context of activation functions for neural networks, we would like to cover some information related to its characteristics, including its derivative.

The softmax function is a generalisation of the sigmoid function. It takes real values as input and maps them to a probability distribution where entry is in the range $(0,1]$. Furthermore, all the entries add up to 1. We know from Chapter 4 that the function is given by:

$$\text{softmax}(z_i) = \sigma(z_i) = \frac{\exp(z_i)}{\sum_{k=1}^{N} \exp(z_k)}, \text{ for } i = 1, \dots, k. \quad \text{(C.1)}$$

We can see that $\sigma(z_i)$ is always positive and is bounded between 0 and 1. If we were to evaluate the function for the elements $[0,1,2,3,4]$ we have that the function will return the values $[0.0116562, 0.0316849, 0.0861285, 0.2341216, 0.6364086]$ which add up to 1. In other words, with this function we find a "soft" version of the maximum, where the maximal input gets a proportionally large contribution compared to the other elements, but all getting part of it.

The characteristics of the function are such that it is suitable to be used for probabilistic interpretation. In cases where we have multiple classes, we can use the function to assign probabilities for an input to belong to each of the classes.

It is bounded between 0 and 1 and the values add up to 1.

In the context of activation functions in neural networks, the softmax function plays an important role, particularly in the output layer and as such we require its derivative so that we can perform backpropagation. The derivative of the softmax function is therefore expressed as:

$$\frac{\partial \sigma(z_i)}{\partial z_j} = \frac{\partial \frac{e^{z_i}}{\sum_{k=1}^{N} e^{a_k}}}{\partial z_j}. \tag{C.2}$$

We can apply the quotient rule to the expression above such that $g = e^{z_i}$ and $h = \sum_{k=1}^{N} e^{z_k}$ and thus:

$$
\begin{aligned}
\frac{\partial \sigma(z_i)}{\partial z_j} &= \frac{\frac{\partial e^{z_i}}{\partial z_j} \sum_{k=1}^{N} e^{z_k} - e^{z_i} \frac{\partial}{\partial z_j}\left(\sum_{k=1}^{N} e^{z_k}\right)}{\left(\sum_{k=1}^{N} e^{z_k}\right)^2} \\
&= \frac{\frac{\partial e^{z_i}}{\partial z_j}}{\sum_{k=1}^{N} e^{z_k}} - \frac{e^{z_i} \sum_{k=1}^{N} \frac{\partial}{\partial z_j} e^{z_k}}{\left(\sum_{k=1}^{N} e^{z_k}\right)^2} \\
&= \delta_{ij} \frac{e^{z_i}}{\sum_{k=1}^{N} e^{z_k}} - \frac{e^{z_i}}{\sum_{k=1}^{N} e^{z_k}} \frac{e^{z_j}}{\sum_{k=1}^{N} e^{z_k}}
\end{aligned}
\tag{C.3}
$$

$$= \sigma(z_i)\left(\delta_{ij} - \sigma(z_j)\right) \tag{C.4}$$

where δ_{ij} is the Kronecker delta function.

C.1   Numerical Stability

WHEN IMPLEMENTING COMPUTATION FOR THE softmax function, we need to take into account the presence of numerical instability for large input values. This is related to the calculation of exponential functions involved in the definition of softmax.

Normalisation of the inputs can be achieved with the introduction of an arbitrary constant C as follows:

$$\sigma(z_i) = \frac{\exp(z_i)}{\sum_{k=1}^{N} \exp(z_k)} = \frac{C \exp(z_i)}{\sum_{k=1}^{N} C \exp(z_k)} \qquad (C.5)$$

Using the properties of the exponential function, we are able to write the expression above as:

$$\sigma(z_i) = \frac{\exp(z_i + \log C)}{\sum_{k=1}^{N} \exp(z_k + \log C)} \qquad (C.6)$$

where $\log C$ is still an arbitrary constant we can choose. One option is $-\max[z_1, z_2, \ldots, z_i]$ which has the effect of shifting the inputs to a range close to zero.

D

The Derivative of the Cross-Entropy Loss Function

GIVEN THE CROSS-ENTROPY LOSS function:

$$L = -\sum_i y_i \log \hat{y}_i = -\sum_i y_i \log \sigma(z_i), \qquad \text{(D.1)}$$

where $\sigma(z_i)$ is the softmax function, we want to obtain the derivative of with respect to the parameter z_j.

$$
\begin{aligned}
\frac{\partial L}{\partial z_j} &= -\sum_i y_i \frac{\partial \log \sigma(z_i)}{\partial z_j}, \\
&= \\
&= -\sum_i y_i \frac{1}{\sigma(z_i)} \frac{\partial \sigma(z_i)}{\partial z_j}. \qquad \text{(D.2)}
\end{aligned}
$$

We need to calculate the derivative of the softmax function, and information about this can be seen in Appendix C.

There are two cases, one for $i = j$ and the other for $i \neq j$:

$$
\begin{aligned}
\frac{\partial L}{\partial z_j} &= -y_i(1 - \sigma(z_i)) - \sum_{i \neq j} y_i \frac{-\sigma(z_i)\sigma(z_j)}{\sigma(z_i)}, \\[2ex]
&= -y_i + y_i\sigma(z_i) + \sum_{i \neq j} y_i\sigma(z_j), \\[2ex]
&= \sigma(z_i)\sum_{i} y_i - y_i = \sigma(z_i) - y_i, \quad\quad\quad \text{(D.3)}
\end{aligned}
$$

as $\sum_i y_i = 1$.

Bibliography

ACE 2004 Multilingual Training Corpus.
   https://catalog.ldc.upenn.edu/ LDC2005T09.

Address Before a Joint Session of the Congress. Barack
   Obama. 44th President of the United States: 2009-2017.
   https://www.presidency.ucsb.edu/ node/286218.

Beautiful Soup.   https://www.crummy.com/
   software/BeautifulSoup/.

Chardet. https://chardet.readthedocs.io.

Cursive Re. https://github.com/Bogdanp/ cursive_re.

re - Regular expression operations.
   https://docs.python.org/3.6/ library/re.html.

Scrapy. https://scrapy.org.

spaCy. https://spacy.io.

Unicode 11.0.   http://www.unicode.org/
   versions/Unicode11.0.0/.

Abadi, M. et al. (2015). TensorFlow: Large-scale machine
   learning on heterogeneous systems. http://tensorflow.org/.
   Software available from tensorflow.org.

Akaike, H. (1969).   Fitting autoregressive models for prediction.   *Annals of the Institute of Statistical Mathematics* 2(1), 243–247.

Al-Rfou, R. et al. (2016, May). Theano: A Python framework for fast computation of mathematical expressions. *arXiv e-prints abs/1605.02688*.

Apache Airflow (2014). Apache Airflow Documentation. https://airflow.apache.org. Accessed: 2019-09-30.

Apple Inc. (2014). Swift programming language. `https://swift.org`.

Apple Inc. (2017a). Core ML. https://developer.apple.com/documentation/coreml. Accessed: 2019-10-01.

Apple Inc. (2017b).   Core ML tools. https://github.com/apple/coremltools. Accessed: 2019-10-01.

Apple Inc. (2019a).   Apple Developer. https://developer.apple.com. Accessed: 2019-10-23.

Apple Inc. (2019b). Core ML. https://developer.apple.com/documentation/createml. Accessed: 2019-10-01.

Archer, S. (2017). Apple hits a record high after crushing earnings (AAPL). http://markets.businessinsider.com/news/stocks/apple-stock-price- record-high-after-crushing-earnings -2017-8-100222647. Accessed: 2018-05-01.

Ball, W.W.R. and Coxeter, H.S.M. (1987). *Mathematical Recreations and Essays*. Dover Recreational Math Series. Dover Publications.

Bapat, R., R. Bapat, T. Raghavan, C. U. Press, T. S, G. Rota, B. Doran, P. Flajolet, M. Ismail, T. Lam, et al. (1997). *Nonnegative Matrices and Applications*. Encyclopedia of Mathematics and its Applications. Cambridge University Press.

Blei, D. M., Ng, A. Y., and Jordan, M. I. (2003). Latent Dirichlet Allocation. *Journal of Machine Learning Research 3*, 993–1022.

Box, G. and G. Jenkins (1976). *Time series analysis: forecasting and control*. Holden-Day series in time series analysis and digital processing. Holden-Day.

Butler, S. (2005). Erewhon; Or, Over the Range. Project Gutenberg https://www.gutenberg.org/ebooks/1906. Accessed: 2019-09-03.

Carroll, L. and J. Tenniel (1897). *Through the Looking Glass: And what Alice Found There*. Altemus' illustrated young people's library. Henry Altemus Company.

Chen, T. et al. (2014). CMXNet: A Flexible and Efficient Machine Learning Library for Heterogeneous Distributed Systems. *arXiv preprint arXiv:1512.01274*.

Cho, K., B. van Merrienboer, et al. (2014). Learning phrase representations using RNN encoder-decoder for statistical machine translation. *CoRR abs/1406.1078*.

Chollet, F. et al. (2015). Keras. `https://github.com/fchollet/keras`.

Continuum Analytics (2014). Anaconda 2.1.0. `https://store.continuum.io/cshop/anaconda/`.

Euler, L. (1736). Solutio problematis ad geometriam situs pertinentis. *Comment. Acad. Sci. U. Petrop. 8*, 128–140.

Fagles, R. (1997). *The Odyssey*. A Penguin Book. Penguin Books.

Fortunato, S. (2010). Community detection in graphs. *Phys. Rep. 486*(3-5), 75–174.

Gabasova, E. (2016). *Star Wars* social network. https://doi.org/10.5281/ zenodo.1411479.

Girvan, M. and Newman, M.E.J (2002). Community structure in social and biological networks. *Proc. Natl. Acad. Sci. USA 99*, 7821–7826.

Github (2018). CNTK: The microsoft cognitive tool. https://github.com/Microsoft/CNTK/. Accessed: 2018-08-13.

Glenberg, A.M. (1997). What memory is for. *Behav. Brain Sci. 20*, 1–55.

Grandjean, M. (2016). A social network analysis of Twitter: Mapping the digital humanities community. *Cogent Arts and Humanities 3*, 1–14.

Greff, K., Srivastava, R. K., Koutník, J., et al. (2017). LSTM: A Search Space Odyssey. *IEEE Trans. Neural Netw. and Learning Sys. 28*(10), 2222–2232.

Hannan, E.J. and Quinn, B. G. (1979). The determination of the order of an autoregression. *Journal of the Royal Statistical Society, Series B 41*, 190–195.

Harrison, D. and D. Rubinfeld (1978). Hedonic prices and the demand for clean air. *J. Environ. Economics and Management 5*, 81–102.

Hinton, G. E. and R. Salakhutdinov (2006). Reducing the dimensionality of data with neural networks. *Science 313 5786*, 504–7.

Hinton, G. E., Osindero, S., and Teh, Y.-W. (2006). A Fast Learning Algorithm for Deep Belief Nets. *Neural Computation 18*, 1527–1554.

Hochreiter, S. and Schmidhuber, J. (1997). Long short-term memory. *Neural. Comput. 9*(8), 1735–1780.

Ioffe, S. and C. Szegedy (2015). Batch normalization: Accelerating deep network training by reducing internal covariate shift. *CoRR abs/1502.03167*.

Jia, Y. et al. (2014). Caffe: Convolutional Architecture for Fast Feature Embedding. *arXiv preprint arXiv:1408.5093*.

Karinthy, F. (1929). Chains in Everything is Different. Online at http://bit.ly/karinthy_chains. Translated from Hungarian and annotated by Adam Makkai. Edited by E Jankó.

Karpathy, A. (2015).   The Unreasonable Effectiveness of Recurrent Neural Networks. https://karpathy.github.io/2015/05/21/rnn-effectiveness/. Accessed: 2019-09-09.

Kingma, D. P. and J. Ba (2014). Adam: A method for stochastic optimization. arxXiv:1412.6980. Comment: Published as a conference paper at the 3rd International

Conference for Learning Representations, San Diego, 2015.

Krizhevsky, A. (2009). Learning multiple layers of features from tiny images. Technical report.

LeCun, Y., Boser, B., Denker, J. S., et al. (1989). Backpropagation applied to handwritten zip code recognition. *Neural Computation 1*(4), 541–551.

Masters, D. and C. Luschi (2018). Revisiting Small Batch Training for Deep Neural Networks. *Computing Research Repository http://arxiv.org/abs/1804.07612.*

McCulloch, W. S. and Pitts, W. (1943). A logical calculus of the ideas immanent in nervous activity. *Bull. of Math. Biophysics 5*(4), 115–133.

McKinney, W. (2012). *Python for Data Analysis: Data Wrangling with Pandas, NumPy, and IPython.* O'Reilly Media.

McKinney, W. (2011). pandas: a foundational python library for data analysis and statistics. Python for High Performance and Scientific Computing: O'Reilly Media, Inc.

Mikolov, T., I. Sutskever, et al. (2013). Distributed Representations of Words and Phrases and Their Compositionality. In *Proceedings of the 26th International Conference on Neural Information Processing Systems - Volume 2*, NIPS'13, USA, pp. 3111–3119. Curran Associates Inc.

Milgram, S. (1967). The small world problem. *Psych. Today 1*(1), 60–67.

Minsky, M., S. Papert, and L. Bottou (2017). *Perceptrons: An Introduction to Computational Geometry*. The MIT Press. MIT Press.

Moody, J. and White, D. (2003). Social cohesion and embeddedness: A hierarchical conception of social groups. *Am. Soc. Rev. 68*(1), 103–128.

Noichl, M. (2017). Relationships between Philosophers, 600 b.c - 160 b.c. https://homepage.univie.ac.at/ noichlm94/full/Greeks/index.html. Accessed: 2019-02-18.

Papachristou, N. et al. (2019). Network Analysis of the Multidimensional Symptom Experience of Oncology. *Scientific Reports 9*(1), 2258.

Paszke, A. et al. (2017). Automatic differentiation in PyTorch. In *NIPS Autodiff Workshop*.

Pedregosa, F., G. Varoquaux, A. Gramfort, V. Michel, et al. (2011). Scikit-learn: Machine learning in Python. *Journal of Machine Learning Research 12*, 2825–2830.

Press, W., S. Teukolsky, W. Vetterling, and B. Flannery (2007). *Numerical Recipes 3rd Edition: The Art of Scientific Computing*. Cambridge University Press.

Pritchard, J. K., Stephens, M., and Donnelly, P. (2000). Inference of population structure using multilocus genotype data. *Genetics 155*(2), 945–956.

Python Software Foundation (1995). Python reference manual. http://www.python.org.

Řehůřek, R. and P. Sojka (2010, May). Software Framework for Topic Modelling with Large Corpora. In *Proceedings of the LREC 2010 Workshop on New Challenges for NLP Frameworks*, Valletta, Malta, pp. 45–50. ELRA. `http://is.muni.cz/publication/884893/en`.

Reitz, K. Requests - http for humans. http://docs.python-requests.org/en/master/.

Rogel-Salazar, J. (2016, Jan). Data Science Tweets. https://doi.org/10.6084/ m9.figshare.2062551.v1.

Rogel-Salazar, J. (2018a, May). Apple Inc Prices Apr 2017 - Apr 2018. https://doi.org /10.6084/m9.figshare.6339830.v1.

Rogel-Salazar, J. (2018b, Jun). Bitcoin/USD exchange rate Mar 31-Apr 3, 2016. https://doi.org /10.6084/m9.figshare.6452831.v1.

Rogel-Salazar, J. (2018c, Sep). Iris Webpage. https://doi.org /10.6084/m9.figshare.7053392.v4.

Rogel-Salazar, J. (2018d, Jul). Sunspots - Monthly Activity since 1749. https://doi.org /10.6084/m9.figshare.6728255.v1.

Rogel-Salazar, J. (2019a, Apr). *Star Wars* Network. https://doi.org/10.6084/ m9.figshare.7993292.v1.

Rogel-Salazar, J. (2019b, Aug). Neural Network - Observation dataset. https://doi.org/10.6084/ m9.figshare.9249074.v1.

Rogel-Salazar, J. (2019c, Apr). Zachary's karate club. https://doi.org/10.6084/ m9.figshare.7985174.v1.

Rogel-Salazar, J (2017).   Boston Pricer.
https://github.com/rogelj/coreml_boston.   Accessed:
2019-10-23.

Rogel-Salazar, J. (2017). *Data Science and Analytics with Python.*
Chapman & Hall/CRC Data Mining and Knowledge
Discovery Series. CRC Press.

Rosenblatt, F. (1962). *Principles of neurodynamics: perceptrons
and the theory of brain mechanisms.*   Report (Cornell
Aeronautical Laboratory). Spartan Books.

Rumelhart, D. E., G. E. Hinton, and R. J. Williams (1986).
Learning representations by back-propagating errors.
Nature 323(6088), 533–536.

Russell, A. (2014).   *Open Standards and the Digital Age.*
Cambridge Studies in the Emerg. Cambridge University
Press.

Schuster, A. (1906). II. On the periodicities of sunspots.
*Philosophical Transactions of the Royal Society of London A:
Mathematical, Physical and Engineering Sciences 206*(402-
412), 69–100.

Schwarz, G. (1978). Estimating the dimension of a model. *The
Annals of Statistics 6*(2), 461–464.

Scientific Computing Tools for Python (2013). NumPy.
http://www.numpy.org.

Simas, T. et al. (2017). Food-Bridging: A new network
construction to unveil the principles of cooking. *Frontiers
in ICT 4*, 14.

Spotify (2014). Luigi. https://github.com/spotify/luigi. Accessed: 2019-09-30.

Stellman, A. and J. Greene (2014). *Learning Agile: Understanding Scrum, XP, Lean, and Kanban*. O'Reilly Media.

Sutskever, I., J. Martens, G. Dahl, and G. Hinton (2013, 17–19 Jun). On the importance of initialization and momentum in deep learning. In S. Dasgupta and D. McAllester (Eds.), *Proceedings of the 30th International Conference on Machine Learning*, Volume 28 of *Proceedings of Machine Learning Research*, Atlanta, Georgia, USA, pp. 1139–1147. PMLR.

van Rossum, G. (2009). Text Vs. Data Instead of Unicode Vs. 8-bit. https://docs.python.org/release/3.0.1/whatsnew/3.0.html.

Vincent D Blondel, Guillaume, J.-L., Lambiotte, R., and Lefebvre, E. (2008, Oct.). Fast unfolding of communities in large networks. *J. Stat. Mech-Theory E 2008*(10), P10008.

Watts, D. and Strogatz, S. (1998). Collective dynamics of small-world networks. *Nature 393*(1), 440–442.

Werbos, P. (1994). *The Roots of Backpropagation: From Ordered Derivatives to Neural Networks and Political Forecasting*. Adaptive and Cognitive Dynamic Systems: Signal Processing, Learning, Communications and Control. Wiley.

Zachary, W. W. (1977). An information flow model for conflict and fission in small groups. *J. Anthropol. Res. 33*(4), 452–473.

Index